Race

and

Ideology

AFRICAN AMERICAN LIFE SERIES

A complete listing of the books in this series can be found at the back of this volume.

SERIES EDITORS

Melba Joyce Boyd
Department of Africana Studies, Wayne State University

Ron Brown
Department of Political Science, Wayne State University

RACE
AND
IDEOLOGY

LANGUAGE,
SYMBOLISM, AND
POPULAR CULTURE

EDITED BY
ARTHUR K. SPEARS

 WAYNE STATE UNIVERSITY PRESS   DETROIT

Pem Davidson Buck's chapter, "Prison Labor," first appeared in a
slightly different version under the title "The Rise of American
Fascism" in *Urban Anthropology* 23:4 (winter 1994).

Lee D. Baker's chapter, "Racism in Professional Settings," first
appeared in a slightly different version as "Forms of Address as
Clues to Power Relations" in the *Journal of Applied
Behavioral Science* 31:2.

Grateful acknowledgment is made for use of the following in
Jon A. Yasin's chapter, "Rap in the African-American Music
Tradition: Cultural Assertion and Continuity." Lyrics from the
song "I'm Not Ashamed," written by Glen Woodward, copyright
1992 Highest Praise Publishing. Reprinted by permission.
Introduction to the song "I Can't Give Up Now," from the album
Gospel from Mt. Nebo, by the Mt. Nebo Choirs.
Reprinted by permission. Lyrics from "Street Corner Hustler's Blues"
by Lou Rawls, copyright © 1996 (renewed) by
Embassy Music Corporation (BMI) and Marvelle Music.
All rights administered worldwide by
Embassy Music Corporation.
International copyright secured. All rights reserved.
Reprinted by permission.

Library of Congress Cataloging-in-Publication Data

Race and ideology : language, symbolism, and popular culture / edited
by Arthur K. Spears.
p.   cm. — (African American life series)
Includes bibliographical references and index.
ISBN 0-8143-2453-3 (alk. paper). — ISBN 0-8143-2454-1 (pbk. : alk. paper)
1. Afro-Americans in popular culture.   2. Racism in popular
culture.   3. Racism in popular culture—United States.   4. Afro-
Americans—Education.   5. Language and education—United States.
6. United States—Race relations.   I. Spears, Arthur K. (Arthur
Kean), 1943– .   II. Series.
E185.615.R16   1999
305.8'00973—dc21   99-38057

Contents

5

PREFACE

My efforts to put together this collection of writings started with my concern about the fragmentary nature of almost all writing on race and related issues. I mean "fragmentary" in the specific sense that particular race topics are not placed within a larger matrix that would relate many of the main issues of race to each other and relate race to oppression in general, thus preventing a realistic assessment of where race relations are going and why racism has been so difficult to eliminate. My scholarly interest in race issues began with Robert Blauner's *Racial Oppression in America* (1972), which, in following in the footsteps of Frantz Fanon's seminal *The Wretched of the Earth* (1968), solidified and buttressed the pillars of an institutional theory of racism, placing the issues of vested interests and privilege in the forefront. Several chapters in this volume foreground also the issue of who profits most from racism.

The literatures on race, ideology, language, symbolism, and popular culture are vast and growing. I and the other contributors have attempted to use selected writings in these areas to construct a clear, coherent narrative that might help those of us who suffer from and are concerned about oppression to see our way clear to some kind of action-oriented understanding of fundamental issues.

The intended audience for this book comprises readers interested in issues of race, racism, and ideology, including students and scholars in most of the social sciences and humanities who share these interests. One of the functions of the introduction is to provide readers unfamiliar with some of the key notions certain critical linkages among them, along with definitions of terms and clarifications of perspectives. Accessibility was an important consideration in selecting and editing the contributions. All of the contributors have been very cooperative in their efforts to keep their work free of unnecessary jargon, which unfortunately detracts from some of the best work in a critical (and noncritical) vein.

I have long felt that individual prejudices and stereotypes, the focus of many specialized works and textbooks on race and ethnicity, lack strong roots. As racial integration spread in the United States in the 1950s and 1960s, it became clear to me that most whites were willing to question their own stereotypes and prejudices, once they were confronted with counterevidence. Reports from grassroots political workers during the course of the Civil Rights and Peace movements supported and focused this observation: whites' racial ideas and political positions could be influenced most starting at the bottom of the socioeconomic scale, with less success as one moved upward, accompanied often by an increase in politeness and a decrease in volume (of talk), but also a decrease in willingness to engage power, resource, and control issues associated with racial hierarchy. What do these experiences tell us? For one, they lead us to think that racism *must* be carefully taught and maintained. Any discussion of the maintenance of inequality puts us face to face with ideology, as disseminated through often seemingly innocent discourses and images in the classroom, in movie theaters, in music videos, in church, and almost everywhere else. This collection attempts to provide answers and explain not only the observations above but also to outline the "logic" of racial categorization and thinking—that is, their internal consistency and functional nature—from the standpoint of those whom they most benefit.

I would like to thank all of the contributors for their patience and conscientiousness, and especially Pem Davidson Buck and Lee Baker for their detailed comments on the introduction. It gives me special satisfaction to point out that two of the chapters (Abalos and Whylie) were written by undergraduate students in my anthropology course on television and film at the City College of the City University of New York. These chapters provide reason for optimism, given my comments concerning the tragic overall state of public education in the United States. Their writings illustrate the importance of encouraging participation in cultural analysis at all levels of the university (and public school systems) in addition to within society in general.

I would also like to thank Faye Harrison and James Houghton for their close reading of and feedback on earlier versions of the introduction, and Marsha Frankel, Karen Projen, and Brenda Price for their assistance in manuscript preparation. Thanks are due to Salikoko Muf-wene and Geneva Smitherman for their support in the early stages of this project, and also to Arline McCord, former dean of the Division of Social Science at City College (CUNY), for arranging research support in part related to this volume.

Finally, and most importantly, I would like to express my apprecia-tion to the Schomburg Center for Research in Black Culture, whose Scholars-in-Residence Fellowship program provided me with assistance for this and other projects. Special thanks go to Schomburg director Howard Dodson and to Diana Lachatanère. Finally, to Verneta Hill, I give special recognition for her continued support.

Arthur K. Spears

RACE AND IDEOLOGY: AN INTRODUCTION

ARTHUR K. SPEARS

PREAMBLE

As Du Bois's (1961 [1903]) words lead us to expect, race has been a major problem worldwide in the twentieth century. Had he lived, he might have come to another conclusion concerning the United States specifically: America cannot be America without racism (cf. Bell 1992). Racism, and its by-product colorstruction (Spears 1992), also termed colorism (color hierarchies in communities of color), is so integral a part of American institutions that an America without racism would be a distinctly new thing, created necessarily by a radical social transformation. This, of course, contradicts many people's view of the United States as a nation fundamentally about freedom and justice for all, one that is meanwhile working out superficial flaws that come to us as part of a historical legacy. In reality, it is the mechanism of racism that has made possible the continuation of the American economic and political system, whose founding documents reaffirm subordination based on race, class, and gender. Racism in the United States, as in all white-supremacist societies, is institutionalized, woven into the fabric of all American institutions (Fanon 1968 [1961], Blauner 1972)—and it is diligently maintained by the economic and power elites who so greatly profit from it.[1] Racism against people of color appeases white working people (that is, working-class and middle-class whites)—and the white underclass, for that matter—who are simply higher in the hierarchy of exploited groups. The leader of the world economic community is also

11

the leader in maintaining and spreading white supremacy in the world. This should not be seen as a cause for despair, but as a call for sober pragmatism and solid work for change.

This book is concerned with the ways in which racism, along with other forms of oppression, is partially maintained by the dissemination of ideology through words, images, and behavior. Racial hierarchies maintain differential access to wealth and power, which is the central reason for the existence of racial categorization. Every U.S. textbook that I have examined obscures the true nature and function of not only racial but also ethnic categorization (cf. van Dijk 1993). Many do not even list the word *racism* in their indexes (though all provide sometimes grossly inadequate definitions and discussions of racism in the text). Most of them discuss prejudice and stereotypes as givens, as though they have a life of their own, largely independent of political and economic factors. Virtually none of them attend to how major mainstream institutions, publishing included, structure racist ("ethnicist," sexist, classist, and heterosexist) discourses and images into their products.

There are many volumes fully or partially devoted to discussions of race and ideology from diverse perspectives. However, there is a tendency for works on race not to relate their discussions explicitly to a macroframework for understanding the dynamics and causes of oppression in general, especially as it affects both nonelite whites and people of color. Almost all of the works on race and ideology lack a macroframework, probably under the often unjustified assumption that the reader brings an adequate framework to the reading.[2] As a result of my conversations with academics in a number of disciplines and with nonacademics, I do not believe this assumption is usually warranted. Many people are very clear and knowledgeable about certain aspects of the big picture, but seem to falter in making linkages and drawing fundamental conclusions. Many serious people seem simply to prefer not to think deeply about race and racism, fearing perhaps that they will be labeled as whining victims or co-conspirators. A brief framework is presented in this introduction in response to such concerns.

Until the post–World War II period, racism was based principally on false ideas of biologically based inferiority. The inferiority it claimed was innate. The more recent neoracism is subtler, in most cases claiming a cultural basis for what is seen as low achievement by people of color. This view is erroneously based on various unproved factors such as cultures of poverty, lack of entrepreneurial traditions, unstable family structures, teenage pregnancy, single motherhood, deficient languages, and anti-intellectualism. However, claims of inferior genetic endowment, for African Americans in particular, still circulate. Neoracism rationalizes the subordination of people of color on the basis of culture, which of course is acquired through acculturation within an ethnic group,[3] while traditional racism rationalizes it fundamentally in terms of biology. Neoracism is still racism, in that it functions to maintain racial hierarchies of oppression. Its new ideological focus on culture has the same function, and provides a vast new field to mine for supposed causes of the lower achievement of groups of color based on dysfunctional attitudes, values, and orientations. As soon as one false theory is overturned by painstaking social science research, another is fabricated. Previous research is frequently ignored. Claims of cultural deficit constitute only one of neoracism's strategies. Another major strategy involves the mass media, which, through selection, emphasis, and omission, portray blacks and other groups of color (not to mention women, the working classes, and other oppressed groups) in negative and stereotyped ways. Finally, the educational system has always played a key role in disseminating racist ideologies; its role under neoracism continues with a shift in content and method. Even university-level academic production has with one hand supported and purveyed racist thought, while with the other it strongly supported antiracism (Baker and Patterson 1994).

New in education in terms of method, or policy if you will, is the systematic miseducation in most public schools of working-class children, white and nonwhite, but more damaging to children of color. The learning abilities of these children are dulled and their senses of self-discipline and self-esteem eroded. It is the perfect educational system for assisting in taming an assertive population that tends to feel strongly about being wronged. Although some students do well in spite of the system, my college teaching experiences offer stunning examples of miseducation. A student asks why Spanish is spoken in South America. Another does not know where South America is on the map. Many students cannot write simple, understandable sentences, among them student teachers who will be teaching in a public school the following semester. Some of them are illiterate, not just *functionally* illiterate: they cannot put letters together to make words, except for the simplest and most common ones, such as *dog*, *a*, and *cat*. Several have told me that they were illiterate when they graduated from high school, and some students I know have graduated from college functionally illiterate.

As part of the neoracist educational strategy, public (and private) schools continue to teach a distorted version of American history. For example, history classes generally ignore the many interconnections among people of color throughout American history, such as those between blacks and Native Americans (Harrison 1995; Forbes 1988) and between Chinese Americans and blacks, to take two examples. Interest-

13

ing in the latter case is the amalgamation and cooperation that occurred in the Mississippi Delta area, particularly before many of the Chinese were able to rise to the status of small-business entrepreneurs.[4] The fact that groups of color have often suffered from the same kinds of oppression is typically not pointed out. For example, Native Americans were enslaved, as were blacks (and whites [Bennett 1987]); both African Americans and Mexican Americans have been victimized by segregated schools, lynching, and debt peonage. Another generally avoided topic is the history of resistance by people of color.[5]

The mass media's role in shaping thought and opinions—and racist ideology—has greatly increased in the postwar period owing to the great growth in their size and reach, attaining monopoly proportions. Monopoly has led to the placement of unprecedented power for shaping thought in the hands of a few conglomerates (Bagdikian 1987; Herman and Chomsky 1988). As Chomsky (1977) has noted, the United States has the narrowest range of mass media political discourse of any of the major economic powers. This can be verified by perusing newsstands in the cities of other countries. This augmented role of the mass media, particularly television and film, which typically present propaganda masquerading as entertainment, makes the study of the media and their impact on popular culture all the more important.

The world problem of racial categorization, and the racism that is an integral part of that categorization, is driven in many ways by the U.S. global presence, through the export of mass media products, fashion, images and standards of beauty, and corporate products and administration techniques. The influx of American (and European) capital into regions of less economically developed countries with no color hierarchies or milder ones has produced comparatively extreme racialization in hitherto relatively uncolor-coded social terrains. The entrenchment and extension of racial segregation in Cuba by American business and crime organizations, which was not abolished until Castro's takeover, is one of the better-known instances. (See Whitten 1974 on Ecuador and Colombia.) The United States is not just another country. Aspects of American society and culture often have worldwide impact. Thus, in learning more about American racial dynamics, we learn more also about something that continues to infect on a global scale.

The purpose of this collection is to explore race and racism as they affect African Americans and other nonwhites in the United States and abroad. The primary emphasis is on African Americans; however, the chapters dealing with other groups serve to underline commonalities in the experience of racism and in the transmission of racist values as they occur in diverse national and ethnic contexts. While there would be no argument that all of the groups discussed in these pages are groups of color, there may be some question as to whether all are nonwhite, particularly if one thinks of *white* as equivalent to the racial term *Caucasian*. There might be some confusion because, for example, at least some of the people of the Indian subcontinent are in racial classifications considered Caucasian, yet they are not normally considered white. This is relevant in the case of the Rom (Gypsies), who trace their origins to India and whose language, Romani, is Indo-European. (It would, however, be a mistake to assume that all of the Rom can trace their biological descent back to India.) In the final analysis, these considerations all amount to a nonissue. The Rom tend to be darker skinned than the whites surrounding them in Europe and North America. Their history of oppression reads like that of the peoples of the African diaspora. The last Gypsy slaves in Europe were freed only in the latter half of the nineteenth century (in Romania); a half a million died in the Holocaust, along with Jews and homosexuals; and their oppression continues (Hancock 1986). Furthermore, the terms *white* and *Caucasian* are not scientific, reliable, or explanatory; whiteness changes through time and space (Gregory and Sanjek 1994; Reynolds and Lieberman 1996), and who is considered Caucasian depends on the particular pseudoscientific model of race that informs one's use of the term. Of course, most people use the two terms interchangeably and subjectively. In this volume, Gypsies are considered nonwhite due not solely to color (after all, some African Americans are fair-skinned, blue-eyed, and blond) but also to their history of oppression resulting from the structural position they occupy in the white-controlled societies they inhabit.

Too often, African Americans and other nonwhites fail to consider their struggles within a broader framework of oppression that would pinpoint common concerns, not solely for other groups of color but also for women, lesbians and gays, and other oppressed groups, especially nonelite whites, including the much-criticized white male heterosexual (who is often presumed not to belong to any oppressed group). Indeed, one of the key considerations that has been almost consistently ignored in the literature on race and racism is that nonelite (i.e., middle- and working-class) whites do not constitute the primary source of racist values. Rather they are led and coordinated in their racism by the policies, discourses, and symbolism manufactured by white elites and their representatives. This point has been made by Gran (1994) and ably elaborated by Du Bois (1969 [1935]) and van Dijk (1993).

Often works that are written either fully or partially by scholars of color, as is the case with this book, are dismissed as being subjective or biased. This is but one tactic in the marginalization of scholars of color.

But why should scholars of color, who have much to gain from a usable analysis of race and racism based on qualitative and quantitative research, be more subjective or biased than white scholars, who clearly, as members of the white group, have something to gain from misrepresenting the true nature of a white supremacist system that licenses them to benefit from skin-color privilege? Moreover, recent critical studies have done much to debunk the myth of the possibility of total objectivity. Many whites find it difficult to confront the fact that their social position, within a white supremacist nation and world capitalist system, may owe more to white privilege than to skills and knowledge. The truly humanitarian impulse in the late twentieth century is to resign from whiteness and all that it entails in order to join the rest of humanity. To resign from whiteness is to reject the inequalities and forms of exploitation for which it serves as the foundation. Resignation from whiteness is indeed possible since whiteness is a state of mind and a regime of behavior. It is a social construction and changes over time in response to political and economic needs.

All of the phenomena indicated by the titles of this book's chapters have commonalities due to their inclusion under the global canopy of race and racism. This is their context, whether implicit or explicit, and they affect and are affected by race and racism. If not at the table, race and racism are the ghost interlocutors. While some chapters are more direct than others, all of them are ultimately about the struggle for cultural freedom in the face of the constraining force of race/racism, both nationally and globally. They approach this struggle, variously, through cultural and ideological analysis and critique. Amilcar Cabral and Frantz Fanon, among others, have instructed us on the centrality of culture in emancipation; this volume continues in the direction they have signaled.

Although most of the contributors to this volume are in anthropology or linguistics (which is itself a major subfield of anthropology), this volume is problem-oriented rather than discipline-oriented. It is more diagnostic than programmatic and is intended to provide information useful in the development of emancipatory theories and practices.

Among the most important goals of this volume is to emphasize, by the juxtaposition of the chapters within it, the necessity for unifying the study of oppression by considering as many fronts as possible, and by considering them within some unifying framework and through the perspective provided by a unifying theme. The theme in this volume is ideology, one side of the coin of oppression. The other side, of course, is coercion, through the many methods of physical force. Consequently, the core interest within these pages is in *an emancipation-oriented treatment of race/racism as illuminated by the concept of ideology.*

16

Below, I present a macroframework for the study of oppression that is intended to aid us in pinpointing both connections and contradictions. The chapters deal not only with discourse, but also with policies, images, institutions, and facets of popular culture.

Another goal is to provide a detailed discussion of cultural self-critique: identifying an aspect of the culture of a people of color, colorstruction, which is a by-product of patriarchal white supremacy. With colorstruction, there is at once a connection to racism and a contradiction—a people struggling against racism but harboring a form of it within themselves. Skin bleaching among people of color is but one example of a behavior reflecting white-supremacist racism directed against the self.[6] People of color cannot simply blame white power elites. Agency is everywhere, and oppressed peoples everywhere are wont to participate to varying degrees in their own oppression. Even the most brutalized slave has options of resistance and accommodation; he or she can always resort to sabotage and revolt, for example, or, to put it bluntly, can commit suicide in revolt. Analyses of white power-elite culpability cannot truly fulfill their emancipatory function unless they are complemented by analyses of internalized oppression within individuals and of cultural domination within groups.

RACE AND RACISM

The concept of race is not scientific. A mountain of scientific research firmly establishes it as pseudoscience (see Reynolds and Lieberman 1996 and the references cited there). It is a sociocultural concept, created and sustained in the minds of humans living in or aware of racialized societies.

Several points can be considered briefly to understand why race is not a scientific concept. Race, again, is based on biological features of humans, but not all of such features. The notion of race has been tied principally to visible human features, primary among them color, facial features, and cranium and skeleton shape and size, which allowed pseudoscientific race studies to take off in the eighteenth century. These features figure most prominently in the popular mind in thinking about race and consequently are useful in a basic discussion.

The first problem with racial classification is that it does not allow for the scientific definition, which minimally must be precise, of discrete groups of individuals. A superficial familiarity with the world's peoples may make it seem that they can be neatly categorized on the basis of features such as hair texture; skin color; and eye, nose, and lip shape. However, a broader knowledge makes it clear that these traits do not vary together. For example, Caucasian is a category including

17

those with pale or olive skin, straight or wavy hair, straight noses or ones nearly so, thinner lips, and eyes without the epicanthic fold. (Eyes with the epicanthic fold are typical of Japanese, for example, and some other Asians, but also of some Africans). Admittedly, this discussion of size, shape, and other traits is somewhat imprecise, but so are racial types.

This Caucasian category presents problems because there are pale people with kinky hair (all over the Americas, for example); very dark-skinned people with straight hair (Dravidians in India, for example); and dark-skinned people with wavy blond hair, flattish round noses, and full lips (Native Australians). Hence, the second problem: the features do not form a stable set. They do not co-vary. "Problem" populations such as Native Australians simply caused race pseudoscientists to create new categories and reorganize their racial systems, leading to the creation of more and more races and subraces.

The third problem is that these "racial" traits are not inherited together. They are inherited separately; thus, we have an extremely wide range of looks due to "race mixing," as witnessed in the Americas, for example. The separate inheritance of genes for physical traits also creates the odd situation of several races existing among the offspring of one nuclear family.

Hence the fourth problem: physical types vary gradually, in clines, as we cross the globe north to south and east to west. The physical traits in question do not allow for the setting up of discrete groups. This makes it impossible to identify racial boundaries. We have only a gradual fading of one type into another. For example, skin color changes gradually as one moves from southern Africa (light-brown to brown) to Equatorial Africa (very dark brown) to North Africa (dark brown, brown to olive and fair), and on up to northern Europe (generally fair).

Fifth, racial traits can change from one generation to the next with a change in environment and/or nutrition. This is notably true of skin color and cranium measurements (Lieberman and Reynolds 1996). Consequently, the rather far-fetched situation can occur in which parents of one and the same race have children of another race—that is, if definitions of race are followed strictly.

Sixth, the physical traits that racial categories are based upon do not tell us anything interesting about people. Negroidness (kinky hair, dark skin color, full lips, etc.), for example, does not allow us to predict either intelligence or the gene for the sickling trait, which can cause sickle cell anemia or simply provide resistance against malaria. Blood type, to take another physical feature, does not vary according to race. Racial groupings that do not reveal anything interesting about people

18

themselves and that relate only to how they are treated by others due to preconceived ideas are otherwise useless.

What some biologists and physical anthropologists refer to as *populations* can be precisely defined (for example, on the basis of blood type), leading to meaningful, scientifically useful results.[7] However, the traits used in defining populations are unevenly spread across racial groups, so one cannot use these features to resurrect racial classification and at the same time continue to identify what are popularly conceived of as races.[8]

Race is a sociocultural category, and more specifically it is ideological in the critical sense that concerns us. Not just any collection of ideas, ideology is a set of ideas put to work in the justification and maintenance of vested interests. Ideology in the critical sense is typically used in reference to power elites, who use ideology to rationalize their power and the exploitation of other groups. Racial categories are integrated into a racial hierarchy arranged on an inferiority-superiority scale, tied principally to presumed intelligence and absence or level of civilization.[9] Race has been the key ingredient in justifying European imperialism, slavery, and more recently the global color order, in which the wealthy nations of Europeans and their descendants plunder the world's resources and exploit to varying degrees all of those, white and of color, outside of national power elites.

Race is and has been used to justify the exploitation of people of color as well as whites. For indeed, racial classification schemes in a number of cases have divided whites themselves into distinct races: Anglo-Saxons defined the Irish as an inferior race. The vilification and degradation of the Irish at the hands of Anglo-Saxons in Great Britain and the United States rivals that of the indigenous peoples of Africa, Asia, Oceania, Australia, and the Americas (Metress 1996; Shanklin 1994, 3–7; Patterson 1994). Consider this description of the Irish, from an 1860 translation of a twelfth-century text by Giraldus Cambrensis:

> But I am haunted by the human chimpanzees I saw along that hundred miles of horrible country. I don't believe they are our fault. I believe there are not only many more of them than of old, but that they are happier, better, more comfortably fed and lodged under our rule than they ever were. But to see white chimpanzees is dreadful; if they were black, one would not feel it so much. . . . (quoted in Curtis 1968, 84; quoted in Shanklin 1994, 3)

As Shanklin points out, the translation was heavily influenced by attitudes of the time and was considerably more derogatory than earlier translations of the same twelfth-century work.

Race has been used to facilitate the exploitation of whites, too, not

19

solely to justify it. This is true historically in the United States (see especially Du Bois 1969 [1935]) and increasingly in Europe. The stigmatization of African Americans and others of color in the United States is used to promote a sense of well-being in U.S. whites, distracting their attention from their own exploitation and creating obstacles for interracial movements for improving the conditions of all. Thus, many working whites (working- and middle-class) find it difficult to identify their own self-interests and end up voting for officials (notably ex-presidents Reagan and Bush) who, once elected, put in place policies and laws that diminish these whites' standard of living while causing income and wealth to flow up the social scale (Chomsky 1994).

As the power of unions is whittled away (despite a few large, successful strikes in the late 1990s), retirement funds are stolen or otherwise dissolved, health and other benefits eliminated, job security diminished, and full-time employment ever more difficult to come by, whites are whipped into fear over crime and drugs, which through the mass media are diligently associated primarily with African Americans and Hispanics (Gilliam 1992; Buck, in this volume). African-American men are falsely presented in the mass media as the prototypical destroyers of family happiness and purveyors of irresponsible public discourse: "it is no coincidence that the issues of sexual harassment, date rape, spousal abuse, . . . child molestation and hate speech reach the height of nationalized ritual via *black* protagonists [in the mass media]" (Giddings 1994). The vilification of these and other populations of color props up the ever growing prison industry, which has awarded to the United States the highest rate of incarceration in the world (Sharff 1995; Morris and Rothman 1995; Buck, in this volume).

Not only are people of color negatively presented to whites to assure the latter's worth (in the face of diminishing rewards for whiteness) and to becloud the income and wealth gap between power-elite whites and ordinary whites (Roediger 1991), others are also served up as whipping boys (and girls): women and gays and lesbians foremost among them. It can be observed, without engaging in an invidious ranking of oppressions, that *in some ways* women and homosexuals fare worse than heterosexual males of color. Sedgwick notes the use of the defense strategy of "homosexual panic," used by gay-bashers claiming that they have received unwanted sexual advances. The success of this defense is based on a tangle of stereotypes and societal pathologies, but corresponding defense strategies using "black panic," "Latino panic," and "heterosexual panic" (for instance, by women protesting unwanted male sexual advances) would never succeed in justifying the acquittal of bashers and murderers using such a defense (Sedgwick 1990, 19ff).

Just as race is sociocultural and more specifically ideological, so also

20

are the dominant constructions of gender, sexuality, and class. These dominant constructions are, too, involved in a tangle of stereotypes, social pathologies, and unwarranted assumptions. Sociological and biological functionalist explanations are often promoted inside and outside the academy in support of theories of universal female subordination and oppression. The anthropologist Eleanor Leacock played a critical role in revealing that female subordination evolved concurrently with the evolution of human societies into states[10] and more recently with European colonialism and its introduction of capitalist private property (Rapp 1993, 89).[11] In other words, female subordination has not existed since the beginning of time.

There is, then, a chain of oppression deflected downward to whoever falls below in the racist, patriarchal, heterosexist society. One of the interesting features of this chain, not discussed enough, is that it is not unilinear in terms of any one particular category, whether it be race, class, sex, sexuality, or whatever. For example, the offspring of upper-middle-class, urban, college-educated African Americans would normally have better life chances than those of poor, rural whites lacking high school educations. However, of all the categories, gender and race are the most predictive in terms of degree of oppression (defined in terms of income, wealth, and quality of life[12]); even whites belonging to nonracial oppressed groups (e.g., white male *homosexuals*) typically do better than blacks not belonging to those nonracial oppressed groups (e.g., black male *heterosexuals*).

Racism can be defined as behaviors which indirectly or directly support the inequality of racial hierarchy. Racists, in this view, are those who engage in such behaviors, which include (1) supporting racial classification and claiming the biological and/or cultural inferiority of races, (2) supporting any other behaviors that support racial oppression, and (3) not doing anything to stop racism. The third results from the reasoning that if one does nothing to eliminate racism, then the racist status quo will continue that much stronger. It also takes into consideration what is referred to as *privilege*. Privilege is the set of benefits that one gains from the racist status quo: better housing, employment, pay, and education, and so on. Privilege is most revealingly discussed in reference to whites, but it is worth noting that accommodationist individuals of color may also derive privilege from racialized societies as a result of co-optation by the racist power structure. In sum, an individual need never have willfully done anything that directly and clearly oppresses minorities; he or she need only have gone about business as usual without attempting to change procedures and structures, thus becoming an accomplice in racism, since business as usual has been systematized to maintain people of color in an oppressed state (Spears

21

1978, 129–30, after Blauner 1972). Racism, being institutional, is only secondarily about an individual's thoughts and actions; it is primarily about the power relations among hierarchized groups and the way in which those relations permeate social institutions and become an integral part of the social structure.

The notion of "reverse racism" is often used to turn reality on its head, frequently in attempts to discredit affirmative action programs, which recognize that due to the history of oppression of peoples of color and women and the contemporary effects of that oppression, something must be done in an effort to assist in creating a level playing field for members of oppressed groups. It is very important to keep in mind that racism, if the notion is not to be semantically gutted, is related to the maintenance of a racist regime in the context of a racial hierarchy. In other words, racism is prejudice (judging people before one obtains information about them) with power behind it.

The primary problem with most discussions of race and racism is that they do not provide a framework or theory that can offer answers to fundamental questions about race and racism. Fundamental questions such as the following can be reasonably answered if they are posed within the framework of an adequate model of race and racism:

1. Why has the United States not been able to eliminate racism, especially in the post–World War II period, when public pronouncements have stated this as a goal? Observe that racial classification and racism must serve important functions for powerful sectors of American society if they are so tenacious. (The same reasoning applies to other societies.)
2. Why has blatant racism in the form of segregation, lynchings, debt peonage, and so on been on the wane during most of the last sixty years?
3. Why was the Civil Rights movement of the 1950s–1970s much more successful than similar previous movements?
4. Why has the issue of instituting a multiracial category recently become so talked about? Had not the one-drop rule (whereby "one drop of black or African blood" makes one black) already been firmly established? Why did the multiracial category not become an issue in the same way in the 1950s, the 1920s, or the 1840s, for example?
5. Will racism ever be eliminated?

In regard to question (1), white privilege is among the principal reasons why racism is so difficult to eliminate. Privilege is not the sort of thing given up easily. It is also true that racism, as dealt with above, facilitates a divide-and-conquer strategy on the part of elite whites in order to keep people of color and working whites from realizing they could improve their condition by uniting. The history of racism in the United States renders it too handy a lightning rod for white discontent for it to be discarded. Thus, the demonization of African Americans and other people of color goes hand in hand with the exploitation, and, since the Reagan administration, the pauperization of working whites.

Consider also the other functions of racism. Racism provides working whites with a sense of well-being that comes from believing that there will always be a group that is lower on the social scale than they are. Secondly, racism creates a reserve labor pool of blacks and other workers of color who can be fired, or left unemployed, during recessions and depressions, but who during periods of economic boom can be reemployed (Marable 1983).

In regard to questions (2) and (3), racism has been on the wane during most of this period, largely for the same reasons that created the conditions for the relative success of the Civil Rights movement: the increasingly glaring hypocrisy of the United States in claiming to represent democracy while significant segments of its population suffered under the world's worst system of racial oppression after South Africa, whose apartheid was itself inspired by Jim Crow laws in the United States. The competition of the (largely capitalist[13]) United States with the (more) socialist Soviet Union and the socialist bloc for the hearts, minds, and especially resources of nonaligned countries (mostly of color) required that the United States improve its image (Dudziak 1995). Not only did the Civil Rights movement benefit from this rivalry, so also did all working people, including whites, who benefited from improved working conditions and better wages in an effort to buy their allegiance to capitalism. Witness the sharp rise in living standards, especially of whites, after World War II. During that period, wealthy elites were willing to forgo some of their profits in favor of the long-term goal of eliminating socialism (Chomsky 1994). Now that socialism no longer appears to be a viable competitor against capitalism, American power elites assume that working whites can now be safely pauperized again.

Many forget that no aspect of the Civil Rights movement of the 1950s through the 1970s was unique in comparison to earlier ones, except for mass media coverage. Of course, common wisdom is that the mass media played a crucial role: the shock of visual images, for example, of the abuse of blacks mobilized whites who might otherwise have remained quiet. This may indeed have played some role, but the ideological conflict between the superpowers suffices to provide a compelling explanation within the more reliable realm of realpolitik. Moreover, whites enjoyed greater privilege during the Civil Rights

23

movement than they do now. It is quite difficult to understand how screen images might have affected their self-interests as they perceived them. In earlier periods, for example during the Reign of Terror against African Americans in the late nineteenth and early twentieth centuries, many whites had witnessed firsthand atrocities committed against blacks without changing their attitudes.

Lynchings and other forms of physical violence against African Americans were a component of the Reign of Terror, aimed at intimidating freedmen and other African Americans into remaining in often near-slave conditions so that wealthy whites could continue to reap the large profits typical of slavery. The violence, then, was an integral part of the slavery-like system of sharecropping/debt peonage/prison labor. Businesses using prison labor today reap similarly huge profits (Sharff 1995; Buck, in this volume). In brief, some of the more blatant forms of racism have greatly diminished or disappeared because they have been replaced by other institutions that accomplish the same goals.

An additional reason for the difficulty in eliminating racism is that it maintains a tripartite syndrome of oppression, guilt, and fear of reprisal. Concerning fear of reprisal, one of the great contradictions of American society (but in some ways expected) is that whites are generally safer in black neighborhoods than blacks in white neighborhoods. Most bias crimes reported in the mass media are against blacks: in New York City, for example, the Howard Beach and Bensonhurst murders, which were actually lynchings, defined as violent murders (outside of the justice system) with the aim of intimidation and behavior control in support of a racist regime. It is not likely that attacks on whites in black neighborhoods would go unreported. One must read the black press to gain an accurate picture of bias crimes against people of color and lynchings specifically, as they sometimes go unreported or hardly reported in the hegemonic press. An example of this is the Central Park lynching by hanging, perpetrated around the time of the Howard Beach and Bensonhurst lynchings and reported in the *Amsterdam News*, but given only slight, back-page mention in the white press, if any mention at all. In spite of all this, black neighborhoods such as Harlem are demonized by many whites in New York City as places of great danger. An important point in all of this, however, one that is hardly ever discussed, is that in all situations of oppression there lurks in the mind of the oppressor the idea that, if the oppressed ever get the upper hand, they will retaliate in kind. This is one of the great unutterables in discussions of racism. This fear surfaces in contexts where people of color come close to or have control (at least over the short term), as, for example, in black neighborhoods. Consequently, whites' seemingly irrational fear of Harlem is not such a mystery after all. The central point is that the tripartite syndrome of oppression, guilt, and fear of reprisal makes it all the more difficult to eliminate racism, since it is racism that maintains the regime that keeps the oppressed from gaining, not only parity, but also the upper hand, which becomes more readily conceivable once parity is reached.

In regard to question (4), the white media's broad support of multiracialism and nearly absolute silence about the movement to abolish the white race (Ignatiev and Garvey 1996) leads one to suspect a hidden agenda. Multiracialism is a movement apparently led by the offspring of parents of different races. Although the parents can be of any two different races (or perhaps "mixed" themselves), I will simplify the discussion by confining my remarks to black-white multiracialism, and follow the main lines of Harris's (1964) theory on American and Brazilian racial configurations.[14]

First, some background. The United States has historically had an officialized two-way racial system, black and white, with in-between mulatto (i.e., multiracial) groups receiving official recognition only in certain areas during specific periods (notably South Carolina and Louisiana), although of course multiracial people existed all over.[15] It is likely that most, if not virtually all, African Americans are now multiracial. Starting in the colonial period, Britain had a surplus population that migrated in significant numbers to North America, while Portugal and Spain did not. This, along with other factors, led to North America's eventually having a white majority, while Latin America had a white minority. As a rule, three-way racial systems, with blacks, whites, and an in-between mulatto group (used here as a cover term for all people in between black and white), have been found in areas with a white minority. (This situation constitutes what Ali Mazrui in a number of public lectures has called the "Latin racial system," as opposed to the "Anglo-Saxon" one, characterizing North America.) The mulattoes, then, serve as a buffer group. Their existence divides those of color into a series, actually, of graded groups who identify up the social scale toward whiteness and serve mediating political-economic functions (e.g., overseeing slaves and military functions). This arrangement allows a relatively small number of whites to maintain control of a much larger population of color.

In areas such as the United States where there has always been a white majority, a buffer group has not been needed. South Carolina and Louisiana owe their exceptional status to demographics and, in the latter case, French racial traditions in Haiti and Louisiana (which received many refugees from Haiti after the Haitian Revolution). These traditions themselves were influenced by demographics, having been formed in white minority conditions.

As the percentage of whites in the U.S. population decreases, the officialization of an intermediate, buffer group becomes increasingly attractive, and thus the very small multiracial movement has been given an inordinate amount of attention by the media. (There are indications that Hispanics are also being groomed for a buffer role, which most played in their countries of origin.) It seems reasonable to assume that the multiracial movement panders to an insecurity and desire to escape the stigma of being black on the part of some offspring of mixed marriages. This assessment is supported by the fact that blackness has the lowest rank in the racial hierarchy. However, the overall political effect of the movement is to aid in keeping whites as the largest single group, by reducing the black population (see Spears in this volume).

It is very important to observe also that a three-way racial system makes it significantly more difficult to organize blacks (that is, non-whites). This is true because in essence three-way racial systems drastically reduce the number of blacks. Blacks are typically defined in these systems as those who have no "white blood" or no visible effects of it. With the degradation of blackness comes the desire of those who have some white ancestry to claim that ancestry and their status as non-blacks—that is, as mulattoes—if their looks do not allow them to claim whiteness. In other words, societies with three-way racial systems in effect have an informal *reverse one-drop rule*: anyone having one drop of "white blood" is not black.[16] (Again, for simplicity's sake, I consider only the black-white dimension of racial systems.) Consequently, when black groups organize in countries such as Brazil with three-way racial systems, those groups have difficulties recruiting persons who in the United States would clearly be considered black but who in their society are not considered black but mulatto. In the United States, the one-drop rule has the effect of forcing dark- and light-skinned blacks into the same camp. Thus, black civil rights movements in the United States have been overall more successful than their counterparts in Latin America (Winant 1994).

The possible effect of the U.S. multiracial movement's reducing the number of African Americans in future census tallies has important, concrete political consequences since the allocation of resources by the federal government is affected by the number of African Americans in the census count.

Thus, the multiracial movement's actual effect will be to aid in maintaining the racial status quo. It will assist in the maintenance of whites as the largest racial block; it will hinder African-American political and economic organizing; and it will reduce benefits from federal government programs.

The movement's professed goal of making it easier for multiracials to claim and express more than one heritage is ill-conceived at best. First and foremost, the problem with multiracialism is that it conflates race and culture. There is not a one-to-one relationship between race, however construed, and culture. The anthropological tradition since Boas has demonstrated this point repeatedly. One can belong to a single racial category, for example, black, and at the same time identify or claim several cultural heritages. American culture itself, like virtually all cultures, is a blend of heritages. Thus, to believe that the existence of a census category of "multiracial" would facilitate the claim and expression of more than one heritage is patently ridiculous. Second, the great majority of, if not all, blacks are multiracial anyway, as are many whites, by virtue of the one-drop rule and white-looking blacks' passing for white throughout American history and intermarrying with whites. Third, leaders in the multiracial movement are themselves not all offspring of mixed marriages, unless mixed blacks marrying mixed blacks constitutes an interracial coupling and produces multiracial children (i.e., multiracialism is construed as inheritable), as some multiracial people have claimed (Marriott 1996). However, in this situation multiracialism becomes entirely meaningless: it becomes a category that includes nearly all African Americans. These observations indicate that multiracialism is merely a front for the desire to escape the stigma of blackness. One wonders whether multiracial activists believe a new census category will exempt them from police brutality, cross burnings, and lynchings.

The propagandizing of multiracialism dovetails with the historical process of promoting nonwhites to whiteness, which can now be defined as the status of the highest ranking racial group, however that group is defined at a particular historical moment. Irish Americans, Italian Americans, and, later in the post–World War II period, Jews (Sacks 1994) have benefited from promotion to whiteness. These promotions have had the effect of expanding the notion of whiteness and increasing the white population. Furthermore, it should be remembered that *blackness is the extreme otherness in white-supremacist racial iconography.* Thus, the one-drop rule and hypodescent (one inherits the status of the lower status parent) have been applied more rigorously to blacks than to other groups of color, creating a situation in which recently and increasingly Native Americanness and some Asiannesses can be bleached out with repeated intermarriages to whites. Observe that whites can claim to be white and at the same time also claim Native American but not black ancestors.[17] The recentness of and increase in these shifts in genealogical principles point not only to blackness as the negative end of a racialized color scale but also to another means of

27

making whiteness more inclusive and thereby strategically increasing the white population.

The status of blackness was also witnessed in April 1997 when Tiger Woods, the golf champion of African-American and Asian parentage, was insulted by a white golfer shortly after Woods won a major tournament. It is instructive that the white golfer insulted Woods with references to his African-American background, not his other backgrounds. The white golfer's wish was that Woods not select "fried chicken and collard greens" (dishes stereotypically associated with African Americans) for the following year's tournament dinner (which he, as that year's champion, was called upon to select). The white golfer did not mine the many Asian cuisine stereotypes available because the best strategy for a joke (or insult) was blackness, not Asianness, owing to the bottom ranking of blackness in the color hierarchy. The white golfer was also probably operating out of the one-drop rule, whereby "one drop" of "African blood" makes one black. Apparently, when situations heat up, multiracialism socially evaporates.

Additionally, there is a tendency to reify the boundaries among groups of African descent (e.g., Latino African Americans, Caribbean-descent African Americans, and U.S.-descent African Americans) in order to divide groups of color as much as possible. (See Spears in this volume.)

Thus, to answer question (5), in view of all the highly important functions racial categorization and racism play in the maintenance of inequality, increasing ever more dramatically since the collapse of the Soviet Union, one can assume that they will not be eliminated in the normal course of events.

In summary, racial categorization and racism are not superficial aspects of the American social system. They are institutionalized, thus permeating all social institutions. They play a fundamental role in the domination by a small white ruling elite of the mass of working people, both of color and white. Racism sets up people of color as scapegoats. Racism leads many working whites to blame working people of color for whites' economic woes, thus directing their attention away from the real causes of their economic problems. Racism, then, involves a divide-and-conquer strategy: whites and people of color in the subordinated classes generally fail to see their common interests and fail to unite to struggle against their common oppressor. Racism is so hard to eliminate because of its crucial role in maintaining domination and the exploitation that it makes possible. The American Civil Rights movement, unlike earlier pre-1950s movements, was able to rid the United States of some of the more blatant forms of official racism primarily because of the United States' embarrassment, due to official racism (notably racial segregation), in its struggle with the Soviet Union for influence in the Third World, consisting mostly of people of color. This struggle was not merely for hearts and minds, but more importantly for resources, many of them critical for industry in the technologically advanced, wealthiest nations and often not available outside of Africa—or at least not at the bargain-basement prices that have been imposed from outside on African resources. Generally, the more brutal and blatant forms of racism such as segregation, lynchings, and debt peonage have decreased in America, due not only to the effects of the Civil Rights movement, but also due to their replacement by other forms of oppression and exploitation. For example, the Drug War and increasing incarceration and the exploitation of prison labor (see Buck in this volume) substitute for some of the earlier forms of control and exploitation. The promotion of multiracialism in the media is a new kind of divide-and-conquer tactic in the white ruling elite's strategy to create smaller blocks of people of color while attempting to keep the white block as large as possible. White working people are intended to continue in their identification, as members of the same race, with ruling elite whites. It is expected, then, that the media will give no support to whites thinking of themselves as multiracial (e.g., those who have "Native American blood," but are still allowed to consider themselves white) or to the abolish-the-white-race movement. Given the overwhelmingly important function of race and racism in the United States, it is highly unlikely that racism will ever be significantly reduced without a change so fundamental that the nation would not be recognizable as we know it. Racism is the foundation that keeps the entire societal structure from tumbling down. Furthermore, without competition from a rival power such as the former Soviet bloc, the United States becomes ever more powerful and spreads its style of racism globally along with its popular, technological, and business cultures. *America* cannot be America without racism. This should not be taken as cause for despair, but as a call for rethinking the fundamentals of liberation strategies.

IDEOLOGY

Without ideology for the shaping of minds, the American power elite, as with all power elites, would have to rely on brute force (the police, the military, and other institutions and forms of coercion) to uphold a nonegalitarian social structure. (Although professed ideals may be egalitarian, wealth and income distribution, the least egalitarian among the wealthy nations, reveal a reality contrary to ideals.) The use

of force is costly and creates resentments that severely compromise social system stability.

In this collection, the term *ideology* is used in its critical sense. So,
while ideology can be thought of as nothing more than a set of ideas,
the true power of the notion lies in the sense that makes possible explanations of the mechanism of power and oppression. *Ideology* used in this
critical sense refers to a set of ideas that functions to justify and support
vested interests. It can indeed be appropriate to talk about ideologies of
various social classes, but my focus is on ruling class ideology, and unless otherwise indicated, the following discussion pertains to this variety
of ideology alone.

Ideology in this sense is a mechanism for the creation of false consciousness, a thought-limiting system that distorts reality, even though
much of it is based on "objective" facts. The real story, so to speak, is
distorted by strategic emphases and omissions. Ideology's effectiveness
varies according to its social context. It roots itself in the consciousness
of its victims through "continuous repetition, in diverse instrumental
domains, of the same basic propositions regarding the nature of constructed reality" (Wolf 1983, 388). In other words, ideology infiltrates
most of the discourses and images with which we come into contact
through the mass media, education, religion, and corporate-produced
popular culture: television, film, music videos, and so on. Ideology seeks
to naturalize, that is, to make the status quo seem to be the natural
order of things, "common sense," rather than the result of diligent
maintenance. It is boundary defining in the sense that it inhibits the
contextualization necessary for the full apprehension and emancipation-oriented interpretation of reality. A useful example of such failed
contextualization is exemplified in the primary currents of working-
class history in the United States. White workers (with the notable exception of the Wobblies, the Industrial Workers of the World) have
often failed to place their own exploitation within the larger context of
the exploitation of labor in general, including African-American labor.
Consequently, the labor agenda has remained largely within the context
of white labor and has lacked the added support that blacks and other
laborers of color might have provided (Dubofsky 1969; Nonini 1992).
This continues to be true today (Buck 1992).

One is tempted to follow Parsons (1959) in stating that the key to
ideology can be found by contrasting it with science—that is, with what
can be established as factually correct. However, it must be kept in
mind that not everything called science is actually that.

Thus, for example, gender biases in medical research mean that
results considered valid for both males and females are often actually
based on research that has focused primarily on males. In this instance,

the interpretation of scientific research is invalid. It can be seen that more gender-specific research is called for by considering just a few gender differences. For example, women are more likely than men to suffer from phobias, depression, and panic attacks, while men are two to four times as likely as women to abuse alcohol and other drugs and to have an antisocial personality (Raymond 1991). In American society, where men, white men, are for ideological reasons taken as the norm, it is not difficult to attribute the bias in medical research to ideological influences.

Consequently, as Wetherell and Potter (1992, 66) note, science is about interpretation as well as data. Moreover, what counts as acceptable data is a matter of interpretation. With interpretation comes the influence of social positions and vested interests. What qualifies as science in the ideal sense is inescapably problematic, and it is question of degree. Observe also that what may qualify as true can be contingent. For example, qualification based on merit as measured by the same standards for all "can be used to justify the exclusion of black groups from some resources and can also be used to oppose racist practices" (Wetherell and Potter 1992, 70–71). Accepting a science-ideology contrast requires seeing science, as a whole, as a work always in progress, to be evaluated according to its ideological effects. All of this is not to deny, however, that there are areas of science such as mathematics that are relatively free of ideological influences.

Often the (neo-)Marxist view of ideology just presented is critiqued on the grounds that it does not account for the stability of capitalism, or at least capitalism's staying power. For example, in their critique of this view, which they include in what they call "the dominant ideology thesis," Abercrombie and colleagues claim that dominant ideologies do "have significant effects but these are primarily on the dominant rather than the subordinate class" (Abercrombie, Hill, and Turner 1990, 2). The foundation of social stability in the advanced capitalist state is not ideological but economic in character. The commitment of subordinate classes to the system is more a matter of "pragmatic acquiescence" than ideological control. Subordinates have an important material stake in the system, and they receive a "stream of rewards" that raises the cost of replacing it with something else. Also, the complexity of the modern division of labor has created a high level of interdependence among individuals, increasing the costs of insurrection-related disruptions in social and economic life. In sum, the "solidity and coercive quality of everyday life" make it appear that society cannot be changed (Abercrombie, Hill, and Turner 1990, 3–4).

Certainly, pragmatic acquiescence plays an important role in the stability of modern capitalist societies, and there has possibly been a tendency among some (neo-)Marxists to overstate the importance of ideology relative to other factors in the domination of subordinate classes. That pragmatic acquiescence is fundamental, however, is doubtful. First, pragmatic acquiescence itself can be seen as a result of ideology. It results from a certain way of thinking, and that thinking itself can easily be assumed to result at least partially from ideological influences. Second, the stream-of-rewards factor in pragmatic acquiescence is certainly affected by class. Those in the lower layers of society have few rewards, so we must account for why they are not constantly in revolt. The class issue forces us to question and investigate the interrelationships among acquiescence, catalysts for revolt, and revolt itself in all sectors of society, not just classes. Third, upon closer scrutiny, we see that pragmatic acquiescence is actually a less specific form of co-optation and clearly must be studied in relation to more specific means of buying people off. These observations build up to a final one, which is that pragmatic acquiescence must be investigated along with ideology, the use of force, co-optation, and other factors that figure in the maintenance of states. The relative importance of each of these factors varies from society to society. In the final analysis, the torture, killing, jailing, and forced exile of many African-American leaders during the U.S. Civil Rights movement, to consider only one period in one country, support the claim by much of the social science literature that the forceful suppression of dissent is necessary, but not sufficient, for maintaining all state societies.

Social inequality, which results from differential access to resources and is tied to social class stratification, is present in all state societies to varying extents. In all state societies there are at least two distinguishable major classes, each, of course, with internal subdivisions: a ruling class, and a class that is ruled. The ruling class owns or controls the "means of production . . . the means of state administration and coercion[,] . . . and the main means of communication and consent" (Miliband 1987, 329); the ruled class does not.

Admittedly, some social scientists prefer to think of American society as something other than a class system: there is too much social mobility, and there are "too many crosscutting factors like race and region and . . . a lot of self-induced false consciousness about where we would like to think we stand" (Hacker 1991, 46). However, this view merely recognizes class mobility, of which there is only a small amount in the United States and other class societies. This view also fails to take into account the major class distinction, just outlined, between the ruling and the ruled, which is based on objective criteria and cannot be denied by reference to people's self-assessment and reference group. Finally, it must be remembered that the concept of class itself is fundamentally about power conflict among economic groups having different interests. To bring lifestyle, subjective self-assessment, and highly limited social mobility into discussions of class can easily and often does lead to muddying our focus on coercion, domination, privilege, inequality, and exploitation.

Exploitation is the root purpose of class hierarchies and thus always accompanies them. Exploitation is also the purpose of racial and ethnic hierarchies, which have, to varying extents depending on the time and place, a class character. By *exploitation* is meant a situation, characteristic of all class-stratified societies, in which the labor of members of subordinate classes is expropriated. This is the function of class stratification. *Super-exploitation* exists when at least some subordinates are deprived of basic necessities while the ruling class diverts critical resources (e.g., in order to supply itself with luxuries). On the level of the nation-state, exploitation consistently involves both senses of the term.

The fundamental issue in such societies, then, becomes one of how an exploitative social structure can be maintained, assuming quite straightforwardly that the exploited will act to the extent they can or feel they can to end their exploitation, while the ruling sector of a society will act to retain its privileged position. There exists, consequently, in stratified, exploitative societies, an inherent tension based on an ineradicable difference in interests. This inherent tension produces a dynamic that calls forth the application of two major mechanisms in attempts to enforce social system stability: force and cultural domination. These are the twin mechanisms of repression, usefully defined by Wolfe as "a process by which those in power try to keep themselves in power by consciously attempting to destroy or render harmless organizations and ideologies that threaten their power" (Wolfe 1978, 6). It is also important to mention a third mechanism, co-optation, which involves buying off leaders, or potential leaders, of resistance movements with offers of well-paid jobs or other forms of financial reward or prestige. However, co-optation can be seen also as a result of cultural domination, the acceptance by exploited groups of the ideology oppressing them. Co-optation is produced by the *mentality* that leads to an individual's throwing in the towel of resistance and accepting what she or he is given.

By *cultural domination* I mean a situation in which members of a subordinated class have to an important extent accepted the ideology of the ruling class. This term, then, focuses on groups rather than individuals. Reserving the term *internalized oppression* for speaking of individuals assists in making the group-individual distinction. Under these definitions, what has been labeled the *bleaching syndrome* (when a black person denies any connection to other blacks) (White 1991) would be

33

an example of internalized oppression: it is not systematically present in African-American communities; it occurs randomly and rarely throughout them.

Cultural domination focuses not directly on ideology, but on the successful dissemination of ideology in one or more classes whose interests it works against. Clearly, as cultural domination increases, the expensive and relatively inefficient routine use of force becomes less necessary. It becomes possible to distract, confuse, divide, and amuse subordinated groups before their actions make the use of force necessary. Harris provides one type of example, drawing on Wadel (1973):

> The poor or near-poor themselves are often the staunchest supporters of the view that people who really want to work can always find work. This attitude forms part of a larger world view in which there is little comprehension of the structural conditions that make poverty for some inevitable. . . . In a study of a Newfoundland community called Squid Cove, Cato Wadel . . . has shown how a structural problem of unemployment caused by factors entirely beyond the control of the local community can be interpreted in such a way as to set neighbor against neighbor. (Harris 1987, 241)

Ideology is a key factor in the maintenance of oppression, but even more important is its successful dissemination.

As noted above, ideology is a set of ideas of a certain type. Various types of behavior may reflect ideology, but in this view are not part of ideology. One of the crucial issues is this: where does ideology exist, in the mental world or in the world of action? It could be said to exist in both places. It, like language, can be fruitfully thought of as a social conceptual structure, one that exists completely in the mind of no one and is continuously in the process of evolution through actual speech behavior. Ideology underlies thought and ideas actually communicated, and action as well. Similarly, language, the conceptual whole, underlies speech, which is, among other things, action. Even if we can say that in certain societies, state societies, there are ideologies, we cannot say that in those societies there exists a statement of some ideology or set of procedures or recipes for action that when followed would produce some enactment of ideological premises. We would do better to say that thoughts are communicated, actions are taken, rituals are performed, routines are engaged in that generally reflect, that are generally in accord with, a set of ideas and principles that nowhere is stated completely and explicitly. Ideology is derivable from all of these since it depends on them for the definition of its nature; ideology is organic and changes as they change—along with their material context. As language, ideology is some kind of entity, but it is not one that we necessarily must be

34

able to apprehend directly or in its entirety. As language also, it contains competing elements, contradictions, and exceptions; a core of relatively more stable content and a periphery of content more noticeably in flux.

First and foremost there are interests, realized consciously to varying extents by various individuals both inside and outside ruling elites. Then there is social discourse and the sociocultural institutions to which various aspects of social discourse are linked. *Social discourse* can be defined as all that which is typically said in a society, group, or an institutional setting or otherwise communicated, for example, via nonlinguistic communication. Both social discourse and actions will reflect ideology to some extent, but we are still left with the question, where does ideology exist?

However, the appropriate question is actually, how is ideology most usefully conceptualized? If ideology is a set of realized linguistic utterances and nonlinguistic communications, then how are we to determine what is ideological and what is not? I would propose that we do so in a way parallel to the way we decide what utterances are part of English, French, Chinese, or any other language. A language, like an ideology, can nowhere be perceived whole. We assign utterances, that is, speech, to a language, I propose, in the same way we assign linguistic and nonlinguistic behavior to articulated ideologies.

Ideology, then, is a structured set of ideas, certain of which are not directly observable, in much the same way that the system of rules that governs the construction of sentences in a particular language is not directly observable in people's speech. Those governing rules of any language must be inferred from actual speech behavior—both from what is said and from what is not said. In the same way, the governing ideas and principles of ideology must be inferred from what is or is not actually said and done. Such actions and statements and their frequency reflect and provide clues to the underlying ideology. Thus, social discourse (defined as all that is typically said or otherwise communicated) is influenced through its relationship to ideology by the interests of individuals both inside and outside of the ruling elite.

However, ideology does not have exactly the same relationship to social discourse as grammar has to language. While all language, basically, is accounted for by grammar, only some of social discourse is accounted for by ideology. When ideology controls all of social discourse, there exists what Gramsci called *hegemony*, the state of affairs in a society in which one view of reality permeates all institutions and informs all communication (Cammett 1967; Gramsci 1971 [1929–35]). Under hegemony, thus conceived, "consent [is] given by the great masses of the population to the general direction imposed on social life by the dominant fundamental group," the ruling elite (Gramsci 1971 [1929–35], 12). Put another way, and more realistically, this is a situation in which the ideology of the ruling elite has no *viable* competitors (Thompson 1984). Although opposing views are definitely expressed and circulated, they are unable to compete successfully with hegemonic views. Obviously, even under hegemony, there are many social discourses, underlain by diverse ideologies, each linked to its own sector of society. Hegemony, like most situations in the real world, is a matter of degree. Indeed, the picture Gramsci painted shows overly passive subordinate (middle and working) classes and has received considerable criticism (see Scott 1985).

Ideology may be expressed in a variety of ways. I will distinguish between *positing* and *constraining* ideologies. Positing ideologies emphasize stating much of ideology directly. Consequently, ideology is manifested in a relatively direct way; however, this does not imply that the entire content of the ideology is made explicit. Some of that content must be gleaned. By contrast, constraining ideologies emphasize constraining social discourse within certain bounds to which explicit reference is not made.

Chomsky, in contrasting the United States (a "democracy") to the former Soviet Union (a "totalitarian state"), aptly illustrates the distinction:

> A totalitarian state simply enunciates official doctrine—clearly, explicitly. Internally, one can think what one likes, but one can only express opposition at one's peril. In a democratic system of propaganda no one is punished (in theory) for objecting to official dogma. In fact, dissidence is encouraged. What this system attempts to do is to fix the limits of possible thought: supporters of official doctrine at one end, and the critics—vigorous, courageous, and much admired for their independence of judgment—at the other. . . . But we discover that all share certain tacit assumptions, and that it is these assumptions that are really crucial. No doubt a propaganda system is more effective when its doctrines are insinuated rather than asserted, when it sets the bounds for possible thought rather than simply imposing a clear and easily identifiable doctrine that one must parrot. . . . (Chomsky 1977, 39)

So, during the Vietnam War, to take one example, the mainstream press restricted itself largely to a discussion of the strategic pros and cons of the war without questioning the assumption that the United States had the right to intervene in the affairs of an independent country.

Bagdikian (1987) makes revealing comments about the media's role in producing a constraining ideology: "Authorities have always recognized that to control the public they must control information. The

36

initial possessor of news and ideas has political power—the power to disclose or conceal, to announce some parts and not others, to hold back until opportunistic moments, to predetermine the interpretation of what is revealed" (Bagdikian 1987, xviii). Also, "It is a truism among political scientists that while it is not possible for the media to tell the population what to think, they do tell the public what to think about. What is reported enters the public agenda. What is not reported may not be lost forever, but it may be lost at a time when it is most needed" (Bagdikian 1987, xx).

The United States is an example of a nation with a constraining ideology; the former Soviet Union, a positing one. Of course, this passage of Chomsky's appeared in 1977 and could not have taken into account the later initiation of the politics of glasnost, the dissolution of the Soviet Union, and the politics of the various post-Union entities. The Soviet glasnost policy, encouraging more openness in public discussion, seems primarily to have been about shifting to a more constraining type of ideology, one more like those of the United States and the countries of Western Europe and Japan, to support the rush to capitalism of the former Soviet republics. If such is indeed what Gorbachev, his allies, and successors planned, using the United States as their prime model, they did not take into account the fact that the success of American constraining ideology in supporting capitalism is based on a large segment of the population, fully employed whites (and, increasingly, more affluent people of color), having a traditionally high level of material comfort (now deteriorating alarmingly [see Chomsky 1994]); a large array of distracting consumer goods (especially electronic pacifiers of various types); a largely narcotizing public education system; and a centuries-old, inculcated fear and loathing of their principal potential allies: their darker-skinned fellow Americans.

I should emphasize that Chomsky is talking about how ideology is communicated—directly or indirectly—not about ideology itself. Ideology itself, I propose, is most profitably thought of as having two components. One component contains conceptual matter that encapsulates the vested interests of a ruling elite. The basic units of this component are propositions. The other component contains ideas or principles concerning how the conceptual matter is to be most effectively communicated and disseminated. Thus, ideology, thought of in this way, incorporates not only a set of propositions and their evaluation but also a set of directives concerning their dissemination.

The conceptual component of all ideologies has just a few fundamental propositions, which generate all the rest. These fundamental propositions could be stated roughly as follows: (1) things are as they should be (for example, this is the best of all possible countries, or this

37

is the best country that it can possibly be); (2) the ruling class (and their agents) deserves to rule because it is better—stronger, more intelligent, more knowledgeable, more industrious, more attractive, and so on; (3) resistance to the status quo is futile. *Ideology is fundamentally about the maintenance of ruling class power, even in racist societies; it is not fundamentally about maintaining white power.*[18] The second proposition could be seen as generating a more specific one in the U.S. context: politicians (agents of the ruling class who are sometimes members also) deserve to rule because they have been duly elected by the people through democratic process. The key word in this "generated" proposition is *democratic*. This word loses its force under critical examination. Important politicians require campaign financing and generally a nonhostile mainstream press. Both of these requirements typically spell out a dependence on support from the wealthy ruling elite since they largely control the media (Bagdikian 1987) and most of the wealth available for political campaigns. Second, many Americans have been historically and continue to be disfranchised by means of the voter registration process, economic debilitation, strategic voting machine malfunctions, and vote-tally fraud, to mention only a few factors. The "breakdown" of voting machines in black neighborhoods in New York City during Jesse Jackson's presidential campaign is one of the better known instances of these informal means of disfranchisement. The proposition that the ruling class deserves to rule is certainly communicated through many mass media channels, notably television and film. When these screen images are analyzed collectively, they show decidedly more positive images of people most like the ruling elite: white, male, wealthy, Protestant.[19]

Referring back to the discussion of race and racism, we see that the most basic premises underlying American racist ideology historically have not changed, but more superficial ones have, for example, those relating to questions of biological inferiority, the content and hierarchy of racial categories, and overt precepts for the treatment of the various races. The more superficial, but still important, ideological propositions of racial and other ideologies can be linked directly to *regime-maintenance imperatives*, or what is necessary for maintaining a political and economic regime.

I have focused primarily on race, but there are at least two regime-maintenance imperatives in the United States: (1) maintain racial hierarchy (as a means of dividing and conquering) and (2) maintain the illusion of democracy. How this is to be done ideologically during different periods is determined by the complex of international and domestic system features. In the foregoing discussion, a basic change of this type was discussed in terms of a change from racism to neoracism.

It is important to note that regime-maintenance imperatives result from weighing the strands of ideology (racism, sexism, etc.) in order to identify which are crucial. Racism, along with sexism, classism, and heterosexism, is a major ideological strand in the United States.

Challenges to existing regimes cannot be undertaken solely in terms of force, just as regimes cannot be maintained by force alone. There must also be (1) a raising of political consciousness and (2) an understanding of regime-maintenance imperatives, as well as the *basic regime imperative* in the case of any regime: maintain control, where *control* is understood as power and wealth. Any attack on existing regimes must attack primordial regime-maintenance imperatives, in our case, not just racism and the other "-isms" but also, for example, the claim of democracy.

To return to the subject of the ruling elite (variously referred to as the elite, the power elite, the ruling elite, and so forth), one of Alan Wolfe's humorous remarks about them is perhaps the best introduction to the subject: "For amusement, they read books (often written with support from their foundations) which 'prove' that no ruling class exists in the United States" (Wolfe 1978, 57). This remark is helpful in that it gets directly at the idea often repeated in American political science discourse. This discourse claims that there are many countervailing power groups in the United States, producing a situation in which no one group has a decisive hand in running the country. Wolfe denies this claim. In looking for the ruling class, it would be a mistake to focus on those in political decision-making positions; rather, the focus should be "on those whose activities define the parameters of the system and reproduce those parameters on a day-to-day basis" (Wolfe 1978, 55). More specifically, the ruling class comprises the politicized members of the upper class. Furthermore, it is

> composed of no more than a few thousand individuals, nearly all of them living in the Boston-New York-Philadelphia-Washington axis. They are all rich. Nearly all are white Anglo-Saxon Protestants or German Jews. They are all either businessmen or descendants of businessmen. They are born to power and grow up in an atmosphere that cultivates power. They recognize each other, and each of them is fully conscious that he belongs to the ruling class. They are chairmen, directors, trustees, vice-presidents, consultants, partners, secretaries, advisers, presidents, members and relatives. They, in other words, are the "they" that people . . . blame for their troubles. (Wolfe 1978, 57)

But what about the American president, whom most people assume to run the country? Again, Wolfe's comments are particularly apt:

> the power of the presidency is not much greater than the power of the president, while the power of the ruling class is much greater than the

39

power of any single member. The collected membership of the ruling class is instrumental in nominating the president, financing his campaign, aiding in his accession to power, and advising him on policies. Its members not only shape the environment in which he makes his decisions, but they also give him all their help when those decisions have to be made. It is he who is more likely to recognize their power, rather than they who will recognize his. There has been no American president in this century who has crossed the ruling class for any length of time. (Wolfe 1978, 61)

Miliband (1987) provides a somewhat different and in some ways more nuanced view of the ruling class, the "power elite" in his terms, and its relationships with other classes and subclasses. The power elite is the top stratum of the dominant class. It is composed of those who control the few hundred largest industrial, financial, commercial, and media enterprises, along with those "who control the commanding positions in the state system—presidents, prime ministers," and the top civil service, military, and police officials (Miliband 1987, 330). The dominant class, at the top of the social pyramid, and the subordinate class, at near bottom (above the underclass), are the two fundamental classes. The subordinate class comprises the great majority of the population and is composed of working people, who get all of their income from their jobs and/or government transfer programs such as welfare. Between the two fundamental classes is another class, the petty bourgeoisie—small entrepreneurs, semiprofessionals, supervisors, ordinary government officials, and so on, who "too are properly speaking part of the subordinate population of advanced capitalist societies" (Miliband 1987, 333). The bottom layer of the dominant class is the "bourgeoisie," comprising upper-level professionals and mid-tier entrepreneurs. In spite of differences and conflicts among the dominant class,

> they usually remain sufficiently cohesive to ensure that their common purposes are effectively defended and advanced. This is particularly true of the power elite. . . . But all . . . differences and conflicts generally pall into relative insignificance when compared with the vast and crucial areas of agreement. . . . For whereas such people may disagree on what precisely they do want, they very firmly agree on what they do not want and this encompasses anything that might appear to them to threaten the structure of power, privilege and property of which they are the main beneficiaries. (Miliband 1987, 331)

Miliband includes high officials such as the president in the top stratum, the power elite, of the top class, his "dominant class." It appears, then, that for Miliband the ruling class would be his dominant class, the top layer of which clearly does more "ruling." Wolfe's ruling class is not really a class, in the sense that there are persons outside the

40

ruling class who have the same relationship as the ruling class to the means and relations of production in society. Wolfe really pinpoints the ruling elite, the ultimate power group, not a class as such. The real problem in reconciling the two authors' views is deciding whether high officials such as the American president are by virtue of their position alone members of the ruling elite, the very top power group. I mostly agree with Wolfe, but I would caution that membership in the ruling elite is by degree rather than being an all-or-none affair. However, most important is that advanced industrial societies, as with all state societies, do have a ruling elite that is usually able to impose its will on society.

We may characterize the dissemination components of ideologies as primarily positing or constraining, and we may also characterize them according to the preferred institutional channels for the dissemination of ideology. While religion is the most important public institution for the dissemination of ideology in the preindustrial state, the mass media and mass public education are the primary institutions in the mature industrial state. The notions of divine right (to rule) and divine descent, buttressed by religious doctrine, are among the more conspicuous examples of religious concepts supporting the interests of a ruler and the ruling group of which he or she is the outstanding member.

With the rise of industrialization, religion and science come into conflict because the system of criteria for belief underlying each is opposed to that of the other. Science, based on empiricism, inevitably collides with religious doctrine, based on faith. Science is indispensable for the modern, industrial state, whose power and ability to survive in a world of competing nation-states depends on the pursuit of science. Science and the technology it makes possible are required for the production of material goods the state needs, notably armaments. Religion, therefore, must lose when it comes into conflict with science. The two mutually contradictory belief systems cannot both be candidates for full support by the state. The advantage of science over religion is what science, in contrast, makes possible: industrialization, commerce, and technologically adequate military institutions. Religion has therefore been replaced as the primary disseminator of ideology by the mass media and mass public education.

Religion, freed from its service to the state, becomes in reality common property, in a sense, free for all to use and exploit as they may. This, of course, does not happen overnight; rather, it is a gradual process. Thus, religion is subject to "private sector" commercialization, as seen especially in the United States with the hugely profitable religion businesses dealing in Christian televangelical fundamentalism. In educational institutions, a strong effort is made to present science as it is—or as it should be—while the social sciences, humanities, and arts typically have a central concern with indoctrination. While free inquiry and creativity are more encouraged in the sciences, narrowness of focus, disciplinary isolation, and credential fetishism are promoted in the humanities and social sciences, particularly in educational institutions other than elite preparatory schools, colleges, and universities. There is, of course a reason for this distinction between institutions: students at elite institutions, being often of the wealthier classes themselves, have the most to gain from the continuation of the current social order and need to be creative and critically sophisticated in order to assume the leadership positions in society held for them. If the students in elite institutions are not of the wealthiest classes, they are at least in a prime situation to be co-opted into the service of the current social order. Students at nonelite institutions, on the other hand, are typically denied the kind of education that could encourage them to document and question oppression. Their creativity, in other words, is held in check. Chomsky provides a revealing comment on the difference of approach that distinguishes the sciences from other fields of study:

> Compare mathematics and the political sciences. . . . In mathematics, in physics, people are concerned with what you say, not with the certification. But in order to speak about social reality, you must have the proper credentials, particularly if you depart from the accepted framework of thinking. Generally speaking, it seems fair to say that the richer the intellectual substance of a field, the less there is a concern for credentials, and the greater is the concern for content. One might even argue that to deal with substantial issues in the ideological disciplines may be a dangerous thing, because these disciplines are not simply concerned with discovering and explaining the facts as they are; rather, they tend to present these facts and interpret them in a manner that conforms to certain ideological requirements, and to become dangerous to established interests if they do not do so. (Chomsky 1977, 7)

LANGUAGE, SYMBOLISM, AND POPULAR CULTURE

The chapters of this book all deal with race and ideology and to varying extents language and symbolism also. The chapters in part 1 take up linguistic, symbolic, and institutional manifestations of race, racism, and ideology. In part 2, the chapters highlight language, symbolism, and ideology as they are intertwined in popular cultural forms that are highly revealing in racial matters. Race is construed in the larger sense that deals with the negative categorizations and hierarchies of the world's peoples based on color and other physical traits. Not all of the groups

42

discussed would think of themselves as a separate "race." Nevertheless, their physical traits, their nonwhiteness, combined with their social history, places them in a disadvantaged position in an increasingly globalized hierarchy of color. Their lifeways unfold in a racialized context; their grouphood is symbolically encoded in racial iconography.

Symbolism in this volume is used in the sense of *nonlanguage* objects, images, and actions that convey meaning that is not inherent in them; they stand for something other than themselves, although what they stand for may well have something to do with their nature. For example, images of blacks in films may communicate subordination, but that subordination is not typically inherent in the images. We are able to attach a meaning of subordination to the images primarily because of the way in which they pattern with respect to one another and because of our knowledge of the sociocultural context of the films, and film itself as an institution. *Popular culture* in these pages refers to cultural products produced for people with whom one has face-to-face relationships and also to what is sometimes referred to as mass culture (Lazere 1987), cultural products for the consumption of mass audiences, distributed through mass media. Consequently, popular culture may have the cultural specificity that is expected in grassroots cultural production, that is, specificity with regard to a particular cultural group such as African-American teenagers in a certain city or African Americans in the northeast. Rap spans both senses of popular culture, but television and film products, of course, are normally produced for mass audiences.

Of the chapters in part 1, those by Spears, Gilliam, Dejean, and Baker investigate language primarily. Hancock exposes externally imposed symbolism on group identity, examining how a group of people, Gypsies (or the Rom, as many prefer to be called), can become symbolic of constructs hardly related to them at all, but fulfilling needs of others. We often find discussions of such symbolic distortion in relation to blacks, Hispanics, Native Americans, and Asians, but seldom do we encounter discussions of subordinate groups such as Gypsies, who have been symbolically banished from the everyday world of work, leisure, and striving to a costumed, carefree shadow world of nomadism and trickery.

In the first of the chapters on language, I deal with how the teaching of language and culture can be used as a forum for combating views of language that support subordination. I use that discussion to put the Ebonics controversy of 1996–97 into context. Baker examines the subtle ways in which (racial) group power relations are reflected in everyday office speech patterns involving forms of address. Gilliam looks at language as resource or hindrance in a developing country. In her chapter, race is the backdrop: she treats a people of color attempting to

43

recover from the trials of colonialism and a contemporary world order structured by a very real color hierarchy. With Gilliam's and Dejean's chapters, it becomes clear that language is usually an issue in developing countries in a way that it is not in wealthy nations such as the United States: the struggle for linguistic equity has extremely important consequences for political and economic development.

I deconstruct terms like *minority* that have much more ideological content than is commonly realized. I show how the study of language, which must be contextualized, can lead students to a critical understanding of their condition and that of their people in society. There are three basic points that students must grasp. First, the prestige of a language or dialect depends on political and/or economic factors, not on any kind of grammatical superiority—for indeed, there is no sense in which one language can be grammatically superior to another. Second, language attitudes are essentially attitudes about people. Thus, the Ebonics controversy was really a masked discourse about blackness, in which derogatory statements that could not be made directly about blacks were made about the language of black people. Third, languages are not simply tools; they are resources. Practically all languages are acquired in a natural context (i.e., growing up in a particular community). Each comes attached to a specific worldview, embedded, so to speak, in what the speakers of that language typically use it to say. One task for students of language and society is to study the languages of oppressed groups in order to discover the discourses to which they are linked, and to locate and amplify those parts of the discourses that can be used in liberation.

Gilliam deals with language and ideology in Papua New Guinea, whose citizens are a people of color. She deals with gender also in her discussion of young male Pure Motu speakers who have attempted with their string bands to adapt traditional culture to modern cultural forms. As English becomes the language of economic development, which, she correctly notes, is not in line with national interests but instead the interests of multinational corporations, there is a corresponding lack of development in the vocabulary of indigenous languages. This "lexical arrest" in indigenous languages corresponds to technological arrest in development for national needs. She makes clear, by implication, that those who select the language of development, that is, true economic development that is in the interest of the country's population, can ill afford to take their task lightly. Implicit in her chapter also is the statement, after Calvet (1974), that language is both superstructure and base, it is a part of the ideological apparatus of the state and the means of production. (See also Devonish 1986; Gal 1989.) Finally, the situation in Papua New Guinea involves ideologies of language (see Woolard and Schieffelin 1994) of a type commonly seen in developing nations of people of color.

Dejean takes a fresh approach to the question of which language should be used as a medium of instruction in Haiti. Both Creole and French are spoken, Creole by all, French by a tiny minority elite. Yet, instruction has been entirely or mostly in French throughout Haitian history, though during the past two decades significant teaching in Creole has begun in public schools. Should the medium of instruction be the child's native language or one she or he arrives at school unable to speak? Common sense tells us that it should be the native language, but a strong trend in language research informs us that in underdeveloped countries such as Haiti, another language is better. In the Haitian case, French, an international language, a "window on the world," is prescribed, when what Haitians actually need is a window on strategies for internally oriented development aimed at putting an end to the misery of its people. Dejean points out that, although experiments have shown that schoolchildren can be introduced to literacy through a nonnative language (in conjunction with use of their native language or not), can learn it, and can go on to perform well academically, it is imperative that the native language be used in order to achieve *mass* literacy. He notes that there have been examples throughout history of elitist educational systems that have provided literacy through instruction in a foreign language, but no mass educational institution has produced *mass* literacy through the use of a foreign language. So, while it is repeatedly recommended that Third World countries use a foreign language in attempts to achieve mass literacy, no one has ever suggested that the developed countries of North America and Europe, for example, use a nonnative language. It is also worth noting that the small countries of Europe, such as Finland and Denmark, maintain their native languages, even though there is widespread use of a second, "world" language or at least one of wider communication.

Wherever mass literacy has been achieved—for example, Cuba, Nicaragua, the Soviet Union, and the United States—the native language of the vast majority of schoolchildren has been the medium of instruction. I hasten to point out that Dejean does not present arguments against bilingual education per se. Rather, he argues against requiring the many Third World children who do not have access to special resources to learn to read and write in a language other than their native tongue. Once they have achieved literacy, of course, they can go on to acquire another language. Many people of color in developing nations encounter the same kind of problem in achieving literacy and continuing their education. Thus, the problems of Haiti and Papua New Guinea are widespread.

Hancock's chapter deals with symbolism and social group identity. It concentrates on the symbolic function of an oppressed group in American society: the Rom, better known as Gypsies. Hancock's remarks on Gypsies recall statements that have been made in relation to several other oppressed, nonwhite groups, notably blacks in the United States. He duly notes the symbolic function of the Gypsy myth, which has little if anything to do with the real people. That myth, rather, serves to define them as scapegoats and to define the oppositional other—all that non-Gypsies are not or should not be. James Baldwin, the African-American writer, stated in much of his nonfiction that a primary symbolic function of U.S. blacks is to define the bottom of the social barrel. Blacks serve to define the bottom level, to which every white can feel fortunate for not having sunk, and in so doing help to perpetuate the fiction that being oppressed is a purely black affair (or one of blacks and other oppressed groups). Hancock's chapter reminds us that oppressed groups have symbolic (and ideological) functions in addition to any economic functions they may have.

In his chapter, Baker asks fundamental questions concerning the relationship between diversity and equality, on the one hand, and cultural patterns and power, on the other. With integration, is there a combining of the cultures of the groups integrated or does the subordinate group assimilate to the culture of the dominant one? In situations where African Americans and whites are integrated, there is generally an unstated assumption that blacks will assimilate to the cultural patterns of whites, the power group. However, sometimes that does not happen. Baker first outlines differences in white and African-American address patterns and then looks at the maintenance of African-American patterns in order to understand how their maintenance is related to the challenging or contestation of power in an entire institution.

Buck's chapter, analyzing the institution of prison labor, treats language and symbolism, but most importantly dissects racism in a growing institution that reflects ominous trends in both the domestic and international business and governmental sectors. Buck makes the telling point that hegemonic discourse on prison labor in the United States is intended to produce the comfortable illusion for those on the outside that prisoners generally deserve to be in prison and benefit from the experience. One of the great ironies of the prison system is its creation of a domestic Fourth World (captive) labor source whose pitifully low wages, minuscule rate of absenteeism, and low rate of drug use make it more attractive than Third World labor. Prison labor, ironically, also takes jobs from whites (and workers of color) on the outside, significant numbers of whom ironically favor higher incarceration rates over the establishment of social and educational programs (if indeed they have the relationship between the two strategies clearly in mind). Obtaining near-slave labor through the penal system is an old American tradition. During Reconstruction and afterward, vagrancy and other types of laws were designed especially for the purpose of indiscriminately jailing blacks. Once in jail or prison, they were leased, whether in chain gangs or otherwise, to plantation owners and other businesspeople at minimal prices. The prison system played a major institutional role in supplying captive black labor that worked under slave conditions. There is strong evidence that today profitability is one of the main reasons for the increase in prison labor.

Buck observes that prison labor cannot be fully understood unless it is related to the racist policies of the U.S. Drug War, which, among other things, criminalizes crack cocaine much more so than the powdered form of the drug. It is also important to observe that high drug use in U.S. inner cities creates in those communities a high level of political passivity and disorganization, making difficult the kind of activism necessary to improve overall conditions there. The domestic Drug War and the increase in prison labor are also related to the international drug war, notably as it unfolds in Latin America, where U.S. agents, U.S.-supported regimes, and revolutionary groups intervene in the drug trade in the pursuit of their own agendas. The drug trade is also used in some cases as a cover for American military involvement in the internal politics of foreign countries. An understanding of prison labor and all of its ramifications is crucial for understanding not only race relations in the United States, but also the evolution of the U.S. economy and the interconnections among the drug trade, prisons, labor relations, U.S. foreign policy, and the shaping of racist discourses and practices for the purpose of control. These interconections may well foreshadow what we can expect to see more of in the future.

The chapters in part 2 look at television, film, and rap. The chapters on television and film examine the content and function of ideology as it is structured into screen products with characters of color and women. The history of stereotyping African Americans and other people of color in television and film is rather well known. Bogle (1973) speaks of five basic black stereotypes in film: toms, coons, mulattoes, mammies, and bucks. The classic tom—servile, docile, avuncular, and asexual—is Uncle Tom of Harriet Beecher Stowe's antislavery novel *Uncle Tom's Cabin*. The model coon is impossibly simpleminded, clownish, and cowardly; Stepin Fetchit comes to mind. Mulattoes are typically female and tragic, the only stock female black character allowed sexual allure—of a kind that positions her to be a white man's throwaway mistress or a counterfeit white lady of leisure. The female protagonist who passes for white in *Imitation of Life* exemplifies a person of

47

this type. Mammies are fat, dark-skinned, older, and enamored of hectoring black people and mothering whites. Hattie McDaniels, the black actress who preferred to play a maid rather than be one, played the mammy role in *Gone with the Wind*, although she managed to bring a modicum of dignity to the part. Bucks epitomize the stereotype of the irrational, penis-driven, hypersexual black male. The most notorious early version of this type was the Negro character who raped a white woman in Eisenstein's filmic paean to white supremacy, *Birth of a Nation*.

Bogle (1991) later added to his list the asexual (or nearly so) sidekick-buddy, a type that has been popular since the onset of racial integration in the 1950s (see also Tasker 1993, chap. 2). Bill Cosby in the television drama series "I Spy" fits this role. The main black character discussed in Abalos's chapter presents an updated version of this type—he does have a sex life, but is unequivocally the junior buddy in terms of actions and imagery. A subtype of this sidekick-buddy type (or the mammy type—take your pick) is the mammy-buddy, an older, fat, sex-appealless (within conventional standards) black man who helps and nurtures a younger, "sex object," white male hero. The original *Die Hard* has this subtype on display. The *Lethal Weapon* series of films does also, but the black actor Danny Glover's role in these films is a "cleaned up" version of this type: only the helping and nurturing remain for the most part, but there is as always an aura of irresistible sexual and combative potency about the white star, while the black one is subtly disrespected and feminized (patriarchy's deepest insult). In one of the *Lethal Weapon* movies, Glover is required to sit gingerly, pants down, on a bomb-rigged toilet, while the white buddy bemusedly goes about rescuing his mammy-buddy in distress. The most extreme example I have seen of the feminization of black men occurred in an episode of the television miniseries "Rich Man, Poor Man," in which a very large, heavily muscled black character is sexually molested by a slightly smaller white villain, after which Nick Nolte's character, a noticeably shorter and slimmer white man (and ex-boxer, for what it's worth), avenges his black buddy.

Other people of color do not fare better. From patriarchal white supremacy's bottomless reservoir of disrespect come humiliating roles such as Tonto, the subservient Indian; Gunga Din, the native itching to serve and die for whites; the China doll, who has the same structural position to white men as the (female) mulatto and thus appears unable to focus on men of her own group, what with all the white adventurers passing through, foraging for receptacles to catch their excess body fluids; and the accented, drug-dealing Hispanics frequently appearing in police and action-adventure dramas.[20]

Abalos, writing on the classic television cop-buddy drama series "Miami Vice," includes a treatment of the representation of a gay man in relation to issues of masculinity. "Miami Vice" has been much applauded for its trend-setting role in television. However, Abalos concludes that the 1980s series was formally novel but in terms of content simply a more sophisticated re-presentation of the premises underlying hegemonic discourse in the United States. She looks at issues relating to sexuality, male and female roles, ethnic casting, and others, demonstrating how contextualization not only makes the meaningful and useful interpretation of screen images as symbols possible, it also allows us better to isolate those units of communication that are indeed symbolic and therefore subject to interpretation. Abalos provides striking informal illustrations of how various qualitative and quantitative approaches to the analysis of symbolic content can reveal what otherwise might remain beneath the level of awareness.

In his reading of the film *New Jack City*, Whylie reveals, with perhaps distressing clarity, how white supremacy infects the minds of those who suffer from it and becomes the mutant virus of colorstruction. This term was formed on analogy with *colorstruck*, the African-American English adjective for people of color (not just African Americans) who at least sometimes show preferences for more "white-looking" people over more "African-looking" people (Spears 1992). I prefer the term *colorstruction* to *colorism* because of this and because of its evocation of *obstruction*, which is what colorstruction is on the road to equality. The most easily accessible example of colorstruction is the before-camera staff at Black Entertainment Television (BET), which is ironically much more allergic to dark-skinned and "African-looking" television personalities than any of the other networks, except, of course, the Hispanic ones, which are draconian in their degradation and marginalization of the dark-skinned Hispanic world.

New Jack City, produced by African Americans with creative control, shows cultural specificity. Other things being equal, "members of a cultural group will produce more compelling cultural products for members of that same group than will an outsider" (Spears 1992, 26). The notion of cultural specificity ties in with that of *redissemination*, which refers to members of an oppressed group incorporating elements of the ideology used against them into the products they create. Redissemination in the typical case is more potent than mere dissemination (by members of the oppressing group) because it will have more cultural specificity: it will be more compelling because of its resonance with the audience's experiences. It is chilling that even African-American filmmakers considered progressive are perpetrators of redissemination, no doubt unawares. Whylie's contribution comes to us in good

49

time. Colorstruction in all communities of color needs to be thoroughly examined in an intense project of continuing culture critique.

Yasin's chapter looks into rap. He exposes the hegemonic media's distortion of the nature and range of artistic production included within rap. The media seem to focus on those types of rap having "gangsta" motifs and uncensored language, usually referred to as profanity or obscenity and seldom understood (see Spears 1998). He notes that rap's beginnings are connected to the Black Power Movement of the Civil Rights era and that it is probably the most vibrant and potent form of grassroots black culture today (also, of course, disseminated though the mass media). These two traits have figured prominently in the internationalization of rap, playing a role in a variety of countries as a model for structures that can serve local, popular cultural production oriented toward liberation. By placing rap, a kind of information mass medium, within the history of the African-American music tradition, Yasin illustrates the continuity, adaptability, and functionality of black culture as well as its historical role in critiquing American society.

Television and film cannot be mentioned without bringing up the important issue of neoracist symbolism in these media. In this connection, it is first necessary to separate language from symbolism and then to separate categorical symbolic patterns from variable ones. A categorical pattern of symbolism is a group of symbols (in television and film, usually images) that all receive basically the same interpretation. For example, if *all* Latinos in a film are presented as unpleasant-looking villains, we then have categorical symbolism; all individual instances in the pattern are negative. If some of the individual instances of a particular pattern, or group of symbols, are positive, while the rest are negative, then we have an example of variable symbolism. Variable symbolic patterns, then, are quantitative. Only a certain percentage of the images have a particular evaluation. Crude, categorical negative symbolism is in effect a slur, an ethnic or racial slur if it involves an ethnic or racial group. Typically, variable symbolism is not received as a slur by audiences because it is much more subtle. Categorical negative symbolism is akin to a spoken slur. In narrative television programs (dramas, comedies—those with a story line) and movies, there are virtually no spoken slurs against African Americans, to take one group as an example. Nor are slurs communicated through categorical symbolism.

However, slurs are communicated through variable symbolism in most television and film products. Some black characters are presented as negative, but some positive ones are presented also and stand ready to serve as counterexamples to any accusations of racism or ethnic misrepresentation.

As a result, one often leaves a movie or comes away from a television program feeling a vague sense of dissatisfaction or discomfiture; or, one may come away feeling that nothing worth commenting on or reacting to has occurred. The second reaction is perhaps the more common and simply underlines the effectiveness of variable symbolism in the maintenance and reinforcement of ideas and the cultural hegemony of which they are a part.

A relevant example of variable symbolism comes from films of the action/adventure genre, typified by movies over the past fifteen years or so starring Sylvester Stallone, Chuck Norris, and Arnold Schwarzenegger, who seems to be the worst offender in this regard. In each of these films, besides the star, there is an array of good characters and villains. One notes that some of the good characters are black,[21] some white; some of the villains are black, some white. However, as many moviegoers are increasingly realizing, even though there are both black and white villains, the worst villain is often black, and accordingly dies the most horrible or violent death. From the standpoint of gore, this villain's death may even be one of the film's showpieces, as is the case in one of Arnold Schwarzenegger's films, *Commando*, in which the black, primary villain, who is also the black in the film with the darkest skin and the most stereotypically black facial features, meets his horrible fate by falling a story or two onto the sharp projectile of a huge machine. The projectile pierces the middle portion of his upper torso, causing an eruption of blood. This was all to the delight of the audience that witnessed this scene when I saw it. (Roughly half of the audience seemed to be African American. In any case, about three-fourths of the audience was non-white, probably mostly American and Caribbean blacks and Hispanics.) Sometimes, it is a good black character who dies a notably horrible death (at least the character is "good" at the time of his death). An example is what happens to Apollo Creed, the black boxer character in Stallone's *Rocky* films. In one of them, Creed is bludgeoned with unusual viciousness in the ring, blood and sweat flying from his body, and dies as a result.

These films as a group seem to have achieved a way of killing two birds with one punch: they pander to the racism of mostly young adult white audiences by furnishing them scenes of violence, included among them vicious killings of blacks; and they pander to similar black audiences by presenting them with some kind of black role model (though definitely less heroic than the white star) as well as heaping quantities of violence. It would appear that makers of this genre of film have discovered—and knowingly use—a viciously racist hook for white audiences that will get past black audiences.

This kind of neoracist symbolism does not flaunt itself. It slips into the consciousness of many of those who view it, simply because it is not blunt enough to be regularly detected. Most important is that such subtle, variable symbolism makes possible the perpetuation of negative stereotyping without significant resistance from the ethnic group negatively affected by it, a group that may otherwise be active in campaigning against defamation. But such campaigns are launched against only defamation by language and through categorical or near-categorical symbolic defamation.

Neoracist negative symbolism, of a variable nature, nourishes among blacks the seeds of self-hate planted continually by an institutionally antiblack society and, among whites, nourishes the white supremacy that promotes the power of a very small ruling elite. The symbolism of the media, not just their language, need to be subjected to constant, conscious interpretation. In a neoracist environment, critique must be based on qualitative and quantitative decoding in order to reveal the media's ideological function. So long as this function remains hidden, it will continue to help maintain differential access to wealth and power, the central reason for the existence of racial categorization and racism.

Notes

1. Du Bois (1969 [1935]) is apparently the first social scientist who realized this and documented it. His work, like that of other independent-thinker scholars of color (and like-thinking whites), has been marginalized in mainstream U.S. academic and intellectual circles.

2. The following works, which are only a few among many, give some idea of the diversity of frameworks and perspectives in circulation: Allen 1994; Bell 1992; Delgado 1995; Montagu 1942; Shanklin 1994; Wallace 1992; Grossberg et al. 1992; hooks 1992, 1994; van Dijk 1993; Diawara 1993; Grimshaw 1992; Marable 1983, 1995; Minority Rights Group 1995; Omi and Winant 1986; Reynolds and Lieberman 1996; Roediger 1991; Smedley 1993; Harris 1964; Wetherell and Potter 1992; Gregory and Sanjek 1994; Smitherman-Donaldson and van Dijk 1988; Tobach and Rosoff 1994; West 1993; Harrison 1991; and *Transforming Anthropology* 5. Du Bois 1969 [1935]; Drake 1987, 1990; *Transforming Anthropology* 2.1 and 3.1; and Blauner 1972 are only a few examples of works mentioned above and others that do attempt to place their discussions within the larger context.

3. Ethnicity is not seen as necessarily involving genetically determined physical characteristics; rather, it is in theory based on the common heritage of a group: shared history, language (which may not be unique to a particular ethnic group), regional origin, and culture. It must be emphasized also that ethnic notions are tied to the position of groups in a social hierarchy and the ideology that assists in propping up the hierarchy. Different ethnic groups can be represented in the same (socially constructed) race and vice versa. See Williams 1989 and Mullings 1978.

4. Most accounts of race in this area focus on the buffer status of the Chinese

Americans (e.g., Loewen 1988). In at least some areas during certain periods, Chinese Americans and African Americans had the same status. Offspring of mixed, Chinese-African-American marriages were considered black, but sometimes passed for Chinese American when and where it was advantageous (personal communication, Rutherford Birchard Edwards, my stepfather, born in 1894, who grew up in the area).

5. This resistance takes both physical and cultural forms. In regard to the latter, see, for example, Guthrie 1996, which discusses African Americans in the Sea Islands.

6. During the 1970s in Kinshasha and other Congolese cities, there was a wave of skin bleaching by women that had several disastrous consequences, one being that it destroyed the skin's elasticity, resulting in the death in childbirth of some who had practiced it.

7. Some biologists, geneticists, and others in the life sciences claim to use the term *race* in the sense of *population* (as characterized herein), and others use *population* merely to resurrect the concept of race.

8. See Marks 1998 and Goodman 1998 for short, excellent reviews of issues concerning biology vs. environment and life experience. They explain why scientists using racial categories produce bad science and thus inhibit deeper understandings.

9. The term *civilization* is not currently used judgmentally in the social sciences. It simply refers to a society with specific traits, namely cities and all they imply.

10. *State* is the term used by most anthropologists to refer to societies with the prominent features of cities, including social stratification involving elites and subordinated groups, occupational specialization, and permanent governmental and bureaucratic institutions.

11. Leacock's oeuvre comprises numerous publications. See Sutton 1993 for a bibliography.

12. In terms of economics, there is strong evidence that sexism is more oppressive than racism. Black males do better than white females in terms of income and earnings. For example, the 1992 median income and earnings of employed black men were $22,369, while for employed white women they were $21,659 (Hacker 1995, 100). When quality of life issues, including health care, are considered, it is harder to tell since quality of life is often difficult to measure and is subjectively determined.

13. The United States has some socialist institutions such as Social Security and welfare, though they would never be called what they are because of socialism's bogeyman status in the United States.

14. See Winant 1994 for a discussion of Brazil's racial struggles during the past decades.

15. The federal census category of mulatto, abandoned in the early twentieth century, did not necessarily reflect local laws and social practices.

16. I am indebted to Charles Hamilton Townsend for stressing this point to me.

17. Ironically, blackness represents extreme otherness and the lowest status in U.S. white-supremacist racial iconography (as indicated by considerations under discussion), but in reality blacks (i.e., African Americans) do not occupy the bottom of the political-economic scale (in terms of per capita income and wealth and other such measures). Native Americans do, and so also do such other groups as Puerto

Ricans and Dominicans. It appears that few U.S. residents are aware of this, due no doubt to the symbolic status of various racial groups. Of course, ranking these (shifting) groups economically or otherwise is fraught with difficulties because some Native Americans, Puerto Ricans, and Dominicans situationally identify as black.

18. Another down to earth way of saying this is that if a group of black humans arrived from outer space with unprecedented wealth and technological power and took over the earth, white elites in Europe, the United States, and elsewhere, once they decided that the new power group was here to stay and that resistance was futile, would start intermarrying (the new power group permitting) with the new power group in order to conserve as much of their power as possible and to insure the elite status of their offspring. Notice also that the new black ruling elite would probably do as such new elites have done throughout history: intermarry with the old elite in order to quickly solidify their power and thereby save expense in putting down rebellions.

19. Students in my television and film courses have done papers actually demonstrating this by analyzing quantitatively the social characteristics of characters and then rating those characters on a positive/negative scale based on how an audience would rate them in terms of other attributes such as looks, personality, sexual allure, possessions, character, morals, leadership, and so on. Most people would expect nonwhites to fare much worse than whites, and they do. What is somewhat surprising is how much worse southern European/Mediterranean (i.e., swarthy or darker-skinned) non-Protestant whites do in comparison to northern European (fairer), Protestant types.

20. See Parenti 1992 for detailed discussions of the stereotyping of groups of color, white "ethnics," and the white working class. See Russo 1987 on the stereotyping of (mainly white) gays and lesbians in film.

21. Sometimes, none of the good characters are black, as, for example, in *Total Recall*, the Arnold Schwarzenegger science-fiction vehicle, where the most positive black character is an air-brained receptionist. The others are an assortment of prostitutes, mutants, and other underworld types.

References

Abercrombie, Nicholas, Stephen Hill, and Bryan S. Turner, eds. 1990. *Dominant ideologies*. London: Unwin Hyman.

Allen, Theodore W. 1994. *The invention of the white race*. Vol. 1, *Racial oppression and social control*. New York: Verso.

Bagdikian, Ben H. 1987. *The media monopoly*. 2d ed. Boston: Beacon Press.

Baker, Lee D., and Thomas C. Patterson. 1994. Race, racism, and the history of U.S. anthropology. *Transforming Anthropology* 5(1 and 2):1–7. (Special issue on Race, racism, and the history of U.S. anthropology.)

Bell, Derrick. 1992. *Faces at the bottom of the well: The permanence of racism*. New York: Basic Books.

Bennett, Lerone Jr. 1987. *Before the Mayflower: A history of black America*. New York: Penguin Books.

Blauner, Robert. 1972. *Racial oppression in America*. New York: Harper & Row.

Bogle, Donald. 1973. *Toms, coons, mulattoes, mammies, and bucks: An interpretive history of blacks in American films.* New York: Viking

————. 1991. *Toms, coons, mulattoes, mammies, and bucks: An interpretive history of blacks in American films.* 2d ed. New York: Continuum.

Buck, Pem Davidson. 1992. With our heads in the sand: The racist right, concentration camps, and the incarceration of people of color. *Transforming Anthropology* 3(1):13–18. (Special issue on Teaching as praxis: Decolonizing media representations of race, ethnicity and gender in the New World Order.)

Calvet, Louis-Jean. 1974. *Linguistique et colonialisme: Petit traité de glottophagie.* Paris: Payot.

Cammett, John. 1967. *Antonio Gramsci and the origins of Italian communism.* Stanford, Calif.: Stanford University Press.

Chomsky, Noam. 1977. *Language and responsibility.* Based on conversations with Mitsou Ronat, trans. from the French by John Viertel. New York: Pantheon Books.

————. 1994. *The prosperous few and the restless many.* An interview by David Barsamian. Berkeley, Calif.: Odonian Press.

Curtis, L. P. Jr. 1968. *Anglo-Saxons and Celts: A study of anti- Irish prejudice in Victorian England.* Bridgeport, Conn.: Conference on British Studies at the University of Bridgeport. Cited in Shanklin 1994.

Delgado, Richard, ed. 1995. *Critical race theory: The cutting edge.* Philadelphia: Temple University Press.

Devonish, Hubert. 1986. *Language and liberation.* London: Karia Press.

Diawara, Manthia, ed. 1993. *Black American cinema.* New York: Routledge.

Drake, St. Clair. 1987, 1990. *Black folk here and there.* 2 vols. Los Angeles: Center for Afro-American Studies; University of California, Los Angeles.

Dubofsky, Melvyn. 1969. *We shall be all.* Chicago: Quadrangle Books.

Du Bois, W. E. B. 1961 [1903]. *The souls of black folk.* Greenwich, Conn.: Fawcett Publications.

————. 1969 [1935]. *Black reconstruction in America, 1860–1880.* New York: Atheneum.

Dudziak, Mary L. 1995. Desegregation as a Cold War imperative. In Delgado 1995, 110–21.

Fanon, Frantz. 1968 [1961]. *The wretched of the earth.* Trans. by C. Farrington. New York: Grove.

Forbes, Jack D. 1988. *Black Africans and Native Americans: Color, race and caste in the evolution of red-black peoples.* New York: Blackwell.

Gal, Susan. 1989. Language and political economy. *Annual Review of Anthropology* 18:345–67.

Giddings, Paula. 1994. Black males and the prison of myth. *New York Times,* 11 September, 50.

Gilliam, Angela. 1992. Toward a new direction in the media "war" against drugs. *Transforming Anthropology* 3(1):19–23 (Special issue on Teaching as praxis: Decolonizing media representations of race, ethnicity and gender in the New World Order.)

Goodman, Alan H. 1998. The race pit. *Anthropology Newsletter* 39 (5) (May): 52, 50.

Gouldner, Alvin W. 1976. *The dialectic of ideology and technology: The origins, grammar, and future of ideology.* New York: Oxford University Press.

Gramsci, Antonio. 1971 [1929–35]. *Selections from the prison notebooks of Antonio*

Gramsci. Ed. and trans. by Quintin Hoare and Geoffrey Nowell Smith. New York: International Publishers.

Gran, Peter. 1994. Race and racism in the modern world: How it works in different hegemonies. *Transforming Anthropology* 5(1 and 2):8–14. (Special issue on Race, racism, and the history of U.S. anthropology.)

Gregory, Steven, and Roger Sanjek, eds. 1994. *Race*. New Brunswick, N.J.: Rutgers University Press.

Grimshaw, Anna, ed. 1992. *The C.L.R. James reader*. Cambridge, Mass.: Blackwell.

Grossberg, Lawrence, Cary Nelson, and Paula Treichler, eds. 1992. *Cultural studies*. New York: Routledge.

Guthrie, Patricia. 1996. *Catching sense: African American communities on a South Carolina Sea Island*. Westport, Conn.: Bergin & Garvey.

Hacker, Andrew. 1991. Class dismissed. *New York Review of Books* 38(5):44–46.

———. 1995 [1992]. *Two nations: Black and white, separate, hostile, unequal*. Expanded and updated. New York: Ballantine Books.

Hancock, Ian. 1986. *The pariah syndrome: An account of Gypsy slavery and persecution*. Ann Arbor, Mich.: Karoma.

Harris, Marvin. 1987. *Cultural anthropology*. 2d ed. New York: Harper and Row.

———. 1964. *Patterns of race in the Americas*. New York: Walker and Co.

Harrison, Faye V., ed. 1991. *Decolonizing anthropology: Moving further toward an anthropology for liberation*. Washington, D.C.: American Anthropological Association.

———. 1995. The persistent power of "race" in the cultural and political economy of racism. *Annual Review of Anthropology* 24:47–74.

Herman, Edward S., and Noam Chomsky. 1988. *Manufacturing consent: The political economy of the mass media*. New York: Pantheon Books.

hooks, bell. 1992. *Black looks: Race and representation*. Boston: South End Press.

———. 1994. *Outlaw culture: Resisting representations*. New York: Routledge.

Ignatiev, Noel, and John Garvey, eds. 1996. *Race traitor*. New York: Routledge.

Lazere, Donald. 1987. Introduction: Entertainment as social control. In *American media and mass culture: Left perspectives*, ed. Donald Lazere, 1–23. Berkeley: University of California Press.

Lieberman, Leonard, and Larry T. Reynolds. 1996. Race: The deconstruction of a scientific concept. In Reynolds and Lieberman 1996, 142–73.

Loewen, J. W. 1988. *The Mississippi Chinese: Between black and white*. 2d ed. Prospect Heights, Ill.: Waveland.

Marable, Manning. 1983. *How capitalism underdeveloped black America*. Boston: South End Press.

———. 1995. *Beyond black and white: Transforming African-American politics*. New York: Verso.

Marks, Jonathan. 1998. Replaying the race card. *Anthropology Newsletter* 39 (5) (May): 1, 4–5.

Marriott, Michel. 1996. Multiracial Americans ready to claim their own identity. *New York Times*, 20 July, 1,8.

Metress, Seamus P. 1996. British racism and its impact on Anglo-Irish relations. In Reynolds and Lieberman 1996, 50–63.

Miliband, Ralph. 1987. Class analysis. In *Social theory today*, ed. Anthony Giddens and Jonathan Turner, 325–46. Stanford, Calif.: Stanford University Press.

Minority Rights Group, ed. 1995. *No longer invisible: Afro-Latin Americans today.* London: Minority Rights Publications.

Montagu, Ashley. 1942. *Man's most dangerous myth: The fallacy of race.* New York: Columbia University Press.

Morris, Norval, and David Rothman, eds. 1995. *The Oxford history of the prison.* New York: Oxford University Press.

Mullings, Leith. 1978. Ethnicity and stratification in the urban United States. *Annals of the New York Academy of Sciences* 318:10–22.

Nonini, Donald. 1992. Du Bois and radical theory and practice. *Critical Anthropology* 12:293–318.

Omi, Michael, and Howard Winant. 1986. *Racial formation in the United States: From the 1960s to the 1980s.* New York: Routledge.

Parenti, Michael. 1992. *Make-believe media: The politics of entertainment.* New York: St. Martin's Press.

Parsons, Talcott. 1959. An approach to the sociology of knowledge. *Transactions of the Fourth World Congress of Sociology.* Milan. Cited in Gouldner 1976.

Patterson, Thomas C. 1994. Racial hierarchies and buffer races. *Transforming Anthropology* 5(1 and 2):20–27. (Special issue on Race, racism, and the history of U.S. anthropology.)

Rapp, Rayna. 1993. Eleanor Leacock's contributions to the anthropological study of gender. In Sutton 1993, 87–94.

Raymond, Chris. 1991. Recognition of the gender differences in mental illness and its treatment prompts a call for more health research on problems specific to women. *Chronicle of Higher Education,* 12 June, A5, A10.

Reynolds, Larry T., and Leonard Lieberman, eds. 1996. *Race and other misadventures: Essays in honor of Ashley Montagu in his ninetieth year.* Dix Hills, N.Y.: General Hall.

Roediger, David R. 1991. *The wages of whiteness: Race and the making of the American working class.* New York: Verso.

Russo, Vito. 1987. *The celluloid closet: Homosexuality in the movies.* Rev. ed. New York: Harper & Row.

Sacks, Karen Brodkin. 1994. How did Jews become white folks? In Gregory and Sanjek 1994, 78–102.

Scott, James C. 1985. *The weapons of the weak: Everyday forms of peasant resistance.* New Haven, Conn.: Yale University Press.

Sedgwick, Eve Kosofsky. 1990. *Epistemology of the closet.* Berkeley: University of California Press.

Shanklin, Eugenia. 1994. *Anthropology and race.* Belmont, Calif.: Wadsworth.

Sharff, Jagna Wojcicka. 1995. "We are all chickens for the colonel": A cultural materialist view of prisons. In *Science, materialism, and the study of culture,* ed. by Martin Murphy and Maxine Margolis, 132–58. Gainesville, Fla.: University Press of Florida.

Smedley, Audrey. 1993. *Race in North America: Origin and evolution of a world view.* Boulder, Colo.: Westview Press.

Smitherman-Donaldson, Geneva, and Teun A. van Dijk, eds. 1988. *Discourse and discrimination.* Detroit: Wayne State University Press.

Spears, Arthur K. 1978. Institutionalized Racism and the Education of Blacks. *Anthropology and Education Quarterly* 9.2(summer):127–36.

———. 1992. Culture critique and colorstruction: Black-produced media images of blacks. *Transforming Anthropology* 3(1):24–29. (Special issue on Teaching as praxis: Decolonizing media representations of race, ethnicity and gender in the New World Order.)

———. 1998. African American language use: Ideology and so-called obscenity. In *African-American English*, ed. by Salikoko S. Mufwene, John R. Rickford, Guy Bailey, and John Baugh, 226–50. New York: Routledge.

Sutton, Constance, ed. 1993. *From Labrador to Samoa: The theory and practice of Eleanor Burke Leacock*. Arlington, Va.: Association for Feminist Anthropology/ American Anthropological Association.

Tasker, Yvonne. 1993. *Spectacular bodies: Gender, genre and the action cinema*. New York: Routledge.

Thompson, John B. 1984. *Studies in the theory of ideology*. Berkeley: University of California Press.

Tobach, Ethel, and Betty Rosoff, eds. 1994. *Challenging racism and sexism: Alternatives to genetic explanations*. New York: The Feminist Press at the City University of New York.

Transforming Anthropology 2(1). (Special issue on Teaching as praxis: Race and ideologies of power.)

Transforming Anthropology 3(1):24–29 (Special issue on Teaching as praxis: Decolonizing media representations of race, ethnicity and gender in the New World Order.)

Transforming Anthropology 5(1 and 2):1–7. (Special issue on Race, racism, and the history of U.S. anthropology.)

van Dijk, Teun A. 1993. *Elite discourse and racism*. Newbury Park, Calif.: Sage.

Wadel, Cato. 1973. *Now, whose fault is that? The struggle for self-esteem in the face of chronic unemployment*. St. John, Newfoundland: Institute of Social and Economic Research, Memorial University of Newfoundland. Cited in Harris 1987.

Wallace, Michele. 1992. *Black popular culture*. Ed. by Gina Dent. Seattle, Wash.: Bay Press.

West, Cornel. 1993. *Race matters*. Boston: Beacon Press.

Wetherell, Margaret, and Jonathan Potter. 1992. *Mapping the language of racism: Discourse and the legitimation of exploitation*. New York: Columbia University Press.

White, Jack E. 1991. Race: The pain of being black. *Time*, 16 September, 24–27.

Whitten, Norman E. Jr. 1974. *Black frontiersmen: Afro-Hispanic culture of Ecuador and Colombia*. Prospect Heights, Ill.: Waveland Press.

Williams, Brackette F. 1989. A class act: Anthropology and the race to nation across ethnic terrain. *Annual Reviews of Anthropology* 18:401–44.

Winant, Howard. 1994. *Racial conditions: Politics, theory, comparisons*. Minneapolis: University of Minnesota Press.

Wolf, Eric R. 1983. *Europe and the people without history*. Berkeley: University of California Press.

Wolfe, Alan. 1978. *The seamy side of democracy: Repression in America*. 2d ed. New York: Longman.

Woolard, Kathryn A., and Bambi B. Schieffelin. 1994. Language ideology. *Annual Review of Anthropology* 23:55–82.

I

Linguistic, Symbolic, and Institutional Manifestations

Teaching "Minorities" about Language and Culture

Arthur K. Spears

In writing of minorities, I have in mind specifically minority groups who are politically oppressed; and, as seen by the quotation marks in the title of this chapter, I cast a sidelong glance at the word *minority* even as I use it. In an African-American cultural context, I might even emphasize my interrogation of the word by making it the object of cut-eye and suck-teeth (actions indicating a negative appraisal [Rickford and Rickford 1976]). I might have used the term *oppressed group* instead, but I believe that there are significant differences between oppressed groups who are truly minorities, to the extent we can pin down the term, and those who are a majority, though I will not argue the point. The crucial point is that the term *minority* depends on how one decides to slice the pie and whose appetite is best served in slicing it in particular ways.

As an example of a so-called minority group, having traits associated with such groups, we can take African Americans in the United States (whom I will also refer to sometimes as *blacks*), who make up from 13 to 20 percent of the American population, depending on one's sources. Blacks are, collectively, victims of a dual labor market that maintains their concentration in less-skilled, lower-paying, and lower-prestige jobs. The group's overall condition has been the subject of numerous mystifications that state effects to be causes. For example, it has often been stated that the poor education of black pupils in the schools—their high dropout rate, their high rates of reading and writing failure—leads to their lowered suitability for better jobs and, as a

61

result, contributes to the continued economic disadvantage that black people face. However, the poor education that so many black pupils receive is actually an effect. It is an effect of the structured inequality in our society. The more basic phenomenon of inequality, then, is what must be examined in order to talk revealingly about education.

Let us look briefly at the unstable semantics of the term *minority*, a term steeped in ideology, and see how, under an alternative ideological regime, African Americans might become part of a majority. Gaining insight hinges on looking at the conceptualization of ethnicity. An interesting fact is that generally all whites are today lumped into the same group, while people of color are subject to finer distinctions. One does not hear about French-Americans or Finnish-Americans spoken of as minorities, nor white Anglo-Saxon Protestants for that matter, though they are. (Sometimes white ethnic groups are singled out, as for example Russians in New York City, but even then they are not spoken of as minorities.) This was South Africa's former apartheid approach to ethnicity: recognizing and reinforcing with "homelands" the maximum number of (divisive) ethnic distinctions among oppressed peoples (various indigenous ethnicities such as Zulu and Xhosa) while rather articifically conceptualizing and constructing one white dominant group, as large as possible, by ignoring real ethnic distinctions when convenient, and by pretending that unstable, shifting, and merging ethnic African identities (Warren Perry, personal communication) were fixed in stone. Perhaps the postapartheid era will see efforts to reconstruct South Africa's apartheid ideology of ethnicity.

The foregoing is clear without even getting into questions involving the shifting foundations of whiteness. Several U.S. European-American ethnic groups (e.g., Italians and Jews [leaving aside black Jews]) have witnessed their ascension into whiteness during the last century, Jews as recently as World War II (Hacker 1995, 9; Gregory and Sanjek 1994; Sacks 1994).

In the United States, for example, Caribbean blacks, both Hispanophone and Anglophone as well as others, by and large, have much in common with American blacks, to the extent that both American and Caribbean blacks, for sound cultural reasons relating to a shared African heritage, should be considered subgroups of the same larger group. This soon becomes clear to any American black living in a neighborhood with many, say, Puerto Ricans and Dominicans, regardless of whether those in the latter two groups were born in the United States or in the Caribbean. Often, a difference in language can hide cultural similarities more extensive than those uniting historically Anglophone American blacks and whites. And, after all, how much do (white) French-American communities in Massachusetts, with some members still fluent in French, have in common with the (white) Russian-Jewish community of Brighton Beach, Brooklyn, where Russian is still vigorous?

Another example is the black/Native American connection, both historical and contemporary. The very close ties between blacks and Native Americans are not widely known. However, we sometimes experience the shock of reality, as for example when we leaf through a newspaper and come upon a pleasant-looking, round-nosed, full-lipped, dark-skinned, woolly-haired Native American staring back at us (Johnson 1996). Many, if not most, American blacks can trace their ancestry to Native Americans. Numerous instances of Native American reservations containing many people who would appear to be black have been observed, not to mention groups of "triracial isolates," mixtures presumably of Native American, black, and white, who have struggled for some time to be officially recognized as Native American (see, for example, Sider 1993). Indeed, we cannot speak profitably of ethnicity without remembering that it is politicized and historical, and therefore not unexpectedly involving changing categories (Sider 1994). The point here is not that Native Americans and blacks should be considered one group, but that there is a close, often ignored, relationship between the two groups such that it might be more appropriate to think of the two groups as really united by an ethnic continuum or cline between them in which one gradually transforms into the other. What is clear is that ethnic boundaries are often based more on politics than on historical and ethnic facts, and that minorities might sometimes become majorities if ethnicity were construed differently.

Going beyond ethnic issues, the term *minority* leaves out groups who should think of themselves in thinking of "minorities." Using instead terms such as *subordinated group* or *oppressed group*, two of a few possibilities, terminologically assists gays and lesbians, women of all ethnicities, and certain physically limited groups (especially those such as the hearing-impaired, who have a distinctive culture and language) in seeing their commonalities.

Members of subordinated groups struggling against societally imposed handicaps have a special need for understanding those aspects of society that contribute to the maintenance of their condition. In stating this, I have in mind especially those political, economic, and communicative (symbolic, linguistic, ideological) aspects of society that do so. I make this introductory comment because so little of what is typically involved in the teaching of the sociocultural aspects of language touches upon the communicative *within* a macropolitical and economic framework that favors the understanding of fundamentals. Nevertheless, language, implicated in the whole of human activity, provides an

63

indispensable vehicle for understanding the dynamics of oppression. Moreover, it provides a particularly useful entry into the study of society and culture because all students, in their capacity as human beings and members of some society, have had intense, lifelong contact with language, a contact that has given them ideas about language, even though those ideas may be mostly impressionistic. Even if ill-founded, students will at least have ideas about what is good language or bad language, or what is corrupt or pure in speech.

It is interesting that the linguistic baggage they bring with them to their first class meeting is usually judgmental. They arrive in a judgmental mode, one might say, and one of the first—and most difficult—tasks of an instructor teaching a language and culture course is to get them to put their judgments aside for long enough to enter an observational mode. (These courses would ideally be referred to as courses on language in society and culture, since language is indeed a part of culture and society.) It is not enough for students merely to set aside their parrotings of injunctions against the use of sentences such as *Me and him went to the store* and their perfunctory approval of sentences such as *He and I went to the store*. They should go on to observe that the sentences that have been labeled for them as "correct" and "incorrect" both have in common that they are said, and that, what is even more interesting, there are sentences quite similar that are not said by anyone (e.g., *Him I and went to the store*), and the reasons therefor lead one to the heart of what language structure is all about.

Yet, the important point is that students bring with them a knowledge of language that is independent of the statements they are likely to make about language. Their knowledge of language is manifest in their ability to speak a language. They know a language and therefore have access to primary data constituting a complete system, but they do not know a political or economic system in the same sense as they do language, nor do they have the same kind of access to such data.

The foregoing remarks are more in the nature of a recommendation for courses dealing with language in society and culture, but if the value of such courses is assumed, one may go on to ask the following: what does the oppressed-group student need to know about language and culture? Indeed, one may ask what the college student, not just those from oppressed groups, needs to know about language and culture, in general and as they relate to the condition of subordinated groups in society. However, the first question is the more pressing one because it relates to matters of survival in a way that the second one does not.

The oppressed-group student, especially, needs to know about the context of language. To go further, it should be observed that the context, the big picture into which language fits, is the semiotic landscape in which language is situated. By *semiotic landscape* I mean the collection of all sign systems, not just language, that the student must confront daily. These sign systems are of diverse types, and are involved in everything from the most basic to the most arcane of activities, including everything from the sign system for pedestrians and automobile drivers to the expressive repertoires used by members of fraternal orders such as the Freemasons and the Knights of Columbus.

However, the important point to make here is not the value of contextualization, but its necessity. Society and culture form a largely coherent whole, although they show discontinuities, changes in progress, contradictions, and permeability. Nevertheless, that whole is very much like a system, in that none of its component elements can be fully understood without some grasp of others. Aspects of society and culture are mutually implicated to varying extents by one another. While one aspect of society and culture such as language can indeed be extracted for examination, that examination can only be preliminary, a methodological convenience, which eventually must come to an end if an adequate understanding is to be reached.

To illustrate why this should be so, let us consider briefly African-American English, also referred to as Black English. A basic, seemingly trivial fact about it is that it exists. It seems trivial because it is so basic. But note, already, that if we raise the question of why it exists, we must venture outside of language per se into history, social structure, economics, and politics. The reason for the existence of Black English is the reason for the existence of the black community that speaks it. Once we begin to understand the distinctness and historical isolation of the black community, we can begin to understand why a distinctive variety of language associated with that community exists.

To take another example, we might also ask why words of West African origin exist in Black English (e.g., *goober* ['peanut'], *cooter* ['turtle'], and *banjo* [Dalby 1971; Dillard 1972]). Few would be surprised by the answer, which relates to the West African heritage of African Americans. In this case, the historical context, at least that part of it relating to the West African heritage, is well known, hence there is little surprise. In other cases, however, the historical particulars might be less well known, with the result that present realities could remain unexplained or mysterious.

Discourse on languages and dialects in the United States highlights the existence of African-American (or Black) English due to the highlighted position of blacks in American society. The overwhelmingly white speakers of the southern coastal California dialect of white English (where *good food* becomes "ged feed") do not find their dialect highlighted in the same way.

I will present and discuss three of the types of facts our students should be aware of, while I recognize that there are other facts that could appropriately be added. I hasten to reiterate that what is valuable in this regard for oppressed-group students is also valuable for all.

1. Prestige languages (or dialects) owe their status primarily to factors that are ultimately political and/or economic, not to any inherent superiority claimed on the basis of grammatical features.

A crucial consideration is the distinction between the terms *language* and *dialect*. First, a word on these terms. It should be noted that there are several linguistic traditions, in both the United States and Europe. There are also linguistic traditions that are independent of those of European and European-derived ones; the tradition of Sanskrit grammarians on the Indian subcontinent is perhaps the best known. The important point is that the status of these terms and other key terms in linguistics may differ according to tradition. I will discuss these terms in what I will refer to, in simplifying, as the American tradition (simplifying because there is more than one).

Among American linguists, *dialect* is evaluatively neutral, although the term is used pejoratively in the everyday speech of many Americans. Among linguists, a dialect is simply a particular variety of a language. On this usage, everyone speaks a dialect, from Queen Elizabeth to the president of the United States, from an Appalachian farmer to a newscaster with one of the national television networks. *Language* is a cover term that subsumes several related dialects. Thus, the English language includes many dialects of English—American English, British English, Australian English, and so on. Each of these dialects could in turn be divided into subdialects; for example, American English includes African-American English (still sometimes called *Black English*), Bostonian English, Midland English, and so on. Often *language* is used where one might expect *dialect*, given what has been stated. The reason for this, however, is that one does not use the term *dialect* unless one is focusing on the fact that a particular variety of language is only one of several related ones. In other words, the use of *dialect* would imply some kind of comparison with related language varieties (or dialects).

In Europe, *dialect* is sometimes used for nonstandard varieties of language or simply those that are not the official language variety of the entire nation. Nonstandards are those that have not been codified, that is, for which there are no grammar books and dictionaries stating which grammatical rules and which forms of words are to be used and when there is a choice. (Codification presupposes that the language variety is written.) Standard dialects are those to which prestige is accorded, while related nonstandard dialects either simply lack prestige or are actually stigmatized. Thus, standard British English (the dialect spoken by Queen Elizabeth) is the prestige dialect in Britain, while Cockney, one of the nonstandards, is not (see Spears 1988, Wolfram and Shilling-Estes 1998 for further discussion).

It would be useful to clarify what is meant by *grammar*. In using this term, linguists refer to the rules for the combination of the units of language. What are the units? Sounds, word roots, (e.g., *fair* as in *unfairly*), word affixes (e.g., *un-* and *-ly* as in *unfairly*), words themselves, phrases, clauses, sentences, and various units comprising several sentences. Some rules of English grammar, for example, prevent sounds from being combined in certain ways: *fbik* could never possibly be an English word because English grammar does not allow the sound sequence "f-b" to begin a word.

To return to the statement concerning prestige languages, let it be noted first that it requires discussion, particularly in that it relates back to what was stated previously concerning evaluative attitudes toward language. The issue here is not whether there are ways to evaluate language; rather, it is the kinds of judgmental evaluation made by the nonspecialist, judgments learned and reinforced through public school systems and other societal institutions.

To understand what kinds of judgment are at issue, we can consider the kinds that are made with respect to sentences such as the following: *He ain't got nothing*, and *Him and her done left already.* Such sentences are typically judged as "bad, incorrect, corrupt, perverse," to mention only some of the labels attached to them. Why these labels and not their opposites?

Sentences from the prestige standard dialects are those that are positively judged; those from the nonstandard dialects are negatively judged. More often than not, these judgments are not based on any kind of reasoning. When they are, the reasons are usually specious: for example, two negatives in a sentence are illogical because they cancel each other out, interfering with the intended message. This kind of reasoning ignores the fact that language is used to express and talk about logic; no type of language-independent logic is encoded into the grammatical structure of language. Each language (or dialect) has its own grammatical logic, which must be distinguished from conceptual logic, which is independent of any specific language. It is often observed that a number of standard, prestige languages (e.g., Spanish) require double negatives in contexts where the standard English translation would not allow them:

Spanish: El no hizo nada. (*no* and *nada* are negatives)

English: He didn't do anything. (*n't* [*not*] is the one negative that standard English allows; compare this with *He didn't do nothing*, with the negatives *n't* and *nothing*.)

In addition to the issue of how sentences from different dialects are judged is that of how one dialect came to be the standard. This is particularly important for persons belonging to subordinated groups to understand, since most speak nonstandard dialects. In fact, the majority of citizens of the United States and comparable modern nations speak nonstandard dialects. The majority of black people in the United States certainly do. Dillard (1972) has estimated this portion of the black population to be 80 percent. From my own experience, a good number of black college students do, at least on some occasions, just like nonblack students. In effect, the dominant dialect of the black community is disparaged, not directly by the appellation *nonstandard*, but in the comments that are usually made about it. This leads to the point that I will discuss in the following pages concerning language attitudes, but the crucial consideration at this juncture is how the dominant form of English in the black community came to be disparaged and what effect that disparagement has had on the student's sense of self and his or her attitudes toward black culture. (Currently, the term most used for this variety is *African-American Vernacular English* [AAVE].)

Students need to know that standard dialects are not in any way inherently better than their sister nonstandard dialects. In other words, they are not more logical and expressive (whatever that means) or better organized (whatever that may mean). Standard dialects do tend to have certain traits, however, that nonstandard ones tend not to have. For example, they are more grammatically conservative—that is, they hold on to some words and constructions after they are no longer widely used. Conservatism and other traits specific to standard dialects are a result of the purposes for which they have been groomed and the uses to which they have been put. As examples of differences, observe that standard English gets better results in the Supreme Court, while on Harlem basketball courts AAVE does. Any variety of language will reflect the uses to which it has been put. Stated differently, all varieties of language can be used for any purpose. The Cockney dialect of English would have, had history chosen it to be the standard, served just as well as any other. Just as standard dialects tend to have certain traits, so do the indigenous language varieties of Native Australians—because of the uses to which they have been put. One of those uses is talking about kinship in what may seem to an average European or American to be unnecessary detail, and this explains their rich kinship terminology.

French and Spanish can be taken as examples of my basic point concerning the connection between economics and politics and standard dialects. What we refer to simply as French is more specifically standard French, one of a number of related dialects spoken in France. The same kind of statement can be made about Spanish. Sometimes referred to as Castilian, Spanish arose in Castile, the region of Spain where the capital, Madrid, is located. French arose in the Ile de France, where Paris is located. The important consideration is that standard French and standard Spanish (Castilian) became the standard dialects of their respective countries due primarily to their position as the dialects of the geographical areas that rose to economic and political prominence. This is not to imply that no "grammatical" concessions have ever been made to other dialect areas. The Real Academia, the language institution responsible for deciding what is acceptable in standard Spanish, has deliberately chosen some non-Castilian forms in order to acknowledge the (lesser) political and economic importance of non-Castillan speaking areas (see Klein-Andreu 1985).[1] Castile's preeminence was partly the result of its leading role in finally reconquering, in the fifteenth century, Spanish territory held by the Moors. The groundwork for French hegemony in France began as early as 1229, when French-speaking seneschals (administrators appointed by princes) were imposed in the Occitan-speaking areas of southern France (Calvet 1974, 172).

We can assume that had other regions outstripped these in political and economic importance, the dialects of those other regions would have eventually become the standards. Economic preeminence leads to political preeminence, and it was the spread of the political power of these regions, political power buttressed by wealth, that led to the spread of their dialects to the rest of the country. There was nothing in the nature of the dialects themselves that caused them to become the standards. Their prestige, today backed by all national institutions, has its origin in factors that are in no way linguistic.

The scenario just presented oversimplifies somewhat, but it does not distort the basic nature of the process that occurred. We might qualify what has been stated by noting that this rather gradual process, whereby the standard, spoken by a power group, emerged and became increasingly codified as the nation-state itself grew and became solidified, does not apply to all countries equally.

Consider briefly the case of Norway, which was ruled by Denmark for roughly four hundred years, until 1814. The official language in Norway was Danish, spoken with a Norwegian pronunciation. There was no standard Norwegian. In 1885, as an outgrowth of nationalist feelings, a kind of Norwegian (called Landsmål) based on several mostly western Norwegian dialects was selected to become the standard, along with the Norwegianized Danish (called Riksmål). Danish was not abolished at that time as a standard because it was still the language of the urban elite, who due to their status exercised considerable influence (see Haugen 1966). It is significant that Landsmål did not become the standard dialect (one of two) of Norway as a result of its being the dialect of a power group. It was not the language of the urban elite. Other factors led to its selection (and indeed to its creation, since it was somewhat artificial, being composed of features from several dialects). Moreover, how much prestige Nynorsk (the contemporary name for the descendant of Landsmål) has is still problematic. Efforts to promote it in Norwegian schools have been regularly sabotaged by teachers, and "there is a powerful presence of traditional riksmål [sic] still being used in the daily press, media, economic life, popular literature, and technology corresponding to Norway's ever-growing industrialization" (Haugen 1985, 262).

Riksmål, or Bokmål (the current equivalent), illustrates our basic theme. Bokmål is basically an artifact of the historical power of Denmark in Norway, and its imposition on Norwegians reflected power realities whose effect can still be felt today.

To summarize, when we speak of prestige dialects in our modern world of nation-states, we are speaking of those that have undergone standardization—a writing system has been provided for them, and they have been codified as explained above—and are, in the typical case, the official variety of some state. Making a dialect official is a political act by its very nature, as is, for that matter, the decision to create a standard. These are the reasons one can present for claiming that prestige language varieties owe their status to political factors, closely tied to economic ones, not to any inherent grammatical superiority. In fact, there is no way to establish in any absolute way the superiority of one language (or dialect) over another.

When the language of minority students is disparaged, they should understand that this disparagement reflects historical and political realities, not their own worth or that of their language and culture. As a matter of fact, understanding the political and economic history of the language situation in their country will help them not only to appreciate their language and culture but also gain an understanding of their current condition. This understanding will, moreover, help them to figure out what to do about changing that condition. This leads to a second point:

2. Language attitudes are basically attitudes about people.

Linguists and other language scholars are sometimes quite surprised by the vehemence with which some people condemn nonstan-

70

dard American English dialects. If we again take AAVE as an example, people who are otherwise reasonable become impervious to reason with regard to this dialect, and this includes both whites and blacks. From one point of view, this is understandable, if not acceptable, behavior in that the negative remarks about black language in such cases can often be interpreted as indirectly negative comments about black people themselves. To put it differently, what cannot be said about black people directly—most people do not want to appear racist—can be said about traits that black people have or behavior strongly associated with them. Degrading comments about the language then become fascinating exercises in metonymy.

Indeed, the interpenetration generally of attitudes about language with attitudes about their speakers is explicitly recognized in empirical research on language attitudes. A standard experimental method in language attitude research is the matched-guise technique (Lambert, Hodgson, and Fillenbaum 1960; Lambert 1967). This technique is interesting because the subjects used in the experiment are asked to respond to items on a questionnaire based solely on language information. The subjects are asked to rate a series of speakers, who have been tape-recorded, in terms of traits such as intelligence, social background, personality, and so on. The speakers recruited for the tape recordings are people who speak two or more languages fluently. The speakers read a passage in one language and then a translation in another language. The translation is controlled for formality of vocabulary and other factors such as tone. Let us say that each speaker records a segment first in English and then in French. Those segments are then mixed up for the subjects, who are to react to the tapes. The subjects hear a particular speaker's English passage followed by passages from other speakers. The passages are mixed up so that it appears to the subjects answering the questionnaires that each passage is recorded by a different speaker. Thus, valuable insight is gained when the subject rates the same speaker differently according to which language she or he is speaking.

Notice that since the subjects are explicitly rating the speakers on nonlinguistic traits, the subjects' responses cannot be taken as attitudes toward language specifically. They can be interpreted only as attitudes toward speakers of particular languages, namely, members of a specific ethnic group. The language spoken merely identifies the ethnic group, in the subject's mind, and the subject then proceeds to record on the questionnaire his or her attitudes toward the ethnic group.

But how do we get directly at language attitudes? The point is that in reality this seems infeasible because the language cannot be attitudinally disassociated, so to speak, from the group that speaks it. To obtain

71

language attitudes uncontaminated by attitudes toward language speakers themselves, it seems that it would be necessary to find a group of subjects who have no knowledge of the group that speaks the language. However, the question then becomes, why conduct that kind of research? After all, language attitudes in a social vacuum are of little use. We study language attitudes not because of their value in and of themselves, but because they tell us something about social structure, teachers' attitudes toward students, and how those attitudes affect students' learning, second-language acquisition, the practice of law and medicine, and employability (Fasold 1984, chap. 6).

The 1996–97 Ebonics controversy elicited many of the virulently negative attitudes toward Black English. (Ebonics is another term used for Black English.) Most of the debate during the controversy was not informed by research in linguistics, the scientific study of language. Although the public at large should debate the full range of issues that concern U.S. citizens, there seems to be a particular willingness on the part of those who have no special knowledge to delve into language issues. Perhaps this is because practically everyone is a native speaker of some language, and that intimate relationship encourages a sense of expertise.

The board of the Oakland (California) Unified School District presented a resolution that ignited the controversy. The resolution sought basically to get teaching staff to use knowledge of African-American Vernacular English (AAVE) as a medium of communication in order to teach standard English better. The schools' responsibility to teach standard English was never questioned, nor was it suggested that AAVE itself be taught. This last point is important because somehow a number of media pundits concluded that the board actually recommended the teaching of AAVE. Indeed, the subsequent changes of opinion and the faulty representations of what the school board had done indicate that some commentators spoke out before they had actually read (or understood) the resolution.

The resolution itself, though basically sound from a pedagogical and linguistic standpoint, contained a few infelicities—enough for raised eyebrows, perhaps, but not justifying the unbridled ridicule that followed. Black English has a grammatical system that is different from that of standard English. It must therefore be studied in its own right and, in teaching, be considered as an entity that, though distinct from standard English, is also closely related to it.

No kind of African-American English is in any way deficient; all kinds serve the communicative needs of their speakers effectively. To characterize any kind of African-American English as nothing more than slang or street language is an insult to the many grandmothers,

72

ministers, adolescents, and others who use it—on at least some occasions. These facts were formally recognized in the Linguistic Society of America's resolution on the Ebonics issue at their 1997 annual meeting.

African-American English is not a collection of slang terms, it is not used only by teenagers who spend much time in the streets, and it is not a corruption of anything—it has its own history and did not spring historically from any one kind of English. *It is a product of the historical blending of mostly English features but also some features of West African languages.* Although some vernacular and standard speakers use slang, and sometimes language unsuitable for the drawing room, this is true of virtually all English speakers in the United States; it is not unique to the African-American community. When linguists speak of particular language varieties, they have in mind structural features, relating to the sound systems (pronunciation) and the matrix of rules governing the construction of words and sentences. Most of the unflattering terms that media pundits have used to characterize African-American varieties of English (e.g., slang, street language, ghetto-speak) are terms defined on the basis of vocabulary, not the fundamental, grammatical structure of these languages.

It is telling that the boundaries of standard English have continually shifted, historically, to accommodate middle- and upper-class whites, but not working-class whites or blacks of any class. Observe that even many college professors fail to follow basic rules of standard English (as opposed to trivial ones of some self-appointed grammarians), as, for example, with rules governing pronoun case. Consequently, we hear nonstandard utterances such as *between he and I* (*between him and me* in standard English), and pleas from grammarians that such expressions be adopted as part of the standard in order to "rescue" the high-status white people who use them (Honey 1995). Of course, some linguists might state that expressions such as these are part of the "informal standard" or the "colloquial standard." The real issue is still that accommodation is made for some speakers, in order to keep their speech within the standard, while other speakers are not accommodated.

African-American Vernacular English is stigmatized because its speakers are stigmatized. Most of the current Ebonics controversy is in the tradition of the frenzied black-threat-to-civilization narrative that we are fed daily by the media. It is deeply troubling that even some African-American public figures participate in it. This media frenzy can be fully understood only within the context of institutional racism and socioeconomic inequality.

An important question is why a small minority of standard English speakers linguistically terrorize nonstandard speakers. We must ask,

73

given the great diversity in standard English throughout the world, why must a line be drawn to reject the entry of some groups into the exclusive standard club? After all, standard speakers can understand their nonstandard-speaking neighbors more easily than standard speakers living far away (ambiguity intended).

The Oakland School Board's decision was fundamentally a sound one, even if it was not expressed in the best way. Virtually all research indicates that children are best taught by taking their native language or dialect into account, and that includes using it as a bridge to the language or dialect they wish to acquire. This view, also, was ratified in the Linguistic Society of America's 1997 resolution on Ebonics.

That said, it should also be observed that language/dialect mismatches are not the major problem in the education of African-American and white students, even though there are important grammatical differences among American varieties of English. Nations with comparatively successful public education, such as Japan, Finland, and Switzerland, have much more far-reaching (i.e., grammatically significant) dialect differences; yet, they have produced vastly better educational systems (see Fishman 1972). The underfunding of public education in the United States is a national scandal, while candid discussions of teacher preparedness are largely taboo.

The true tragedy is that language differences are not the major problem for African-American students. In dealing with the low scholastic achievement of too many African-American students, we must confront a number of issues, both broad and narrow:

• the structure of deliberately maintained inequality
• the manifestation of racism and internalized oppression in the "Ebonics" debate
• the nature and function of white-supremacist racism in American society
• the debilitation of educational institutions serving most African Americans in the wake of the Civil Rights movement
• the reasons why the wealthiest nation on earth has the worst distribution of wealth and income of all the major industrialized nations

The third point that students need to be aware of is the following:

3. Language is more than a set of grammatical rules. It is not just a tool, it is a resource, permeated with psychology and society.

The obvious corollary of this is that when a group is deprived of its language, it loses an important resource.

Upon first inspection, this may seem to be false. After all, if all languages have the same expressive potential, that is, any thought can be expressed in any language, then why should it make any difference in which language a group communicates? Why shouldn't Gaelic-speaking Irish, for example, be just as happy and productive if they are forced to speak English (assuming that they all learn to speak it well)?

The answer takes us back to what was stated above concerning the fact that languages reflect the purposes to which they have been put. Thus, if a society such as that of Native Australian groups attaches great importance to kinship relations, the kinship terminology of the language they speak will usually reflect this. To put it differently, specialized vocabularies are developed for special interests. The Arabic of Bedouins has many words for different types of camel, which are especially important in their desert environment.

Consider Eskimo speakers. (I use *Eskimo* because more people are familiar with this term. Some prefer *Inuit*.) They can speak in Eskimo about nuclear physics, but it would be harder for them to do so than it would be for English speakers because English has a highly developed, specialized vocabulary for talking about nuclear physics. English speakers have been more interested historically in nuclear physics. So, if English-speaking nuclear physicists, say, were for some reason forced to learn and carry forth in Eskimo, they could do so but at a great cost in efficiency. No doubt, over time they would push their Eskimo language to develop a specialized terminology for nuclear physics, such that one day an ethnically Eskimo Eskimo-language-speaker could point his or her finger at ethnically American Eskimo speakers as members of a group that speak a distinctive dialect of Eskimo, much in the same way that blacks who speak a distinctive dialect of English are pointed at. Actually, the Americans would most likely code-switch into English when they needed a nuclear physics term. But, over time, the net effect would be the same. The English words would become an integral part of the distinctive dialect of Eskimo spoken by the erstwhile English speakers.

The important observation, however, is that speakers develop their languages to suit their distinctive communicative needs as well as they can. They put their own cultural stamp on the language(s) they speak, and the kind of stamp is determined by the purposes for which the language(s) is/are used.

Consider the full bilingual, a person who has full control of two languages. This type of speaker typically code-switches—that is, he or she goes back and forth from one language to the other. Why the switches, when he or she is perfectly capable of holding forth in either language alone? One of the several reasons for code-switching is simply that certain things are better said in one of the languages because that language has been used, or used more, to say those things—and one is simply in the habit of speaking a certain language to certain people, in certain places. The message, to be sure, can be communicated in both languages, but in one language the message can be communicated more simply, with more pizzazz, with certain apropos allusions to related matters, due perhaps to a word's multiple meanings in one language but not the other. Using one language, a person can express the message with a short direct sentence. The other language might well require paragraphs. A French word, for example *pain* ('bread'), probably does not for any French-English bilingual have the same associations— smell, texture, memories—that the English *bread* has. *Pain* can be used to talk about Wonder Bread, monkey bread, and corn muffins just as *bread* can be used to talk about loaves of bread and baguettes. Both words have the same meaning, roughly speaking.[2] However, they are not psychologically equivalent: neither evokes the same range of thoughts, memories, and references as the other.

All languages have what I refer to as culture capsules, words or phrases that require an understanding of an entire area of culture for their correct interpretation and use. The word *camp* is a culture capsule, such that Susan Sontag (1966) could write an entire essay on it. When something is said to be camp, what is it? First, of all, it has to be something human-made, a piece of furniture, a flower arrangement; it cannot be a mountain range or a riverbank. It usually cannot be too new or too old; it has to be able to fit into that never-never land that is removed from the present but not old enough to be of antique value. An aura of kitsch is almost a necessity. But what does one have to know in order to identify kitsch? How does one acquire the requisite discernment? In a word, no short, simple definition of this word would suffice for its correct use and interpretation. A table is a table. Use of the word *table* requires little or no understanding of American culture. Any foreigner learning English can learn to use it easily, but learning to use *camp* correctly is a different matter. We can talk about camp only in a sociocultural setting in which mass consumption and the institutionalization of trendiness and fashion allow still-useful objects to be discarded on the grounds of tastelessness—and then taken up again because their particular brand of tastelessness has been reclassified as being of special interest.

Another example is provided by the Navajo word *hózhǫ*. The approximate translation: that which is good, true, beautiful, harmonious, balanced, just, and so on (Witherspoon 1977). The average speaker of English in the United States would probably think, even if English had a word such as *hózhǫ*, what on earth would we use it to talk about? It certainly would not be appropriate for talking about New York City politics, but neither would it do for modern art or the California coastline. Our culture does not predispose us to think of anything positive in so many ways: aesthetically, juridically, ethically, and so on.

It is rather obvious that the term *hózhǫ́* allows the Navajo to speak efficiently and effectively about the Navajo worldview and to perform efficiently and effectively rituals that tie in directly to that worldview. If Navajos lost their traditional language, Navajo, they would no doubt have to reshape their new language in order to express efficiently and effectively that which is deep within their collective psyche. In other words, they would have to reshape English so that they might speak in English about Navajo things, just as, for example, African Americans have reshaped English so that they may speak about African-American things.

Different peoples may speak the same language (perhaps with minor dialectical differences, such as those differentiating white and black American dialects of English) but in doing so not communicate the same set of messages. That is, their discourses may well be different. (Lavandera [1984] demonstrates this with a detailed, quantitative analysis showing that women use a higher percentage of grammatical forms considered polite than men do.) The Catholic discourse on God is not the same as the Quaker discourse on God. The result is that, for someone to communicate effectively with a person of another group speaking the "same language," it is sometimes necessary to learn to produce another kind of discourse. One can speak a language without being able to communicate effectively to its speakers. This is why sociolinguists draw an important distinction between linguistic competence, knowledge of a language's grammar, and communicative competence, knowledge of how to *use* the language, as, for example, to produce efficient, effective discourse.

To take an example, suppose one traveled to Kirundi-speaking Burundi to help with the preparation of census data. Among other things, one would have to find heads of households and ask them how many children they have. Now suppose one does what seems logical—simply translate the English question "How many children do you have?" into Kirundi. Let us assume our census-taker has a flawless linguistic command of Kirundi and translates perfectly. She asks the father of a family the question, and he says five. Just to check, she asks the wife, who says ten. To make matters worse, the census-taker has on good authority that all of the children are now at home. She goes there; she counts them (they are all sitting in the same room with the parents); and there are only eight. What on earth can be the matter? She could take the ethnocentric road and condemn the people of Burundi as incorrigible liars. Or, she could be more reasonable and acknowledge that there must be a language/culture issue.

77

The problem is that the census-taker has learned the language, but not how to use it in order to produce effective discourse. In Burundi, the culturally determined practice is for the father to count sons only; the mother, daughters only. Furthermore, since parenthood is highly valued, and valued numerically, parents count both living and dead children. For our census-taker to get the correct answer to the culturally loaded question, she would have to ask, "How many children, now alive, do you and your husband (or you and your wife) have?" (Albert 1972, 100). The answer to this question would be eight.

Once, while I was having a conversation with an apparently white student enrolled in one of my courses, that student told me he was "black" (African American). He said it in a rather matter of fact way, since it was clearly information that would be helpful for us in pursuing the topic at hand productively. Ironically, by telling me he was black, he made it clear to me that he most probably was not black. Blacks who look white have a number of ways of informing other blacks that they are black, but a direct statement is highly unlikely (at least in the black communities in which I have spent time). The means that are used include nonverbal behavior; references that only a black person could understand; a black expression (preferably one that has not been much discussed in academic publications and the mass media); or an indication of membership in a black fraternity or sorority, or even better, some indication that all of the men or women in one's family belong to a particular black fraternity or sorority. There are literally thousands of such indicators. Evidently, there is a black sociocultural and linguistic rule that constrains one from claiming blackness directly, greatly favoring a demonstration of it through the display of in-group knowledge or behavior.

This student had been raised, during part of his adolescence, by an African-American family. Apparently, as a result of his very close identification with them, he came to consider himself black. Whatever his relationship with the black family, his overall relationship with black people in general was not deep enough for him to be sufficiently steeped in black culture to be black in a meaningful way, that is, culturally black. During our conversation, he said nothing "black." No distinctively black messages or expressions were communicated. No typically black reactions to events were communicated. In the same situation, a white-looking black person would have suffused his or her conversation with distinctively black remarks, not only to indicate that she or he was black, but to prove it, just in case doubt lingered.

Most of us acquire a language naturally—that is, through social interaction in a particular cultural setting. There are only a very few people who have the talent to acquire fluency in a language in an artificial way (e.g., in the classroom or through self-teaching). In acquiring a language naturally, we learn, for the most part subconsciously, the abstract rules that underlie the discourse that we must master in order to function effectively in the society that uses the language. Underlying this discourse is, in essence, a philosophy or worldview. Thus, in learning a language—and doing so naturally, as the overwhelming majority of people do—we are in reality learning a language/worldview. We may conceive of this worldview as a set of discourse-generating principles, assumptions, and texts of relatively fixed structure, such as old sayings, stories, proverbs, and verbal routines of various kinds.

One of the most important explorations that can be undertaken in a language and culture course is that of the worldview that comes inextricably attached to specific languages. It is especially important for subordinated-group members to understand their own language/worldview because it is their very own; that worldview is, among other things, a resource, a source of supply, support, assistance—and an obstacle to full emancipatory thinking. All groups, in their language/discourse (i.e., the combination of the grammatical rules making up that language and what those rules in practice are typically used to say) have a collective wealth and wisdom, a theory of their condition, showing coherence and contradiction, recipes for coping, compendia of past solutions to problems (in folktales and proverbs, for example), a self-image, and programs for progress, stagnation, and retrogression. It has not been ordained that worldviews be entirely positive; however, a group's own view appears normally to be better for it than that of any other group. Needless to say, there are always significant differences between the language/worldview of the subordinated group and that of the oppressing group (membership in which is a matter of changeable degree).

As an example of several of the above points, observe an aspect of African-American English discourse. In my Black English courses, I ask the (mostly black) students why, if one wants to insult someone using strong language, one could say

> Look at that yellow (light-skinned) fool. Look at that black (dark-skinned) fool.

but not

> Look at that brown/brown-skinned/tan fool. (Anomaly is indicated by the crosshatch.)

Why does the last simply not work as an insult? *Black* is unfortunately for many African Americans still an insult and reflects the internalization of oppressive ideas about blackness stemming primarily from European colonialism and imperialism in the modern period. Its use reflects an accommodation to and collaboration with white supremacist ideology. But *yellow* (and related words such as *high yellow*) is an insult, too, and represents a mediated form of the rejection of whiteness—as connected to white supremacist ideology and oppression—through its put-down of blacks closest to whites. Brownness occupies a middle, neutral ground in the tug-of-war between two black consciousnesses, between resistance and collaboration, between emancipatory thinking and internalized oppression, which Du Bois (1961 [1903]) saw as threatening to tear the black psyche asunder. From our postmodern vantage point almost a century later, it is clearer that within all psyches, as within all societies, there are opposing wills and contradictory influences. This situation, though at times quite uncomfortable, represents business as usual. However, the level of oppositionality may be particularly severe in societies such as the post-slavocratic United States.

Like any resource, language/worldview must be examined, evaluated, purged, and protected. It must be improved over time through changes wrought by cultural critique, "the examination of received values, institutions, practices, and discourses in terms of their economic, political, social, and aesthetic genealogies, constitutions, and effects" (*Cultural Critique* 1:5, Fall 1985). Cultural critique assumes the existence of some degree of cultural domination effected by a dominating group on a subordinated one. By *cultural domination* (i.e., internalized oppression) is meant the acceptance, by an oppressed group, of ideas that are not in their best interest—that is, ideas that serve to mystify the true nature and causes of their condition and thereby impede their efforts to improve their condition. The subordinated group's self-image must also be protected from the negative one with which the oppressing group would replace it. The institutions providing the behavioral context for the maintenance of self-affirming discourses must be nourished.

Thus, to take an example from African-American communities, churches (usually fully controlled by African Americans) must be protected to the extent that they serve as behavioral contexts for positive discourses (e.g., those which accord to church members positive identities, which in turn serve to lessen the demoralizing effects of the degrading roles these same church members are often forced to assume outside the black community).

The fundamental purpose, then, of a language and culture course should be to start students on the road toward gaining a critical understanding of the position of their people (however many ways defined) in the world through the structured exploration of language as it has been and is being used.

Notes

1. As a result of the Constitution of 1978, the Spanish linguistic situation has become more complicated in terms of a standard. The country is administratively organized into seventeen Autonomous Communities, and in five of them Spanish, the only official national language, shares co-officiality with a regional language. The three regional languages are Basque, Catalan (co-official in three communities), and Galician (see Azevedo 1996).

2. Actually the French and English words cover bakery goods in different ways. English speakers (limiting themselves to English) would call *bread* what the French speaker would distinguish by the words *croissant*, *pain*, and *brioche*. And even in one language, semantics can be fuzzy. Observe: *We'll have corn muffins instead of bread*, which implies that the two are not the same thing. However, one might also, in response to *What kind of bread are you having?*, answer *Corn muffins*. Notice that Marie Antoinette's famous "Let them eat cake!" translates from the French "Qu'ils mangent de la brioche" ("Let them eat *brioche*"). *Brioche* is a slightly sweeter, softer form of bread—as American English speakers would call it—typically eaten with special meals (e.g., on Sundays). Nevertheless, *cake* translates the import of Marie's impolitic remark. For an excellent discussion of meaning and language in the real world, around the world—as opposed to sterile theoretical models—see Hanks 1966.

References

Albert, Ethel M. 1972. Culture patterning of speech behavior in Burundi. In *Directions in sociolinguistics: The ethnography of communication*, ed. John Gumperz and Dell Hymes, 72–105. New York: Holt, Rinehart, and Winston.

Azevedo, Milton M. 1996. Review of *Lingua inicial e competencia lingüística en Galicia*, by Mauro A. Fernández Rodríguez and Modesto A. Rodríguez Neira. *Language in Society* 25:305–7.

Calvet, Louis-Jean. 1974. *Linguistique et colonialisme: Petit traité de glottophagie*. Paris: Payot.

Cultural Critique. 1985. 1:5.

Dalby, David. 1971. Black through white: Patterns of communication in Africa and the New World. In *Black-white speech relationships*, ed. Walt Wolfram and Nona H. Clarke. Washington, D.C.: Center for Applied Linguistics.

Dillard, J. L. 1972. *Black English: Its history and usage in the United States*. New York: Random House.

DuBois, W. E. B. 1961 [1903]. *The souls of black folk*. Greenwich, Conn.: Fawcett Publications.

Fasold, Ralph. 1984. *The sociolinguistics of society*. New York: Basil Blackwell.

Fishman, Joshua. 1972. What has the sociology of language to say to the teacher? In *Language in sociocultural change*, ed. Anwar S. Dil. Stanford, Calif.: Stanford University Press.

Gregory, Steven, and Roger Sanjek, eds. 1994. *Race*. New Brunswick, N.J.: Rutgers University Press.

Hacker, Andrew. 1995. *Two nations, black and white, separate, hostile, unequal.* New York: Ballantine Books.

Hanks, William F. 1996. *Language and communicative practices.* Boulder, Colo.: Westview Press.

Haugen, Einar. 1966. *Language conflict and language planning: The case of modern Norwegian.* Cambridge, Mass.: Harvard University Press.

———. 1985. Review of *Talemålet i skolen: En studie av drøftinger og bestemmelserom muntlig språkbruk i folkeskolen (fra 1874 til 1925),* by Ernst Håkon Jahr. *Language in Society* 14:259–62.

Honey, John. 1995. A new rule for the queen and I? *English Today* 11(4):3–7.

Johnson, Kirk. 1996. Moonface Bear is dead at 35; Led a tribal uprising in '93. *New York Times,* 23 May, D25.

Klein-Andreu, Flora. 1985. What standard? Paper presented at NWAVE 14, Georgetown University.

Lambert, Wallace. 1967. A social psychology of bilingualism. *Journal of Social Issues* 23:91–109.

Lambert, Wallace, R. Hodgson, and S. Fillenbaum. 1960. Evaluative reactions to spoken language. *Journal of Abnormal and Social Psychology* 60:44–51.

Lavandera, Beatriz. 1984. *Variación y significado.* Buenos Aires: Hachette.

Rickford, John R., and Angela E. Rickford. 1976. Cut-eye and suck-teeth: African words and gestures in new world guise. *Journal of American Folklore* 89:294–309.

Sacks, Karen Brodkin. 1994. How did Jews become white folks? In Gregory and Sanjek 1994, 78–102.

Sider, Gerald M. 1993. *Lumbee Indian histories: Race, ethnicity and Indian identity in the southern United States.* New York: Cambridge University Press.

———. 1994. Identity as history: Ethnohistory, ethnogenesis and ethnocide in the southeastern United States. *Global Studies in Culture and Power* 1(1):109–22.

Sontag, Susan. 1966. Notes on "camp." In *Against interpretation and other essays,* by Susan Sontag. New York: Farrar, Straus, and Giroux.

Spears, Arthur. 1988. Black American English. In *Anthropology for the nineties,* ed. Johnnetta B. Cole, 96–113. New York: The Free Press.

Witherspoon, Gary. 1977. *Language and art in the Navajo universe.* Ann Arbor: University of Michigan Press.

Wolfram, Walt, and Natalie Schilling-Estes. 1998. *American English: Dialect and Variation.* Malden, Mass.: Basil Blackwell.

LANGUAGE AND LABOR
IN PAPUA NEW GUINEA

ANGELA GILLIAM

The analysis of language and linguistic characteristics cannot be separated from other cultural processes. Indeed, language is at once a mirror and a constituent element of politics, economics, social life, and the mind (Goodwin and Duranti 1992). Certainly connected to language issues and problems, then, is the question of political economy and the relationship production has to the growth or decline of a particular language.

The objective of this chapter is to continue the exploration of the relationship between language and the state power in Papua New Guinea, with special reference to two languages: Pure Motu and Hiri Motu.

First, some background information is in order. Papua New Guinea, located roughly north of Australia and New Zealand, has a population of almost four million people. Since it is a new nation, having achieved independence from Australia in only 1978, the country has suffered from the same kinds of externally oriented (i.e., metropole-benefitting) economic development and cultural domination typically borne by other subordinated regions. Though there is great variety in the phenotypes of the various demographic groups in the country, the population was considered "black" and "native" in the colonial era. My students at the University of Papua New Guinea were quick to remind the visitor that they have thirty thousand years of documented existence in the Pacific, even though the majority of population "types" may re-

83

mind one of African Diasporic or Asian/Pacific peoples in other parts of the world.

It is estimated that there are approximately 750 distinct languages spoken in the country. With colonialism, two contact, trading languages arose: Hiri Motu (which used to be known as Police Motu because of its use and spread by Papuan police officers around the turn of the century) and Tok Pisin (formerly known as Neo-Melanesian or New Guinea Pidgin). Tok Pisin is especially interesting because it is a creolizing language, one whose resources have been developed to the extent that it is now used in Parliament. (A *creolizing* language is one that has gone from being a pidgin language, spoken by no one as a native [first] language, to being the native language of a portion of the population, though for most it is a second language. Pidgin languages arise from contact situations and can be considered a sort of compromise form of speech among speakers sharing no common language.) Tok Pisin's rise in the world of affairs underlines a point that linguists take for granted, but that many nonspecialists are unaware of: all languages are equal in terms of their expressive potential. If a language does not have at a particular stage, say, suitable vocabulary resources for the discussion of physics, that language has nevertheless the structural (i.e., morphological, syntactic, and semantic) resources for development into a code that is adequate and efficient for such a purpose.

Pure Motu, sometimes called just "Motu," is spoken by Papuans in the coastal area in and around the capital city, Port Moresby. The country's three official languages are Hiri Motu, Tok Pisin, and English. In contrast to the situation in most Third World countries, the language of the people who traditionally inhabited the capital zone did not become the language associated with urbanization, national integration, and modernity, a language whose acquisition is considered highly important. Tok Pisin serves this purpose. It is the common language in all cities, not just the capital. Consequently, it is the language that people from different ethnic groups and language backgrounds use for intergroup communication. One recent estimate had 26 percent of all Papuans able to speak Tok Pisin, with 12 percent able to read and/or write it. A more recent estimate has over half the population speaking it. (See Gilliam 1984 for further details.) In spite of the status of Tok Pisin, English is the language of the greatest power-wielding institutions of Papua New Guinea. It is interesting, however, that the national Parliament is for the most part conducted in Tok Pisin because many of the elected representatives do not speak English.

The goal of this writing is not to attempt to reproduce the important record of classical linguistic work done by Taylor (1978), Dutton

84

and Voorhoeve (1974) or Chatterton (1970) on the origins of Motu and Hiri Motu, but to raise new questions.[1]

Indeed, some of the subjects still being debated are whether Hiri Motu is expanding or shrinking, whether language planning and intervention can alter a linguistic trend, and whether Pure Motu is a private language of solidarity to be used only in situations of ethnic intimacy. For all of these issues, the question of the historic struggle to confront colonialism and changing economic conditions is key to the answer. The question of just what impact social relations and historical processes have on language itself is an important one.

It is the position of this chapter that since the lexicon reflects the material condition—or the base—of a given society, and lexical arrest accompanies technological arrest, one must investigate the socioeconomic situation of Pure Motu and Hiri Motu speakers and how that situation reinforces what occurs with those languages.

But first, let us define the situation. Papua New Guinea was divided one hundred years ago, during the same period that the African continent was carved up at the Berlin Conference in 1884. According to Amarshi, Good, and Mortimer, direct colonization became the pattern in Melanesia. Imperial Germany annexed the northern half of mainland New Guinea and the smaller islands to the north and east in 1884. In response to Australian appeals, Britain in the same year took over the southern portion, known as Papua (Amarshi, Good, and Mortimer 1979). But Papua, the region that is home to Motu speakers, did not move in the same direction or at the same speed as German New Guinea. This was to prove both a problem and a godsend for coastal Papuans at a later point. On the one hand, the lackadaisical British approach to Papuan administration meant a slower penetration of capitalism than in the northern part. On the other hand, this very feature was to enable Motuans to hold on to their customs, including the precolonial barter trade. "Until 1942, governments in British New Guinea had to fight persistently to obtain sufficient funds to maintain basic administrative services" (Griffin, Nelson, and Firth 1979, 11). Furthermore, the type of big business interests already established in German New Guinea were virtually absent in Papua. This explains the smaller amount of export-oriented plantation production in Papua, a feature Amarshi, Good, and Mortimer have defined as characterizing the "ultra-periphery" (Amarshi, Good, and Mortimer 1979, 12).

This type of economic construct carried with it a tradition of bonded labor—similar in some ways to the situation in apartheid South Africa. Papua was the source of indentured migrant workers who were paid "single man" low wages, which were not enough for the worker's family. This situation meant that, in effect, the village community subsidized the capitalist sector, in that the continuance of coastal barter trade and local production still remained the basis of village existence. Nonetheless, some subsistence agriculture became historically marginalized during the early colonial period, and much of the agricultural work was left to women.

Colonial conditions throughout the world have engendered racialist attitudes toward the labor force; Papua was no exception. The laws applying to workers involved in the cash economy included a historical "colour bar" that was so pervasive that a "Papuan could not wear clothes above the waist unless he belonged to a special group . . . he had to be indoors from 9 p.m. to daylight" (Amarshi, Good, and Mortimer 1979, 181–82). This type of social context is part of an overall situation in which people are no longer producing for their own culture but where the fruits of their labor benefit another society.

Furthermore, the colonial situation involves the imposition of an export-oriented economy, which is accompanied by the introduction of a language that will be seen as representing the more powerful foreigners. Production reflects a linguistic stratification relegating the language of the workers at the lower end of the spectrum to informality and affective usage. This is part of a process that we can call *lexical arrest*—the situation in which lexical specialization and creativity is diminished in the speech of first-language (L1) speakers. "If the speakers of a language move to a situation in which the tasks and labor they perform in their society are progressively restricted by a reduction in their productive lives, gradually the lexicon of labor specialization will also be reduced" (Gilliam 1984). The skills the workers are directed to develop "are geared towards serving the same ends of the world market rather than towards development of an internal material, with the result that technologically, and in relation to the developed world, we move backward rather than forward" (Babu 1972). This technological arrest is usually part and parcel of economic underdevelopment. A people who labor under an economy that strips away the condition for increased participation of all sectors of the society will ultimately suffer linguistic underdevelopment.

This process had to be well under way by World War II, and was reinforced by the fact that Papua New Guineans carried a good part of World War II "on their backs" and in their gardens (mines still explode and maim Papua New Guineans.)

Australia occupied German New Guinea from the end of World War I until 1945, when Papua and New Guinea became jointly administered. Though Papua New Guinea received its independence in 1975, Australia still controls much of the economy. Given Australia's own history of dependent "down under" capitalism, there was little capacity for building the kind of infrastructure in the south that the Germans had started to build in the northeast. Indeed, Ali Mazrui was "to one day charge Australia with having denied Papua New Guinea an infrastructure for nationhood" (Griffin, Nelson, and Firth 1979, 147). This perception is contradictory for Papua, for as we shall see below, it is in the area of language and culture that this history presented benefits to a people struggling to hold on to their customs and dignity.

Nonetheless, the port-city-metropolis configuration whereby the language of the ethnic group living in and around the capital becomes the lingua franca of the working class does not apply in Port Moresby, the capital of Papua New Guinea. Tok Pisin (previously called Neo-Melanesian by foreigners) serves this purpose. Indeed, Pure Motu is reserved for one's speech community exclusively. As Renagi Lohia (personal communication 1991) maintains, Pure Motu speakers always learn the "other's language," in order to save Pure Motu for the home. Indeed, Papua New Guinean scholars must ultimately ask themselves if the drive for the separatist movement, Papua Besena, was not reinforced by these linguistic habits. Spokespersons for Papua Besena sometimes reflected ethnic chauvinism and the "we-were-contacted-before-you" attitude toward other groups.

Yet the language that has more chance to grow and expand is Hiri Motu, a distinct language from Pure Motu, because it is one of the country's three official languages. As noted above, Hiri Motu is a traditional language of trade and exchange in the Papuan region, and has been referred to as Police Motu. Taylor's thorough compilation of available research on the origins of Hiri Motu has this interesting data from a turn-of-the-century missionary: Motu speakers used pidgin forms when speaking to foreigners, but reserved Pure Motu for themselves (Taylor 1978).

At some point, the Australian colonial government tried to encourage English among Papuans. In 1929 government anthropologist F. E. Williams started a newspaper for "natives." Started during the same year as the passage of the White Women's Protection Act, the paper is revealing in its approach to both the projected reader and language:

> This paper is for the people of Papua. . . . It is for the brown men, and it will tell you about the things that belong to you. . . . The paper is written in English because the Government want you to learn the white man's language. There are many languages in Papua—Kiwai, Namau, Motu, Suau, Binandele and many others—more than a hundred of them. The white man cannot learn them all. It is better then for the Papuans to learn the white man's language. Then he will understand you; and you will understand him. And that will be a good thing, for he can teach you a lot that is new. (*The Papuan Villager* 1:1, 1929)

Thus, the stage was set for many linguistic contradictions, and English began to serve functions of class and to become "linguistic capital" with a profit-related benefit. Hiri Motu developed in the contact situation characterized by bonded labor and a male-exclusive work context. Finally, village labor became increasingly marginalized and female. Did Pure Motu become almost a "private" language by the efforts of females primarily? (Taylor notes a similar solidarity function for Hiri Motu among southern coastal "rascals" in today's Papua New Guinea who "exclude" the police from their own conversations.) Women clearly insisted on teaching their children Pure Motu, though it had lost its currency in the contact situation. The issue of gender is rarely considered when looking at the interface between Pure Motu and Hiri Motu. However, the current situation is that Motuans of both sexes are trying to spread Pure Motu while government resources are rarely given over to that effort.

In addition, the power of English speakers is reproduced by the fact that it is very difficult to find secular material in either Hiri Motu or Pure Motu. This is directly related to the fact that the English language "produces privilege in which value is tied to its rarity or exclusivity of use and access to acquisition" (Gilliam 1984).

But there is a phenomenon that bears mentioning here. Contrary to the situation of some Papua New Guinean languages where the youth are choosing *not* to speak the language of their speech communities (Nekitel 1980b), there is indication that young people are attempting to spread Pure Motu through the expansion of traditional music and popular string band. This unusual linguistic intervention demonstrates Pure Motu's power as a symbol for linguistic authenticity while at the same time it lacks the expanded usage required to be some type of "cultural capital"—which would allow increased access to employment.

The "string band" phenomenon is a uniquely current Papua New Guinean response by young male Pure Motu speakers to adapt traditional culture to "modern" cultural forms. In this, the string bands become an activity that partly answers the problem of the high unemployment rate among Papua New Guineans. The string band and its popularity, even in other island countries, is a source of pride for Pure Motu speakers who are increasingly ambivalent about other features of traditional culture. Indeed, there is often a cultural contradiction between Papua New Guinean traditions and newly received cultural norms.[2] This is exacerbated by an educational policy that does not have universal literacy as a goal or an accomplishment. And the late Margaret Nakikus, deputy director of the National Planning Office, maintained that the capital's high crime rate was due to an anger directed toward well-off expatriates and Papua New Guineans because "the system has not allowed them to get the same kind of jobs and opportunities those in government have had."[3] Papua New Guinean linguist Otto Nekitel goes further: "In view of the mounting social problems and the present state of lawlessness, one has been prompted by these circumstances to question the validity and relevancy of the apparent pro-English trend" (Nekitel 1980a).

The string band is a way around this problem for young men who use the phenomenon as a source of upward mobility as they leave, disaffected, village life and try to become part of "modern" city life. But this expansion of music in a language that in normal usage is reserved for the home and village cannot reverse what appears to be a trend toward shrinkage of Pure Motu. The private use of language rarely promotes its expansion—indeed, it restricts such growth—particularly if there is not transference of usage from private to public space. Language use in public space provides a structure for growth and the acquisition of new words, the collective transformation of grammar in a wide arena, and new applications in civic life. Additionally, in most nation-states an essential aspect of linguistic expansion is the updating of the language through access to government resources.

Speakers of Pure Motu are consciously attempting to critically assess other parts of their culture as well. Lohia affirms that traditional bride-price exchange generates more revenue circulation in Motu villages than export-oriented development projects for rural areas (Lohia 1981). This type of confidence in traditions is not limited to Pure Motu speakers alone, but can also be found throughout Papua New Guinea. However much linguistic and cultural resistance form part of a community's response to colonialism, direct linguistic intervention is necessary to further development. In addition, first-language speakers from a broad base of a given speech community must be involved in the language expansion. Restricted use of Pure Motu turns it into a type of Latin. Hiri Motu is still a viable "regional lingua franca," but available research shows that Tok Pisin is expanding at a greater rate (Taylor 1980). Tok Pisin is a vehicle for nationalistic expression of the country as a whole; Hiri Motu has become a rallying cry for regionalism. One language leads to national unity; the other has been used to engender separatism.

The neocolonial situation is such that it is imperative to ask certain questions within the context of linguistic work. Yet many of the social scientists who have done work in Papua New Guinea have contributed to the continued exotification of that country. Their goal has been to describe Papua New Guinean reality in such a way as to enhance their own careers rather than to demonstrate the need for a sound language policy. The current language policy seems designed to forever create the need for English-speaking experts, whose differential "expatriate" salary ranges drain the nation's economy.

The most intriguing and as yet unanswered questions are the following. To what degree has the "ethnography of speaking" both Pure Motu and Hiri Motu been a response to the "cultural invasion" that usually accompanies colonialism? What role have women played in linguistic resistance of Motu speakers? How can both Pure Motu and Hiri Motu arrest the shrinkage that appears to exist in those languages without pandering to separatist goals?

For one thing, it is not enough to work toward linguistic standardization; there must also be a struggle for universal literacy. As Bob Litteral communicated to Taylor, real language planning progress is more likely to come from the "lower" levels than the national government (Taylor 1981). This reinforces our position that first-language speakers of a given language must be involved in its expansion.

Also, Hiri Motu should be required for public service professionals. How is it possible for Papua New Guinean lawyers and doctors to get degrees without having had to take courses in the nation's official languages? The work of Renagi Lohia when he was head of the Public Services Commission was directed toward that end.

The relationship between language and state power exists everywhere. This power is also related to internal and external economic factors. It must be a part of any analysis of language change in "contact" situations.

Notes

1. I am indebted to the assistance and collegial support provided by Professor Andrew Taylor, whose work is respected by Motuan scholars. In addition, this analysis could not have been written without the "insider's scholarship" and guidance of Ambassador Renagi R. Lohia, a Pure Motu and Hiri Motu speaker, who is currently the Permanent Representative of Papua New Guinea to the United Nations.

2. One example of this contradiction was provided by Rennie Lohia in regard to body decoration. Traditional Motu tattoos have made way for Western fashions of body decoration (e.g., anchors or ships, snails, etc.). Once a young high school student in New York City noticed the tattoos that Mr. Lohia had put on his body and asked why he was not using traditional Motu designs. Mr. Lohia replied, "If I did that, I would not fit in with my friends when I return to Papua New Guinea."

3. This information came as a result of an interview with Margaret Nakikus for WBAI-FM radio in New York City, September 1983.

References

Amarshi, Azeem, Kenneth Good, and Rex Mortimer. 1979. *Development and dependency: The political economy of Papua New Guinea.* Melbourne: Oxford University Press.

Babu, A. M. 1972. Postscript. In *How Europe underdeveloped Africa,* by W. Rodney. Dar Es Salaam: Tanzania Publishing House.

Chatterton, Percy. 1970. The Origin and development of Police Motu. *Kivung* (Journal of the Linguistic Society of Papua New Guinea) 3:95–98.

Dutton, T. E., and C. L. Voorhoeve. 1974. *Beginning Hiri Motu.* Canberra: Dept. of Linguistics, Research School of Pacific Studies, Australian National University.

Gilliam, Angela. 1984. Language and "development" in Papua New Guinea. *Dialectical Anthropology* 8:303–18.

Goodwin, Charles, and Alessandro Duranti. 1992. Rethinking context: An introduction. In *Rethinking context: Language as an interactive phenomenon,* ed. Alessandro Duranti and Charles Goodwin, 1–42. Cambridge: Cambridge University Press.

Griffin, James, Hank Nelson, and Stewart Firth. 1979. *Papua New Guinea: A political history.* Sydney: Heinemann Educational Books.

Lohia, Renagi R. 1981. Impact of regional brideprice on the economy of Eastern Motu Villages. In *Post-Independence economic development of Papua New Guinea,* ed. P. A. S. Dahanayake. Proceedings of the Institute of Applied Social and Economic Research (IASER) Conference Monograph Series, no. 19, 27–29 October.

Nekitel, Otto. 1980a. Our first linguist. *Post-Courier* (Port Moresby), 17 October.

———. 1980b. What is happening to vernaculars? Paper presented at the Waigani Seminar, University of Papua New Guinea. *The Papuan Villager* (Port Moresby), 15 February.

Taylor, Andrew. 1978. Evidence of a Pidgin Motu in the earliest written Motu materials. In *Proceedings of the Second International Conference on Austronesian Linguistics.* Canberra: Australian National University.

———. 1980. The future of Motu. Paper presented at the Waigani Seminar, University of Papua New Guinea.

———. 1981. Current media development of Hiri Motu. Paper presented at the annual congress of the Linguistic Society of Papua New Guinea.

THE NATIVE LANGUAGE
AS A MEDIUM OF INSTRUCTION:
AN ISSUE REVISITED

Yves Dejean

There is a large population of non-English-speaking students entering the American school system every year. What language or languages should be used with these students as the medium of instruction?

Some possible answers to this question might involve practical considerations that do not necessarily parallel sound theoretical principles. For example, consider a family moving from Romania to a small city in upstate New York. Suppose the family has a six-year-old child who has never been to school before and is going to enter the first grade in an English-only American school. No one is able to communicate in Romanian, and the only available medium of instruction is English. A concerned teacher would no doubt accept this situation as an inevitable fact of life. Nevertheless, the concerned teacher does not have to abandon sound principles of general application. Such a case does not preclude questions such as the following. What language would be the best medium of instruction? Would it be preferable for this child to learn to read and write first in Romanian, rather than starting the process of reading without the important condition of fluency in the oral language represented by the written symbols?

Suppose an unbiased observer wishing to learn something about language and education were to tackle the general issue of language and education. Suppose he or she began by looking into how particular languages have functioned in particular educational systems over the last eighty years.

1. He or she would notice that, in all so-called developed societies where there is mass education, the medium of instruction is the language familiar to the majority of children and adults.
2. That person would also notice certain school systems, for example in African countries and in Haiti, where the medium of instruction is not a language familiar to the majority of children and adults of these regions. Furthermore, the researcher would notice that in such so-called underdeveloped societies, mass education is not a reality.
3. The researcher would find some instances of the use of two languages as media of instruction, one being the native language of children involved in so-called bilingual programs, and the other being another language that the same children are trying to acquire.

Our observer would undoubtedly come across a monograph published in Paris by UNESCO (Rotherberg 1953), *Vernacular Languages in Education*, which accepts the principle that the best medium for teaching is the mother tongue of the child or adult student.

The observer would relate this principle to his first observation and ponder the fact that the practice of so-called developed countries is a reflection of it. In other words, where mass education has succeeded, the medium of instruction has been the mother tongue of the majority of children and adults of the community. The observer would no doubt not take such a finding lightly, perhaps even being surprised by a disturbing contrast in scholarly practice. On the one hand, there is a propensity among scholars to use both carefully planned experiments and common sense in their research on school systems serving linguistic majority children in wealthy countries. On the other hand, there is an inclination among the same scholars to neglect common sense when experimenting with linguistic minorities and/or underdeveloped countries.

In 1975, Patricia Lee Engle reviewed the literature related to the use of vernacular (or home) languages in education, assuming that the many studies she examined addressed themselves to two straightforward questions: "(1) Will a child learn to read more rapidly in his second language if he is first taught to read in his primary language? and (2) Will the child achieve greater general knowledge of other subject matter areas in his second language if he is taught these subjects first in his native language?" (Engle 1975, 1).

The primary purpose of her paper was "to evaluate the evidence bearing on the issue of what language to use in teaching minority children in a bilingual culture." She did not find the surveys conclusive, and for her, "the question, then, is as yet open to debate."

94

In January 1982, Nadine Dutcher surveyed eight case studies in seven countries with the aim of answering the following questions: "In a multilingual society, what is the best choice as the initial language of instruction for the child in primary school? Is it a second language, or is it the first language? Which will result in greater access to secondary school?" (Dutcher 1982, 40). She found out that "there is not one universal answer. . . ." (iii).

In May 1982, Iris C. Rotberg linked the choice of the language or languages of instruction in the United States to the question of whether or not a particular approach is "the most effective way to teach children English and other academic skills" rather than to the issue of whether or not it is the most effective way to provide limited-English-proficient children with a complete education meeting their intellectual, affective, psychological, social, and physical needs (Rotberg 1982, 155).

It is remarkable that these writers never related the question of "what language to use in teaching minority children" to the issue of what language to use in teaching majority children. The obvious relationship between the two seems to be overlooked even in the 1953 UNESCO monograph. Although for the UNESCO experts it is axiomatic that the best medium for teaching is the mother tongue of the pupil, the monograph never relates the principle suggested for Third World and minority children to the accepted practice of using the mother tongue as the medium of instruction in Europe, North America, and other "developed" areas. The education of Third World children and linguistic minority children should be based on the same essential principles as the education of children from more privileged communities.

One must assume that the basic link that exists between the thinking processes and a spontaneously acquired first language is the same in all children of the world. Equal educational opportunity does not mean the same books, the same teachers, the same methods, and the same curriculum. Rather, it means the acceptance of the same basic principles of education when dealing with linguistic minority children: the same attitude of respect for what they bring to school, for their established first language, for their right to free self-expression through the only channel of thought they already possess, for their right to understand and be understood in a classroom, and for their right to meaningful participation in the educational process.

The question is not whether it is possible or feasible to educate a group of children in a foreign language, but whether it is natural, or most efficient, to do so. One should not confuse the issues of naturalness and feasibility. That something is possible or feasible does not mean that it should be done. Astronauts can be trained to move and work in a vacuum. Nobody would jump to the conclusion that ordinary people should be trained to move and work in a vacuum. A good example of such a confusion is found in Russell Campbell's (1970) paper "English Curricula for Non-English Speakers." He accepts as a fact the well-known, widespread educational failure of most Mexican-American and Navajo children and comments on the usual explanation: "To explain these results, the most common assumption has been that it is unreasonable to expect a child to acquire the fundamentals of education in a language he does not understand" (Campbell 1970, 305).

Campbell thinks that this assumption should be reexamined and he states, "It apparently is not the fact that it is unreasonable to expect children to acquire the fundamentals of education in a foreign language. *Once one accepts this as a possibility* [emphasis mine], additional evidence in its favor can be brought into focus" (Campbell 1970, 306).

Notice how the value of the statement can be modified if words like "a child" are replaced by something like "most children"—in other words, if the issues of feasibility (a child, some children, even many children) and naturalness (most children) are carefully distinguished, and also if one approaches mass education and individual education differently.

Modern school systems in different parts of the world suffer from many shortcomings. Every year people are reminded of the low reading level of one half of the ninth-graders in New York City. These poor readers are, by and large, monolingual English-speaking children. Although educators are rightly alarmed and are tempted to find a scapegoat, common sense will prevent them from attributing this failure to the fact that the medium of instruction is English—that is, the native language of the majority, rather than a foreign language. (There are, of course, dialect differences in the "monolingual" student population, but they are inconsequential compared to the actual language differences I deal with here.) Nobody would say that the reading problems of many young monolingual Americans could be solved by introducing Hindi or Arabic as the medium of instruction in American schools. Although many things are malfunctioning even in schools having a population of monolingual students, it is not because their native language is the medium of instruction.

What is natural, or most efficient, for the majority should also be presumed natural for minority groups. If the use of the mother tongue as the medium of instruction is accepted and advocated as the natural thing to do in the education of majority children, then in principle the use of the mother tongue as the medium of instruction should be accepted and advocated as the natural thing to do in the education of minority children.

96

The burden of proof rests on the shoulders of whoever advocates the use of a foreign language as the medium of instruction. No one is expected to prove that Japanese, Germans, Frenchmen, Englishmen, Americans, and Russians have been wrong and are still wrong in using the native language of their majority in the education of the native speakers of those languages. If a scholar were to suggest that Chinese should be the medium of instruction in Japan, Germany, France, England, America, and Russia, then he would have to present solid and convincing evidence that this foreign language would be a better medium of instruction for non-Chinese-speaking children. It is surprising that the advocates of foreign languages as media of instruction in many African countries, in many underdeveloped countries, and for many linguistic minorities, have never submitted a serious proposition to the governments of the aforementioned countries (or others like them) to make use of, say, Chinese or Hindi or Spanish as the medium of instruction in their school systems.

Our unbiased observer would take a fresh look at some questions underlying a number of language teaching experiments conducted in the Philippines (Alatis 1970, 282–83; Engle 1975, 6–9; Dutcher 1982, 6–9).

Do Filipino children do better from the third grade on, when they shift to an English curriculum, if they are first taught in their native language, in English, or when both languages are taught simultaneously?

Why should experiments be conducted to answer such questions? Does one need an experiment to know in advance that monolingual English-speaking students in America would do very poorly after two or three years of schooling in English, their native language, if they had to shift to a French curriculum in the third grade? Why should one give up common sense when dealing with linguistic minorities or with countries formerly colonized by foreign powers that forced their languages upon them?

The observer would take a close look at the well-known St. Lambert experiment (Lambert and Tucker 1972) and would notice several points:

1. In the middle-class St. Lambert suburb of Montreal, in 1963, a group of English-speaking Canadian parents showed concern for the failure of a variety of traditional foreign language teaching and learning techniques to provide a useful knowledge of French among students, even after years of study.

2. These English-speaking Canadian children were not failing in their schooling but receiving a high-quality education by the general standards accepted in Canada.

3. With the help of specialists from McGill University, a group of committed parents obtained funding for a kindergarten class conducted entirely in French by a competent bilingual teacher for monolingual English-speaking children in a monolingual English-speaking school.

4. Great care was taken to make sure that the children of the experimental group would feel free to express themselves in English. Regular tests were administered to ensure that these children in the French-language kindergarten would in no way suffer any impairment in the development of their English skills.

5. The experiment was continued in the following grades.

6. The progressive introduction of English language arts courses began in the first grade and was intensified thereafter.

7. The declared and carefully pursued goal was to provide these children with as good a general education as their peers in other English-only classes and schools of the St. Lambert suburb, although their education was geared toward French-English bilingualism.

8. The program was monitored by specialists and conducted on a voluntary basis with the full approval and active participation of parents and many members of the community.

9. The St. Lambert suburb was half English-speaking.

10. The experiment lasted several years and was successful in providing the participants with both an excellent general education and bilingual ability in French and English.

The St. Lambert experiment revealed that it is indeed possible for children to acquire a second language when the first years of their formal education are conducted in that language.

This was nothing new in world history. For centuries education has been conducted in Latin in Europe for non-Latin-speaking children with success both in acquiring Latin as a second language and in developing academic excellence. For a long period of time, education has been conducted in Hebrew for Jewish children having no previous knowledge of the Hebrew language. Education has been conducted in Sanskrit for Indian children speaking another language. Education has been conducted for the last 170 years in French for native speakers of Haitian Creole in Haiti. In all these cases, communities were dealing with a variety of elitist education and not with any form of mass education. If we consider the history of the modern, technologically advanced countries of today—Germany, the United States, England, Canada, Japan, and so on, we find no instances of successful mass education conducted in a language that is foreign to the vast majority of school-children. The St. Lambert experiment confirmed what has been known for a long time: it is possible to educate small groups of children in a foreign language. The St. Lambert experiment does not address the issue of mass education for majority or minority children.

The UNESCO monograph (Rotberg 1953) made a statement concerning adult education: "the great majority of adults will not have the time to master a foreign language sufficiently for it to be used as an effective medium of education" (58). This applies to many secondary school students moving to a foreign country, as, for example, many teenagers entering the American school system every year from non-English-speaking countries like Haiti, the Dominican Republic, Cape Verde, Greece, and Italy. The UNESCO statement can be considered with respect to most elementary school, limited-English-proficient children if educators ask themselves seriously what it is "to master a foreign language sufficiently for it to be used as an effective medium of education."

No research has been conducted casting doubt on, let alone refuting, the generalization expressed in the UNESCO statement quoted above. Therefore, a cogent argument can be made for instruction in a student's native language. In contexts in which a second, nonnative language is important, for example, those involving language-minority students, an argument can be made for bilingual education, in that it, too, uses the student's native language in instruction, in addition of course to a second language to be acquired. An argument for bilingual education in such a context follows:

• Every thinking person possesses one main channel of thought which is expressed through the particular language(s) that person acquired natively.
• The use of that channel is necessary for the kinds of thinking required in educational settings, as long as it is not replaced or supplemented by another linguistic channel, that is, a sufficiently well-mastered other language.
• The average child entering an American school with little or no knowledge of English, who uses another language natively, will rely on his native language for months and probably for more than a year.
• Nobody would deny that an important goal of formal education is to favor, encourage, promote, and develop thinking ability in children.
• No school can in good conscience oppose, hamper, or ignore several months in the development of the thinking processes of any group of students; and a curriculum which deliberately impedes or ignores such processes is inadequate.

• Any school dealing with the education of children whose cognitive processes depend upon and are linked to a language other than the principal school language (i.e., English in the United States) must face the problem of at least preserving the cognitive ability of those children. That cannot be done only by providing a very good English as a Second Language (ESL) program since the best ESL program cannot enable children to function in English and sufficiently master the English language in a matter of weeks or even months to the point of using it freely as an ordinary channel of thought.

• A cognitive instrument cannot change overnight or in a few weeks, months, or even years. A new channel of thought cannot be built overnight or in a few weeks, months, or even years.

Since the UNESCO statement of 1953, linguistics has made interesting progress, notably in the subfield of psycholinguistics, which deals with language acquisition and the relationship between languages and cognition. Although little is known about the exact relationship between language and thought, at least linguists have a better idea of the complexity of the native language acquisition process during early childhood. They know that the mastery of a first language is a remarkable feat, something that educators should not take lightly. In the past twenty-five years, as many linguists have become involved in the study of language as a social and cultural phenomenon, they have become more aware of the importance of the child's native language as a crucial link with a segment of society. In the case of children, this link cannot be severed without significant psychological damage.

Valdman and Stephan (1980, 84) take exception to the UNESCO monograph of the early 1950s and claim that it presented a new dogma, "an article of faith." This ironic statement is a reflection of an ideology that hampers our understanding of the real needs of the Haitian population. In spite of a strong and accurate statement by Valdman (1984, 77) that Haiti "is in essence a monolingual country" where the whole population, from the landless peasant to the richest city dweller, shares in the everyday use of Creole, he nevertheless draws a conclusion that, given mass education as a goal, flies in the face of logic and common sense:

> Notwithstanding the fact that Creole is the only language shared by all Haitians, there is no inherent principle of language planning that compels its use as the primary school vehicle or as the official language. Nor, contra the celebrated UNESCO article of faith (1951), has it been convincingly demonstrated that in a multilingual country, in all situations, literacy is most effectively imparted in a child's mother tongue. (Valdman 1984, 84)

100

Notice the inaccuracy of the expression "a multilingual country," applied to a country Valdman himself has described as a "monolingual country."

Perhaps Valdman should publish a statement directed to American boards of education, teachers colleges, university departments, schools of education, and others involved in education, with the following claims: Notwithstanding the fact that English is the only language shared by over 200 million Americans, there is no inherent principle of language planning that compels its use as the primary school vehicle. Nor has it been convincingly demonstrated that in the United States literacy is most effectively imparted in the monolingual English-speaking child's mother tongue.

Modern education requests an active student participation in the classroom and in the learning process. In the past students were supposed to keep silent, to listen to the instructor. Today, students are encouraged to speak their minds, to question, to answer freely, and to express their feelings, beliefs, and thoughts. How is it possible for the average child of an average class with an average teacher to freely participate and talk while using a language unknown or unmastered? Fluency in the medium of instruction is a prerequisite to active participation in class. For a meaningful education, fluency in the medium of instruction should be a point of departure rather than a goal. Although fluency in a second language can be an important goal for native speakers of another language, it should not be the only goal.

It is important to clearly distinguish two quite different issues in the field of bilingual education and keep them separate.

First, for millions of limited English proficient (LEP) students in the United States, bilingual education is a *need*. The main concern of their educators should be to take care of this crying need among linguistic-minority children.

Second, bilingual education can be viewed as an ideal, a desirable goal, for all children. This is a different issue, the issue of providing a dramatically richer education for everyone. This second issue may be a dream, not likely to become a reality even in a distant future. The first one is a *right*, the full recognition of which is long overdue.

By now the question of using the native language of LEP children in the United States should have been settled. The problem is how to implement bilingual programs using both English and their native languages; how to create the necessary educational materials; and how to properly train teachers, both bilingual and monolingual, to deal with the bilingual education of these children.

The UNESCO experts of the early 1950s were on the right track. Their major preoccupation was with *how* to use vernacular languages, not whether to use them. And their concern was how to alleviate the inconvenience of an education conducted in a foreign language in the unfortunate case in which the use of the natural medium of instruction, the native language, would be impossible. Here in the United States, educators should have similar concerns. In isolated instances, one single child or just a handful of children cannot be provided a bilingual program using their native language. How can such children be protected and helped? How can educators spare them the hardship of cultural shock? How can their teachers alleviate their bewilderment at what is going on in the classroom? It is the teachers' responsibility to study the means of coping with such problems.

The proposal of this chapter is to approach the issue of choosing a proper medium of instruction for linguistic-minority children, keeping in mind common sense, naturalness, and mass education as the goal.

It is not by chance that during this last century of compulsory education, modern societies that were able to wipe out illiteracy (or nearly so) and to provide all their citizens with formal schooling did so by using the native language of the majority, not an unfamiliar language.

It is not by chance that a shift from the exclusive use of Swedish, the language of the politically dominant minority in Finland up to the nineteenth century, to the use of Finnish, the language of the majority, permitted Finland to become one of the most advanced modern societies as far as general education is concerned. Up to the mid-nineteenth century, the majority of the Finnish population was illiterate.

It is not by chance that the Soviet Union successfully dealt with mass education of its large illiterate population (70 percent of the population as a whole) between 1915 and 1940 by using Russian for Russian-speaking people and more than sixty indigenous languages for its linguistic minorities.

It is not by chance that the successful literacy campaigns of Cuba, in 1961, and Nicaragua, in 1980, were conducted in Spanish and that the remaining pockets of illiteracy were mainly among the non-Spanish-speaking minorities.

A country that has an immigration policy must also develop an education policy based on sound educational principles to deal with the needs of school-age immigrants.

Educators must reject the double standard that has crept into their educational practice. While monolingual teachers accept as axiomatic that the best medium for teaching monolingual English-speaking students is the mother tongue of the children, how could they deny the truth of the same statement when applied to minority children? To do so is to accept uncritically an ideology pervading the thinking of most educators, scholars, and researchers. The contradictions, fallacies, and

102

inconsistencies observed in the treatment of the issue of the best medium for school instruction are to be explained by the influence of certain assumptions and the interests they serve.

One of these assumptions is that it makes sense to treat problems of oppressed groups one way, those of the dominant classes of a society, another. What immediately comes to mind in thinking of education is that mass education in the eyes of dominant groups can be dysfunctional, literacy in particular, if it has the effect of making restless a normally dormant mass of people. Ignoring sound principles of general application when dealing with oppressed groups is but one manifestation of this same assumption.

References

Alatis, J., ed. 1970. *Bilingualism and language contact.* Washington, D.C.: Georgetown University Press.

Campbell, Russell N. 1970. English curricula for non-English speakers. In *Bilingualism and language contact,* ed. J. Alatis, 301–12. Washington, D.C.: Georgetown University Press.

Dutcher, Nadine. 1982. *The use of first and second languages in primary education: Selected case studies.* World Bank Staff Working Paper no. 504 (January). Washington, D.C.: World Bank.

Engle, Patricia Lee. 1975. *The use of vernacular languages in education: Language medium in early school years for minority language groups.* Bilingual Education Series no. 3 (June). Arlington, Va.: Center for Applied Linguistics.

Lambert, Wallace E., and Richard G. Tucker. 1972. *Bilingual education of children: The St. Lambert experiment.* Rowley, Mass.: Newbury House Publishers.

Rotherberg, Iris C. 1982. Some legal and research considerations in establishing federal policy in bilingual education. *Harvard Educational Review* 52:2. Paris: UNESCO.

———. 1953. *Vernacular languages in education.* Monographs on Fundamental Education no. 8. Paris: UNESCO.

Valdman, Albert. 1984. The linguistic situation of Haiti. In *Haiti—Today and Tomorrow: An Interdisciplinary Study,* ed. Charles R. Foster and Albert Valdman, 77–99. Lanham, Md.: University Press of America.

Valdman, Albert, and Georges Stephan. 1980. Vers la définition d'un modèle d'enseignement bilingue et fonctionnel pour haïti. In *Créole et enseignement primaire en Haïti,* ed. Albert Valdman, 48–74. Bloomington, Ind.: Indiana University Press.

THE SYMBOLIC FUNCTION OF THE GYPSY MYTH

IAN HANCOCK

It is evident that there are aspects of the dominant European-derived cultures that are perceived as threatening: groups seeking escape from them were well represented among the early settlers in North America. Others have more recently sought to drop out and establish alternative societies; the hippie communes of the 1960s, and the new-African and new-Islamic colonies that have sprung up since the Civil Rights movement within the United States are examples of this. For the most part, such breaks with the mainstream have been initiated by individuals who were originally participants themselves, and who have only subsequently become disenchanted by it.

Perhaps the most vigorous rejection of the dominant culture, however, is typified by those groups who have been insulating themselves from the world around them from the very beginning (that is, those that have not grown as societies alternative to, and derived from, the mainstream). Whereas none of the eighteenth- and nineteenth-century immigrant utopian societies survive today, and very few of the dropout communes, people such as the Amish or the Doukhobors continue to maintain their isolation successfully here in North America.

One ethnic minority that belongs in this latter category is the Romani, or Gypsy, population. Numbering about one million in North America, until very recently Gypsies have existed unobtrusively here, seldom attracting national attention and in fact not even recognized by most of mainstream society as real people at all. Commenting on this, journalist Nikki Meredith wrote that "the secrecy of the Gypsies makes the Mafia look like an open society" (Meredith 1983, 9).

The history of the Gypsy people can hardly be matched in terms of oppression and injustice. Since their very entry into Europe from Asia seven and a half centuries ago, they have been the victims of slavery and genocide, deportation and torture. No other single human population has endured suffering so widely and so consistently as have the Rom. At first incarceration, then expulsion, sterilization, and finally extermination were techniques employed by the Nazis to deal with Gypsies, treatment civilized individuals now regard in retrospect with horror. Yet within the past few years, since the late 1960s, all four have been proposed by different European governments as means of solving the "Gypsy problem." And with the rise in ethnic nationalism since the collapse of socialist governments in Eastern Europe, anti-Gypsy sentiment has risen with increased vigor.

Although there were three Gypsies with Columbus on his second voyage in 1498, Gypsies began to reach the Americas in greater numbers in the sixteenth century as transportees shipped here to work in plantations. Others came to the United States at the end of the nineteenth century, fleeing slavery in Europe. However, victims of discriminatory immigration policy, they were turned away at Ellis Island. Those who managed to come in across the Mexican or Canadian borders met anti-Gypsy laws, some of which are still on the books today, and which are still periodically put into effect. No other ethnic minority in this country is the target of repressive laws that name them specifically and forbid (or require a license for) them to establish homes or to work in different counties and states. No other ethnic minority has special police bureaus monitoring its movements or specialists compiling a computerized file of its names, addresses, and genealogies.

Facts such as these contrast starkly with the idealized picture that the *gajikano*, or non-Gypsy, population has of Gypsies. I recently bought a lapel button bearing the slogan "Free the Gypsies." This, and another with the wording "Free the Unicorns," was on sale in a novelty gift shop. Its intent was to amuse. After all, in the popular mind, Gypsies are the very epitome of freedom. There are hundreds of literary pieces, either novels or poems, as well as a great number of songs, that have a Gypsy theme; and the theme has overwhelmingly to do with freedom: freedom from nine-to-five jobs, freedom from having to attend to personal hygiene, freedom from sexual restrictions, freedom from the burden of material possessions, freedom from responsibility, freedom from the law. The August 1996 issue of *Disney Adventures*, a magazine for children, wrote about a condition called "gypsyitis," the symptoms of which are "an urge to run away from it all and dance among the dandelions" and being "footloose and fancy-free." In Black's *Gypsy Bibliography*, which includes nothing written after 1914, there are 133 ballads, 199 plays, 351 novels, and 262 poems listed that have been written about, or include, Gypsies in the English literary tradition.

In the book *The Pariah Syndrome* (Hancock 1987), I document in detail the facts of Romani history from the perspective of the Roma being a targeted population. What emerges is a picture of centuries of almost ceaseless oppression. Whatever periods of freedom may have existed during that time were short-lived, and were the result of the idealizing of the Gypsy population by the writers and philanthropists of the time, people whom Dougherty (1980, 273) called "superficial sentimentalists or genteel snobs looking for a feudal relic to coddle and patronize" in his study of the Gypsy image in literature. Without doubt, there exists an extraordinary discrepancy between the real and the perceived state of the Gypsy.

When we examine the reasons for this, a number of possibilities present themselves. Part of the stereotype includes the belief that Gypsies are a "mysterious" people with an unknown, perhaps otherworldly, past. This is alluded to repeatedly in the content and even the titles of books and articles about Gypsies. This would suggest that the reason lies simply in ignorance of the facts. And yet a great deal is known about Gypsy origins and history. It has been documented for over two centuries that Gypsies trace their linguistic and cultural heritage to India. A hundred and twenty years ago, Simson (1865, 8) called the fictitious image of the Gypsy as wanderer "very erroneous," pointing out that "nomadic Gypsies constitute but a portion of the race, and a very small portion of it." In 1902, American romanologist Albert Sinclair wrote in his journal, "How little people, even those who are much interested, learn about the American Gypsies! They do not know they own real estate, lend money, join the churches, how many or how few there are, etc. In fact, they know little about them" (quoted in Salo 1993, 42). More recently, Okely (1983, 125) has made the same point: "Gypsies do not travel about aimlessly, as either the romantics or the anti-Gypsy suggest." Scholarly treatments of Gypsies are numerous and readily available, and lack of information cannot be the reason for the perpetuation of the myth. But the *idea* that a lack of information exists has become a part of that myth. The reasons for its persistence must, then, be sought elsewhere.

More recently, there have been signs of a grudging acknowledgement of the legitimacy of Gypsy identity and history, but a resistance to it—as though it were driving away something more valuable. Even when discounting the fictional image, it is reinforced by being repeated;

even when none of the trappings of that image are a part of the reporter's actual experience, they are alluded to. In August 1986, one Boston newspaper ran a six-page feature on one of that city's Romani families, claiming on the first page that from their appearance, they could have been "Spanish, or French, or Italian, or Irish," but by the second page calling them "Glitter and gold, decked out in bright babushka of legend. They are exotic women in colorful skirts, dancing in sensual swirls. They are dark men with smoldering eyes. They are carefree spirits playing the tambourine. The entire image is crowned with a halo of mystique, shrouded in a cloak of mystery. And there is some truth to all of it" (Brink 1986, 5).

It is clear that Gypsies give fledgling journalists a chance to exercise their skills in creative fiction, but truth is distorted considerably in the process. Despite showing two pictures, one inside and one out, of the *house* of the Gypsy family it discusses, another article is entitled "Hustle, hustle aboard the caravan." Crystal balls, nonexistent in the community described, are alluded to in the headline, "Authorities gaze into Gypsy con-game." Despite its serious intent, a twenty-minute documentary film about a Romani school in California closed with the observation that "Although Gypsies still dance around the campfire, the fire is slowly flickering out as Gypsy life gradually fades into oblivion. . . ." The film dealt with education, and it included no dancing and no campfires.

Most writers about Gypsies still get their information from books rather than from firsthand experience. Those who do manage to win the confidence of actual Gypsies, and thereby gain temporary entry into the Romani environment, quickly find their preconceptions shaken. There are no campfires and tambourines, no crystal balls and violins. Yet their nonexistence is not interpreted as evidence of the inaccuracy of the Gypsy image—but rather as a sign that true "Gypsy life" is disappearing.

A student of mine came to me at the end of a course I give on Romani history to thank me for what she had learned. However, she admitted to some disappointment because I had made Gypsies become real people for her. She preferred the image she had had of them before taking the class, she said.

In 1973, Cohn (1973, 61) suggested that Gypsies themselves survive as a people because they "are needed in [non-Gypsy] culture," the implication being that Gypsies exist because of non-Gypsy sufferance. There is a need, presumably in all cultures, for an avenue of escape for those individuals who cannot function fully in their own society, either because of personality traits or a genuine grievance against its standards. Cohn's statement is misleading, however, because he does not make the point that what attracts the "hippies and fanatics" he speaks of are not, in fact, Gypsies but the imaginary popular image of Gypsies that those same individuals help to sustain.

A number of alternative reasons have been suggested, by sociologists and others, as to what motivates such people to be attracted to the Gypsy image; these have been discussed at more length in Hancock 1976. One possibility is that the normalizing pressures of mainstream, Anglo-dominated American society have robbed some of those in it of their identity; ethnicity for such people becomes a precious commodity, and since (unlike for Italian, Irish, Serbian, and other Americans) there exists a tangible, mythical Gypsy identity to which "hippies and fanatics," musicians, actors, flower children, and others apparently belong, it serves as a useful, all-purpose ethnic receptacle. Since it exists quite independently of Gypsies themselves, there is never a conflict with the actual ethnic community who, as will be shown, make use of it in turn for their own purposes.

Fantasy projection harms the Romani people by keeping the stereotype alive, and by making it difficult to convince the media of more serious Gypsy-related issues. But another reason for the maintenance of the Gypsy image by the establishment has been more harmful in the past, though it is far from dead: the Gypsy as scapegoat.

Since the fourteenth century, Gypsies in Europe have existed as a people without a geographical homeland, and without any kind of political, military, educational, or financial strength. They have been an easy target for the application of blame. Gypsies have been accused of theft, poisoning wells, poisoning cattle, spreading diseases, stealing children, and even cannibalism. The most recent charges of the latter crime were made in Slovakia as recently as 1928.

Kephart has recently suggested that prejudice against Gypsies is based in their being perceived of as a countercultural population—a refinement of the notion of Gypsy as scapegoat:

> American Gypsies too, continue to face prejudice and discrimination. Some observers contend that it is a matter of ethnic prejudice, similar to that experienced by blacks, Chicanos and other minorities. However, it is also possible that the Rom are perceived as a *counterculture*. . . . If people *perceive* of Gypsies as a counterculture, then unfortunately for all concerned, prejudice and discrimination might be looked upon as justifiable retaliation. (Kephart 1982, 43)

Yet another explanation, and an attractive one for this writer, has been proposed by Sibley. He believes that there has been an intrinsic manipulation of the Romani population by the establishment, which, for its own purposes, keeps the Gypsy myth alive and resists efforts to adjust it to something more realistic. Since that image is the antithesis of all of the values of that establishment—morality, work ethic, hygiene, and so on, it serves a useful purpose in helping to define the boundaries of the dominant culture:

> It is notable that myth contributes in a significant way to the shaping of images of groups that do not fit the dominant social model. The possibility that the characterization of social groups like Gypsies may be based on myth is rarely considered, particularly in governmental circles, probably because these myths are functional—they serve to define the boundaries of the dominant system. Accounts of non-conforming behavior assume the form of a romantic myth, or they involve imputations of deviancy, which are also largely mythical; the romantic image, located at a distance or in the past, necessarily puts the minority on the outside. (Sibley 1981, 195–96)

Romani reactions to their treatment by non-Gypsies have taken two main directions. There has, on the one hand, been a withdrawal from all unnecessary social and physical contact with non-Gypsies. Cultural pressures to remain aloof have existed since before the exodus out of India, and no doubt have their origins in the Indian caste system. Among contemporary Gypsies in the United States, their actual manifestation differs from group to group, being most strongly maintained by those who came here directly out of slavery. But children are taught from the beginning that a clear-cut division exists between people who are Gypsies and people who are not, and that it must be maintained at all costs. This is reinforced by notions of cleanliness, eating habits, the handling of animals, sexual behavior, and so on. The desirability of being a Gypsy is emphasized; and, while there are no illusions about the difficulties of maintaining Romani values in a non-Romani environment, very few Gypsies would want to be anything else. At the same time, great lengths are gone to in order to protect the ethnic identity; it is still the case that only a handful of Gypsies admit their ethnicity publicly, one reason for the apparently tiny number of identifiable Gypsies in the professions.

On the other hand, there has been an internalization of the stereotype, and a regurgitation of it for the public: if this is what fascinates the non-Gypsy, and if this is what they are willing to pay for, then they shall have it.

Media attention of this sort can in fact harm the whole community. Police routinely step up their harassment of all Gypsies in an area, even when just one individual or family is under investigation. Nevertheless, an image is usually projected that can mislead the public, and thereby protect the community. Sometimes this seems to be done instinctively: in the article by Brink mentioned earlier (assuming that she did not put words into his mouth), her interviewee claimed that Gypsies do not work like other people, and that there were no Gypsies in the professions, no Gypsy doctors. And yet the individual involved had attended a World Romani Congress in Europe and had met its leaders, all Rom, who numbered among themselves physicians, professors, politicians, and engineers. His own nephew was majoring in computer science at the University of Colorado. In the same way, outsiders are discouraged from learning the Romani language and may be told that it is Greek or Spanish. This misleading representation from within the Romani community serves as a shield; it is believed that if inquisitive non-Gypsies are busy pursuing the myth, they will leave the real thing alone. The myth is a mechanism of liberation that allows a minimum of interference from outside. The function of this, however, is beginning to be affected by contemporary changes affecting the Gypsy community.

In the past few years, the American Romani population has begun to organize itself in ways previously nonexistent in this country. For example, they now have a representative at the United Nations. Some have called such efforts "fantastic," others "a mere toying, a waste of energy" and "artificially contrived" (Lípa 1983, 4). In an article that appeared in 1984, a leading Hungarian scholar of Romani studies wrote that "it is a grave mistake to suppose that either racial factors, or the idea of ethnic identity, unite the different Gypsy groups" (Vekerdi 1984), although a report by a team of geneticists working at the Boston General Hospital and published in *The Lancet* in August 1987 made it clear that the analysis of blood groups, haptoglobin phenotypes, and HLA types has established Gypsies as a distinct population with origins in the Indian region of the Punjab; this finding is supported by the worldwide Gypsy language, Romani, which is notably similar to Hindi (Thomas et al. 1987).

Romani self-determination is a threat to those scholars whose investment in Gypsies is in their value as anthropological subjects. We are taking their toys away, and they react accordingly. Like Inuit [Eskimos] without igloos or Indians without tepees, Gypsies without wagons cheat the investigator of something. While Anglo-Americans can progress from horse and cart to automobile, "exotic" minorities are seen to be losing something of their identity if they do too.

New conflicts for American Gypsies are becoming evident as these movements grow: since obtaining permanent representation in the United Nations in 1979, the Romani Union has entered the international forum; trans-Atlantic communication is on the increase; with the ongoing demand for more Romani representation on the U.S. Holo-

111

caust Memorial Council, Washington has become very well aware of the Romani presence in this country. Indeed, a congressional hearing on human rights abuses of Gypsies was held in Washington on April 14, 1994. It is not possible to remain invisible and to be involved in such matters. More and more Romani Americans are seeking legal recourse and challenging discrimination in the courts, and winning. There is an increasing rejection of the word "Gypsy" and all of the negative connotations that go with it. This is slow going; it was only in November 1992 that the *New York Times* bowed to pressure to begin spelling the word *Gypsy* with a proper noun's capital initial letter. But if the existence of the Gypsy myth is to be eradicated in Euro-American society, both Gypsies and *gaje* are going to have to find alternatives to fulfill its functions, and this is not likely to be accomplished soon.

References

Black, George Fraser. 1971. *A Gypsy bibliography*. Ann Arbor, Mich.: Gryphon Books.

Brink, Susan. 1986. Lost in the city. *Boston Herald Sunday Magazine*, 10 August, 4–7, 16.

Cohn, Werner. 1973. *The Gypsies*. Reading, Penn.: Addison-Wesley.

Conner, Randolph. 1985. She takes Halloween spiritually. *Images*, 25 October, 5.

Dougherty, James. 1980. The Gypsy in literature. Ph.D. diss., University of Chicago.

Grumet, Joanne, ed. 1986. *Papers from the sixth and seventh meetings of the Gypsy Lore Society*. New York: North American Chapter of the Gypsy Lore Society.

Hancock, Ian. 1976. Romance vs. reality: Popular notions of the Gypsy. *Roma* 2:7–23.

———. 1987. *The pariah syndrome: An account of Gypsy slavery and persecution*. Ann Arbor: Karoma.

———. 1991. The East European roots of Romani nationalism. *Nationalities Papers* 19(3):251–67.

———. 1992. The roots of inequity: Romani cultural rights in their historical and social context. *Immigrants and Minorities* 11(1):3–20. Special issue entitled *Gypsies: The forming of identities and official responses*.

———. 1993. Anti-Gypsyism in the new Europe. *Roma* 38/39:5–29.

———. 1996. Standardization and ethnic defense in emergent non-literate societies: The Gypsy and Caribbean cases. In *Language, Blacks, and Gypsies*, ed. T. Acton and M. Dalphinis. London: Karia Press.

Kephart, William M. 1982. *Extraordinary groups: The sociology of nonconventional lifestyles*. New York: St. Martin's Press.

Lípa, Jiři. 1983. Commentary on priorities in Romanological studies. *Newsletter of the North American Chapter of the Gypsy Lore Society* 6(1):3.

Meredith, Nikki. 1983. The fortunes of the Gypsies. *California Living Magazine*, 24 April, 9–15.

Okely, Judith. 1983. *The traveller Gypsies*. Cambridge: Cambridge University Press.

Salo, Sheila. 1993. Sinclair meets the Rom. *Journal of the Gypsy Lore Society* 5(3):35–44.

Sibley, David. 1981. *Outsiders in urban societies*. New York: St Martin's Press.

Simson, Walter. 1865. *A history of the Gypsies*. London: Sampson, Low, Son & Marston.

Thomas, James, M. Doucette, D. C. Thomas, and John Stoeckle. 1987. Disease, lifestyle, and consanguinity in 58 American Gypsies. *The Lancet* 11:377–79.

Vekerdi, J. 1984. The Vend Gypsy dialect in Hungary. *Acta Linguistica* 34(1,2):65–86.

Racism in Professional Settings: Forms of Address as Clues to Power Relations

Lee D. Baker

In 1985 Ronald Reagan reconstituted the U.S. Civil Rights Commission by appointing Clarence Pendleton Jr. as chair. Pendleton made the number one priority of the Civil Rights Commission the investigation of "reverse discrimination." Pendleton reassured Reagan that the Commission was "working on a color blind society that has opportunities for all and guarantees success for none" (quoted in Omi and Winant 1986, 1). The revamping of the Civil Rights Commission was a benchmark in the erosion of strides made by people of color during the Civil Rights movement. Ironically, the efforts of Republicans during the 1980s to eliminate race-based preferential hiring, promotion, college admissions, and contract procurements were couched in the rhetoric of the Civil Rights movement. After all, it was the Rev. Dr. Martin Luther King Jr. who had had a dream that his children would be judged solely on the "content of their character."

From Reagan's Civil Rights Commission in the 1980s to the proposed California Civil Rights Initiative in the 1990s, neoconservatives have rearticulated the notion of racial equality by conflating it with "traditional" American and family values.[1] Simultaneously, less conservative interests have failed to attack structured racial inequality systematically (Winant 1994; Edsall and Edsall 1992; Gregory and Sanjek 1994). While conservatives have been dismantling affirmative action programs, liberals have been consumed with promoting notions of multiculturalism and furthering ethnic diversity. Developing multicultural curriculums for the public schools and fostering or managing di-

115

versity within the workplace are exceedingly important endeavors. However, even if ethnic diversity is embraced and racial parity (in the aggregate) is achieved, one cannot lose sight of the fact that these efforts do not eliminate racial inequality or equalize the disparity of power and economic relations between people of color and whites. Legal scholar Derrick Bell explains that "Black people will never gain full equality in this country. Even those Herculean efforts we hail as successful will produce no more than temporary 'peaks of progress,' short-lived victories that slide into irrelevance as racial patterns adapt in ways that maintain white dominance" (Bell 1992, 12).

Regardless of efforts to "integrate" the workforce, systemic racism remains within the larger society and within particular work sites. Political scientists, sociologists, and legal scholars have all demonstrated that institutional racism often persists within various work- and market-places, legislative bodies, and courtrooms, despite efforts to manage or institute ethnic diversity (Edsall and Edsall 1992; Guinier 1994; Grofman, Handley, and Niemi 1992; Terkel 1992; Shull 1993; Winant 1994). In professional office settings, racism does not take on the virulent form of racist slurs, violent acts, or even overt discrimination, yet racial as well as gender inequality persists. Despite great strides made in hiring people of color and women within the managerial and professional sectors, they remain scattered in lower-level positions and grossly underrepresented within the top ranks (Shull 1993).

The question I have posed is, what can linguistic anthropology offer to help explain the menacing problem of the color line as well as help to manage diversity?[2] One effective approach is to draw from the discourse of anthropologists interested in issues of political economy who employ ethnographic methods to interrogate how culture is woven into social structure and how culture affects people as social agents. On the one hand, peoples' everyday lives are shaped by legal, economic, bureaucratic, political, or state structures; but on the other, people shape their everyday lives to resist or manipulate the structural forces that oftentimes repress them. This delicate balancing act is done through the learned behavior of culture—sometimes consciously, other times not.[3]

By analyzing subtle sociolinguistic and cultural rules through ethnographic inquiry, I will make an argument that an ethnically diverse workplace, by itself, does not constitute a change in the structural power relations or how that power is culturally signified. Yet, work sites are often contested spaces, and when an organization's hierarchy is challenged, aspects of the cultural signification of power shift. It is incumbent upon anthropologists and other behavioral scientists to help executives and personnel managers understand that ethnic diversity it-

116

self does not change structured inequality or directly confront the new face of racism. Lerone Bennett Jr., executive editor of *Ebony Magazine*, reminds us that "We hear people say, 'We tried integration and it failed.' That isn't so. Integration has never been tried in this country. It has not even been defined. What is integration? If you put two, three blacks in an all-white institution, it's not integrated. It requires a complete change in the way you think as an institution. Real integration involves a change in values" (Terkel 1992, 380).

NEW FACES OF RACISM

African Americans have been engaged in an incipient class-formation process as a consequence of the Civil Rights movement, affirmative action programs, and rising numbers of African-American college graduates (Brooks 1990). This process began precisely at the point when the U.S. economy moved from an industrial and manufacturing base to one motored by finance, information, and service (Harvey 1989). As the economy became increasingly deindustrialized, cities lost hundreds of thousands of manufacturing jobs and billions of dollars in federal funds. These trends have been augmented by a general pattern of uneven development that has been systematically decimating many inner cities. This has led to an increase in crime, infant mortality rates, high school dropouts, and drug trafficking (Kennedy, Gastón, and Tilly 1990).

The combination of decomposing inner cities and the loss of high-paying union, manufacturing, and industrial jobs has driven an invisible wedge between the more mobile clerical and professional African Americans and the structurally underemployed, underpaid, or unemployed African Americans in the inner cities (Myers-Jones 1988; Edsall and Edsall 1992; Wilson 1978). The structural rift within the African-American community has been accompanied by the construction of two competing images within the "black" racial construct, which is perpetuated primarily by the media.

The first image—a positive image—is primarily formed on prime-time television sitcoms such as the Bill Cosby show and through genuinely positive media personalities such as Oprah or newscasters. In addition to television personalities, there are a myriad of elected and appointed African-American public officials that are ensconced within the vehicles of popular culture and contribute to the image that "blacks have made it." This image is reified by an even larger number of upwardly mobile African Americans who are part of the professional middle class (Brooks 1990; Davis 1992).

The second image of African Americans—a negative image—is

117

framed by crime and ideas of "the underclass." This image is produced at the movie theater, on the nightly news, and by pundits and politicians who view "illegitimacy" and crime in terms of an individual's lack of traditional values (Gingrich and Armey 1994). This image of the "underclass" is almost always couched in the criminal activity of people of color (Williams 1994). As a *Time Magazine* cover story put it, "The universe of the under class is often a junk heap of rotting housing, broken furniture, crummy food, alcohol and drugs" (Franklin 1991, 98). To round out this image, one merely needs to envision the black male gang member contemplating his next carjacking on a dimly lit street corner riddled with graffiti and littered with garbage, forty-ounce beer bottles, and crack vials.

These two competing images of successful minorities and "gangster/welfare mother" serve to bifurcate prejudice along class lines, which circumvents allegations of individual racial discrimination.[4] This occurs because the construct of race that is imposed upon poor blacks is often juxtaposed with the construct used for and by the black middle class. If one begins to isolate the inequality within the criminal justice system along racial lines, one needs to look at only the burgeoning black middle class to assume that members of the so-called underclass could have made it or pulled themselves up by their bootstraps.

Yet, members of the black middle class still are faced with racism that is sophisticated, subtle, and often unnoticed by its perpetrators. Often this form of "racism with a smile" occurs in the workplace and cannot be readily identified or prosecuted.[5] For example, cultural and social isolation, lack of promotion, last-hired first-fired policies, disaffection, stress, and discrimination accompanied by nonracial factors[6] are some examples of institutional racism that contribute to disempowerment in the workplace (Brooks 1990).

POWER *PLAYS:* HEGEMONIC FORMS OF ADDRESS

While power in the workplace is most often articulated structurally, economically, or interpersonally, it is also often signified culturally by subtle cultural patterns that dominate specific settings or permeate entire organizations where people work. The cultural patterns that govern how people interact with each other in a specific factory, institution, corporation, or office can be used as a window to view how ethnic or racial groups dominate or contest the structural and economic power relations within in each context. One way of getting at the dominant culture of a particular work site is to observe how language is used. A revealing use of language in the workplace is the *form of address* that managers and staff use with one another. Significant clues about power relations in the workplace are provided by the way managers and staff address one another formally or informally using titles, first names, given names, or nicknames.

My research demonstrates a simple pattern: certain sociolinguistic rules that are unquestioningly observed within the workplace correspond with the cultural rules of the racial group that holds the top positions within an organization. The rules that govern usage of forms of address signal cultural ascendancy at the work site. For example, white staff members employed within an organization run primarily by African Americans unquestioningly observe African-American forms of address. Similarly, black staff members who are employed within organizations run predominantly by white Americans unconsciously use Euro-American forms of address. (It should be noted, however, that in the United States, teasing out what *is* "American culture"[7] and what *is* distinctively Euro-American culture, African-American culture, Latino-American culture, and even "corporate culture" is exceedingly difficult. These sociological categories of ethnic groups' cultures are themselves exceedingly problematic.)

Robert Rydell's loose interpretation of Gramsci's notion of hegemony is useful to introduce here. Hegemony denotes the exercise of economic and political power in cultural terms by the established leaders of American society and the

> consent given by the great masses of the population to the general direction imposed on social life by the dominant fundamental group; this consent is "historically" caused by the prestige (and consequent confidence) which the dominant group enjoys because of its position and function in the world of production (Gramsci 1971). Hegemony, moreover, is the normal means of state control in a pluralistic society. (Rydell 1984, 4)

Prestige and confidence are thus markers of hegemony. Hegemonic forms of address are the forms used within white-dominated work sites such as IBM Corporation, New York Life Insurance Company, and Harvard University. My observation of forms of address in offices of these institutions revealed that *first name (FN) reciprocity* was overwhelmingly used to address organization members, regardless of ethnicity or role. I will call this the hegemonic form of address. This typical conversation at New York Life Insurance Company between the general manager and the assistant manager is an example of first name reciprocity, which makes them seem to be peers.

Manager: Billy, how's the monthly plan coming? We need it tomorrow.
Ass't. Mgr: Rick, you know I'll have it.
Manager: So it's done!
Ass't. Mgr: Done!

119

If the traditional African-American pattern for addressing peers is the general pattern used in a professional setting, by both whites and blacks, then the cultural milieu of that site challenges the ascendancy of Euro-American cultural hegemony. This is the case at some historically black colleges and universities (HBCUs). Conversely, the power to control the language pattern can be linked to contesting structural and economic power relations in a larger context than the work site. This is the case, I will show, in the African-American studies department at Temple University.

TRADITIONAL AFRICAN-AMERICAN RULES OF ADDRESS

Unlike the hegemonic (FN) form of address shown above, the traditional African-American form of address used within a structured setting such as a church, fraternity, social club, office, grade school, and so on, is *title + name (T + N) reciprocity*. The following phone conversation at Lincoln University, an HBCU, is typical of a traditional African-American form of address. Although only one side of the conversation was recorded, the title + name reciprocity is clear.

> *Staff 1:* Hello, may I please speak with Mr. Foley?
> [Pause]
> *Staff 1:* It's Ms. Johnson.
> [Pause]
> *Staff 1:* Mr. Foley, it's Ms. Johnson in Admissions. I would like to know . . .

Within this form of address there are a host of patterns that emerge, and they are contingent upon everything from generational distance to academic credentials. Similarly, titles and names can range from fictive or real kinship designations to terms of endearment. The general impetus of title + name reciprocity is respect and deference. The impetus is *not* demarcating social hierarchies (e.g., military ranks), which is the pattern associated with Euro-American use of T+LN in "status marked situations [which] are settings such as the courtroom, the large faculty meeting, and Congress, where statuses are clearly specified, speech style is rigidly prescribed, and the form of address of each person is derived from his social identity, e.g., 'your honor' or 'Mr. Chairman.' " (Ervin-Tripp 1986, 220).

The important issue here is that the traditional African-American form of address is a different cultural and language pattern than the general pattern employed at corporations imbued with hegemonic prestige. If African-American forms of address are used at a work site, then, at the cultural level, we can assume that African Americans have power.

120

SETTINGS AS CONTESTED SPACE

There are two terms that need to be defined before proceeding: *setting* and *locale*. Dell Hymes provides the most important description of setting for this investigation. In Hymes 1986, he suggests that the "setting refers to the time and place of the speech act and, in general, to the physical circumstances" (60). I argue that the ethnic group that has structural power over the setting provides the contextualization cue that signals the form of address. Implicitly then, the forms of address used signal who has power over the setting where work is done. If the setting is the physical space of the site where work tasks are executed, the *locale* is the larger cultural and geographical context in which the organization is located or embedded. Although the term *setting* has been used here to describe the work site, neither setting nor situation have been consistently defined within the sociolinguistic literature. Blom and Gumperz 1986 provide a nuanced distinction between setting and locale, and it helps to better understand that delicate differences in sociolinguistic rules are sensitive indicators to power in the workplace. Blom and Gumperz state that they "use the term *setting* to indicate the way in which natives classify their ecological environment into distinct locales. This enables us to relate the opportunities for action to constraints upon action provided by the socially significant features of the environment" (422).

I have observed how forms of address were used in a number of office settings. These include a branch office of IBM Corporation in Portland, Oregon; a branch office of the New York Life Insurance Company in Philadelphia, Pennsylvania; Howard University in Washington, D.C.; an administrative office at Lincoln University in Oxford, Pennsylvania; a Puerto Rican community development organization in Philadelphia, Pennsylvania; an administrative office and an academic department at Temple University in Philadelphia, Pennsylvania; and the W. E. B. Du Bois Institute for Afro-American Research at Harvard University in Cambridge, Massachusetts. I have also made casual observations of how people address each other in various churches, fraternal organizations, parties, and conferences. In all but two locales, the sociolinguistic rules of each setting corresponded with rules of the locale. I call these corresponding settings. I will provide only two examples to illustrate the office settings that typify the concept of corresponding settings (settings where the ethnic majority sets the cultural rules). The first example is the nonprofit Puerto Rican community development organization in North Philadelphia; everyone speaks Spanish. If anyone calls the organization to do business, as a vendor or contractor, he or she must speak Spanish. This organization is predominately Puerto Rican, and Puerto Ricans have power. Another example of the correspondence of power to the ethnic majority's cultural patterns and rules from my observations is a branch office of IBM in Portland, Oregon. The language that is used in this setting is English and the forms of address are also Euro-American. Not surprisingly, the majority of the employees are Euro-American. No ethnic minority group has any significant power in the larger organization, even though the branch manager is black. These two examples demonstrate the uncomplicated understanding that language and cultural rules correspond with the ethnic group that occupies the majority of the positions and has power within the organization. What becomes interesting and provides an entrée into the power and ethnic relations of an organization is when language patterns do not correspond with the ethnic majority of the workers in the organization.

NONCORRESPONDING SETTINGS

I looked at the problem of noncorresponding settings (where language use does not correspond with ethnic majority) in two locales and three settings. The first locale was Temple University. This organization is a large Pennsylvania Commonwealth university with over thirty thousand students. Just over half of the Temple student population is Euro-American, plus there is also a relatively large African-American, Latino-American, and Asian-American student population. The administration and the faculty of the university are overwhelmingly Euro-American, but the university is located in the African-American community of North Philadelphia. Therefore, much of the staff employed by the university is African American.

The other locale was Lincoln University. This organization is one of the 117 HBCUs, and it is a small Pennsylvania Commonwealth university of about 1,700 students. The vast majority of Lincoln students are African American; however, there are some Euro-American and Puerto Rican students. The administration and the faculty of the university are overwhelmingly African American, but the university is located one mile from Oxford, Pennsylvania, a predominantly white, rural farming community in southeastern Pennsylvania. Therefore, much of the staff employed by this university is Euro-American.

I investigated three settings at these two locales. At Lincoln, I observed forms of address in the office of admissions. In that office, there were three Euro-American secretaries, two African-American admission counselors, and two African-American work-study students. In addition, the director of admissions was African American. At Temple University, I explored two settings. The first was the office of the Graduate School, which was predominantly African American. The African-American workers in this office included three secretaries, two coordinators, four work-study students, and a computer programmer. The Euro-Americans in the Graduate School office of Temple University included one coordinator, one office administrator, and the dean for graduate studies. The ethnic makeup of the structure of these two settings reflected their respective locales: the staff reflected the makeup of the surrounding community, but the management represented the ethnic group that had power within the organization.

The second setting at Temple University that I explored was the Department for African-American Studies. The staff, faculty, and administrative personnel in this department were entirely African American. In this setting the ethnicity of both staff and management was representative of the surrounding community. The ethnicity of the people in power within this department was not representative of the ethnic group that held power within the overall organization.

PATTERNS OF FORMS OF ADDRESS

For this investigation, the administration offices are the speech situations, a request to see an application of a particular student is a speech event, and the addressing of the interlocutor to request the scores is a speech act. It became obvious that in each one of these settings the same style of standard business English (SBE) was spoken. There was no evidence during routine office speech events (i.e., answering telephones, granting and accepting requests or discussing plans, budgets, recruiting trips, test scores, policies, etc.) in each office for code-switching, diglossia, or co-occurrence of style repertoires. At the Lincoln University admissions office, the form of address consisted of title plus last name, (T + LN); at the Temple University Graduate School office the form of address was first name (FN); and at Temple's African-American Studies department both forms were employed.

At Temple's Graduate School office there were no rank, generational, gender, or ethnicity decision sets that were considered before the speech act of an address was made. Therefore an African-American undergraduate work-study student called the Euro-American dean, who had a Ph.D., by her first name. Conventions when answering the telephone varied. Some individuals addressed themselves as FN + LN and others just as FN, but titles were never used in telephone conversations, or in face-to-face conversations. Furthermore, status (which re-

123

fers to their position in the office—i.e., secretary, coordinator, work-study) was also not considered. The hegemonic form of address previously identified as FN reciprocity was the form used in this office. A typical example of first name reciprocity is this exchange at the graduate school.

> *Secretary:* Michelle, I sent off the memo you requested yesterday.
> *Dean:* OK, thanks. Tell Mary [a coordinator] to keep a soft copy and file the hard.

In this dialogue, both FN reciprocity and SBE are evident.

Within the admissions office at Lincoln University, there were no status or ethnicity decision sets considered before the speech act of an address was made. However, rank, gender, and generational considerations were made before the form of address was used. T + LN reciprocity was the general rule of address. Therefore, a Euro-American secretary referred to the director of admissions as Dr. + LN, and addressed other secretaries and the admission counselors as Mr. + LN or Ms. + LN. The secretaries and admissions counselors addressed each other as Mr. + LN or Ms. + LN, but the director as Dr. + LN. The director addressed himself on the telephone as Dr. + LN and each of the other members of the office addressed themselves as T + LN on the telephone, except the work-study students, however, who addressed themselves and were addressed as FN. There was no marital status consideration for the women. For example, no woman was addressed as Mrs.; all were addressed as Ms. The conversation between a Euro-American secretary and one of the African-American admissions counselors provides a general description of the T + LN reciprocity that was the rule of address at the admissions office at Lincoln University, although there was some variation to this rule in other departments at Lincoln.

> *Counselor:* Ms. Collings, can you make twenty copies of this and give ten to Dr. Brown?
>
> *Secretary:* Sure, but doesn't Mr. James need some?

The description of the address forms in either setting does not consider personal telephone conversations, break conversations, lunch conversations, or gossip conversations. Nor does it consider written communication, in which forms of address and specific speech styles differed.

Some interesting decisions were made in forms of address in the African-American studies department at Temple University. Generally, T + LN reciprocity was used. However, some of the staff and faculty had names that were explicitly African. Rarely did the T + LN reciprocity occur with an African name, unless both the first and last name were

African or a faculty member was addressed, in which case the form was Dr. + [African] LN. Otherwise the address was simply [African] FN or [African] LN. The administrative assistant had an African name, but she was rarely called Ms. + [African] LN. However, the secretary, who had a European name, was generally addressed as Ms. + LN. Graduate students who were close to their advisors or other faculty called their soon-to-be colleagues by their first names. However, male graduate students more often used first name reciprocity with faculty than female graduate students did. Faculty members sometimes used FN reciprocity and at other times did not. The cultural pattern of addressing peers was not as clear-cut in the Department of African-American Studies as it was at Lincoln University. However, a cultural pattern emerged in the Department of African-American Studies that was different from that of the graduate school and in the larger Temple community. This was clearly demonstrated by staff members in the graduate school who conformed to the African-American rules of address in conversations with staff members in the Department of African-American Studies. An explicative situation was when a staff member from the graduate school had to hand deliver a confidential fellowship nomination to the chairs of both math and African-American Studies. Two different forms of address were decided upon. The same individual, in incidents taking place five minutes apart, engaged in two different forms of address.

Math Department

Staff: Is FN in? I need to deliver these nominations to him.
Receptionist: I'll see, let me buzz him.
Receptionist: FN, FN + LN is out here and she has your nominations.
Staff to Chair: Here are the nominations. I need for you to review them . . .
Chair: OK, I'll have them first thing tomorrow. Tell FN [the dean] that I need to speak with her before the meeting Tuesday.

Five minutes later and about a half a block away, the same staff member had to deliver the same packet to the chair of the African-American Studies department.

African-American Studies Department

Staff: FN [African Name], is Dr. + LN [African name] in? I have to hand deliver the nominations.
Secretary: Yes, one moment.
Secretary to Chair: Ms. + LN, from the graduate school, is here to see you.
Chair to Staff: Oh hello Ms. + LN, I have been waiting for these.

125

I asked the staff member, "Why did you address people differently in the African-American studies department and the math department?" She shrugged her shoulders and replied, "I didn't even realize that I addressed anyone differently."

What's My Cue?

What are the subtle differences between these two settings that made the graduate school staff member decide to address people differently? The answer to this question must be prefaced by a brief explanation of the rules of alternation and co-occurrence. Susan Ervin-Tripp (1986) explains that alternation refers to the choice made in implementing alternate styles (from a repertoire, e.g., Black English, Urban American Spanish, or Pidgin English) within a situation, setting, or a speech event. Co-occurrence refers to the rules that govern to what extent alternate styles can co-occur within a situation, setting, or speech event. For example, within the situations described in this analysis, there is a restriction on any co-occurrence. The only style that occurs within "an office situation" is SBE. However, at lunch, on break, or during a personal telephone conversation, other styles may co-occur, and the interlocutor may choose from his or her repertoire of styles and engage in a different style of discourse. Therefore, within the office setting, while speaking to fellow peers (the office situation) there are rules that restrict any co-occurrence of styles. The same sociolinguistic rules for the co-occurrence of style apply to speech acts within a given style. For example, within the style of SBE, a repertoire of various acceptable forms of address may co-occur. However, there are sociolinguistic rules that govern which form the interlocutor implements, and to what extent they can co-occur.

In the settings described, the only co-occurrence of forms of address ensued within the African-American studies department at Temple (excluding work-study students at Lincoln). Co-occurrence was restricted to all forms except T + LN at Lincoln's admissions office, and FN at Temple's Graduate School office and the larger Temple community. But the co-occurrence of address forms was allowed in the African-American studies department. People in this department contested the hegemonic form of addressing people (FN), which was the general rule in other Temple departments and offices.

Therefore, in a larger context, the cultural rules were the same, but in a narrow context there were cultural rules that applied to making decisions about what form of address to use.

The subtle differences between these two settings were obvious enough to make the staff member from the graduate school make an unconscious decision to address people differently in settings that were only half a block away. These differences are linked to the power of an ethnic group over the space or setting where work is performed. The only variable that was markedly different was the ethnicity of the people in power in each setting. The empowered ethnic group that dominated each setting provided the contextualization cue, which mandated an alternate form of address or allowed the co-occurrence of forms. Conversely, the forms of address used signaled that a particular ethnic group was empowered and/or was contesting larger power relations.

Gumperz highlights this idea of signaling within a context. In *Discourse Strategies* (1982), he describes a contextualization cue as "any feature of linguistic form that contributes to the signalling of contextual presuppositions. Such cues may have a number of such linguistic realizations depending on the historically given linguistic repertoire of the participants . . . lexical and syntactic options, formulaic expressions, conversational openings, closing and sequencing strategies can all have similar contextualizing functions" (131). One can justify the setting of the situation as a contextualization cue that dictates the form of address employed, because context cues carry information and implicit meanings that are conveyed as part the communicative process and are rarely talked about. These cues are taken for granted and tend to go unnoticed when the participants comprehend and notice them as relevant cues within interpretive processes.

However, when a person does not react to a cue or is unaware of its meaning or function, the interpretation of the missed cue can lead to misunderstandings. Often these misunderstandings are couched in attitudinal terms: "A speaker is said to be unfriendly, impertinent, rude, uncooperative, or to fail to understand" (Gumperz 1982, 132). Therefore, miscommunication due to failed interpretation of context cues is regarded as a social faux pas and leads to misjudgments of speaker's attitude or intent, and is not likely to be identified as a mere linguistic error. The explanation of "misjudgment of attitude" corresponds to the reaction of the staff at each setting if the dominant pattern is not followed in their setting.

At Lincoln's admissions office, when asked about their interpretations of people who use the FN form of address within the office, the general response of workers (regardless of ethnic affiliation) was that the person would be seen as being disrespectful. However, at Temple's graduate school, when people were asked about their interpretation of an individual who used the T + LN form of address, they generally responded (regardless of ethnic affiliation) that T + LN was too formal and if someone expected to be called by T + LN, he or she would be considered "uppity."

Subtle Differences = Power

These subtle cultural differences do relate to power in the work-place. The ethnic group that has power dominates the cultural milieu of the setting. Although the majority of the staff members at Lincoln University are Euro-American, they generally conform to traditional African-American forms of address, because African Americans have power at this locale. Similarly, the majority of the personnel at Temple University are African American, but they consent to the Euro-American forms of address, because Euro-Americans have power within this organization. However, in the African-American studies department at Temple, the workers generally conform to African-American rules of address and do not consent to the hegemonic Euro-American forms of address. Within this particular setting, the smaller department is challenging the cultural ascendancy that dominates the larger organization. For the most part the staff members at each one of these settings were oblivious to their conformation, or lack thereof, to the language patterns in each setting. Most people conformed or consented to the cultural rules in each setting without even being aware of it.

One can see that these delicate differences in sociolinguistic rules are sensitive indicators of cultural differences and differences in ethnic minority empowerment in different settings or work sites. The control of the cultural context of the work site is important, because it is often contingent upon the ethnic group that is empowered in that workplace. However, if that work site or setting is on the periphery of the organization or otherwise marginalized, as one can argue is the case for the African-American studies department at Temple, then the use of different rules of address can be indicative of a counterhegemonic struggle against the larger organization. Similarly, if the whole organization or institution is marginalized (for example, Lincoln University could be considered marginal, with 1,600 students compared to Temple's 20,000 + students in the same system of higher education), this can be reflective of an entire organization that is engaged in a counterhege-monic struggle against institutionalized racism.

When the African-American workers do not challenge and simply consent to the dominant culture of an organization, even if they are the majority, then, chances are, they still do not hold, or have easy access to, structural power. Similarly, rural working-class whites at Lincoln University conform to the traditional African-American form of address. Within this organization, they do not have easy access to structural power.

Looking at the struggles that are mediated culturally is important in the wake of "diversity policies," affirmative action, and halfhearted commitments against racism, because these can blur historically contingent forms of institutionalized racism. In many organizations, there is ethnic diversity, but ethnic minorities still do not have easy access to power, and when and if they do obtain a powerful position, they must, at least in the context of work, assimilate into the hegemonic culture and reproduce its relations.

Ultimately this sociolinguistic analysis confirms the pessimistic thesis Derrick Bell advances in *Faces at the bottom of the well: The permanence of racism* (1992): that racism is an integral, permanent, and indestructible component of U.S. society. This data confirms that structural power relations are often signified through subtle cultural rules within specific organizations. These cultural rules within specific organizations are only emblematic of larger social relations within society. Programs and efforts to manage diversity cannot change historically contingent patterns of oppression. They can, however, confront these patterns by recognizing that members of underrepresented subordinate groups must have access to the very top leadership positions within any organization. I do not want to suggest that the presence of traditional African-American forms of address should be seen as a test for African-American empowerment, because the logical extension would entail segregated or Balkanized organizations where one groups controls one organization and another group controls a different organization. I want to provide a unique approach to demonstrate how organizations where nontraditional staff members are well represented often maintain inequitable power relations. By any criteria, Temple University is a model for diversity efforts. However, the structural inequality and racial disparity remain so pervasive that they are systematically articulated by subtle cultural patterns.

Ann M. Morrison in *The new leaders: Guidelines on leadership diversity in America* (1992) has also recognized this issue. She suggests top managers must "make diversity a pervasive part of the culture," and argues that "When diversity is institutionalized in an organization, support has a better chance of continuing even after personally committed top executives leave" (193). Her approach to these issues is consistent with this study because she asserts that the only way an organization can confront racial inequality and manage diversity effectively is to change the racial composition of the board of directors, insure the commitment of the CEO, and employ stringent but balanced diversity policies. Her emphasis on a balanced approach to managing diversity is paramount for its effectiveness.

While efforts to manage diversity must be orchestrated from powerful positions, programs and strategies cannot be authoritatively dictated because subordinates will find strategies to resist such mandates, which will only increase racial animosity. This balance is difficult but fundamental. It is increasingly difficult within the context of palatable arguments for a "color-blind society." Proponents of a "color-blind" society are simply turning a blind eye to white supremacy and the intractability of racism.

Notes

1. An excellent example of this dynamic is welfare reform as it was outlined in the Personal Responsibility Act for the *Contract With America* (Gingrich and Armey 1994; Edsall and Edsall 1992).

2. Eric Wolf suggests that "each endeavor to understand humankind works with a set of characteristic ideas that orient its inquiries and justify its existence, and for anthropology ideas about race and culture . . . have played that guiding and legitimizing role" (Wolf 1994, 1).

3. George E. Marcus and Michael M. J. Fischer suggest that investigating the political and economic relationship between state structures and the everyday life of people is grounded in work "pioneered during the 1960s by such scholars as Eric Wolf, Sidney Mintz, June Nash, and Eleanor Leacok" (Marcus and Fischer 1986, 84). Other examples of this genre include Taussig (1980); Fay (1982); Willis (1982); Sabel (1982); and Williams (1994).

4. Many people structure their racist attitudes and prejudice along class lines. Since they don't feel any animosity toward middle-class people of color they feel that they are exempt from allegations of racism. This dynamic is clearly demonstrated in *Race: How Blacks and Whites Think and Feel About the American Obsession* by Studs Terkel (1992).

5. In recent years, the strides made to alleviate discrimination and empower people of color have eroded, in part because the Supreme Court has devised difficult definitions of employment discrimination under title VII of the 1964 Civil Rights Act. These definitions are *disparate treatment* (requiring proof of racial motivation) and *disparate impact* (requiring statistical analysis of the impact of discrimination). Both definitions are burdensome, time consuming, and expensive to prosecute (Brooks 1990). One of the biggest hurdles in prosecuting disparate impact cases is the lack of statistical significance for promotion cases or discrimination in higher levels of management. Often there are so few people in top management positions that attorneys can't substantiate the statistical impact. On the other hand, to prosecute disparate treatment cases, attorneys need "smoking gun" evidence or overtly racist discrimination, which is difficult in the light of the subtle patterns of racism prevalent in many workplaces (Omi and Winant 1986, 120). In short, the Supreme Court (i.e., *Regents of the University of California v. Bakke [1978]*) has made a concerted effort to relax or eliminate the Justice Department's efforts to enforce affirmative action. Securing power in the workplace, for African Americans, has been and continues to be a struggle. The struggle is for ownership and access to power.

6. *John Henryism* is another form. This is a description of a personality type that is derived from the fictional African-American laborer of legendary strength.

In the legend, John Henry died while pitting his sledgehammer against a steam drill. The term *John Henryism* is used to define a syndrome of stress and hypertension found within the African-American middle class.

John Henryism manifests itself when one struggles to get into the mainstream. It is said to be characterized by the belief that one can triumph despite the odds. "Unlike the aggressive 'type-A' personality the John Henry personality 'shows extreme patience and tends to suppress anger in order to deflect white hostility' "(Brooks 1990, 40).

7. I understand "American hegemonic culture" to be those aspects of culture that are promoted by the state and capitalist interests, and are shared across ethnic, racial, and class lines in the United States. This gloss of American hegemonic culture is informed by Davis 1992; Gramsci 1971[1944]; Omi and Winant 1986; and Winant 1994.

References

Bell, Derrick. 1992. *Faces at the bottom of the well: The permanence of racism.* New York: Basic Books.

Blom, J. P., and J. Gumperz. 1986. Social meaning in linguistic structure: Code-switching in Norway. In *Directions in sociolinguistics,* ed. J. Gumperz and D. Hymes, 407–34. New York: Basil Blackwell.

Brooks, R. L. 1990. *Rethinking the American race problem.* Berkeley: University of California Press.

Davis, M. 1992. *City of quartz: Excavating the future in Los Angeles.* New York: Vintage Books.

Edsall, T., and M. D. Edsall. 1992. *Chain reaction: The impact of race, rights and taxes on American politics.* New York: W.W. Norton.

Ervin-Tripp, S. 1986. On sociological rules: Alternation and co-occurrence. In *Directions in sociolinguistics,* ed. J. Gumperz and D. Hymes, 213–50. New York: Basil Blackwell.

Fay, S. 1982. *Beyond Greed.* New York: Viking.

Franklin, R. S. 1991. *Shadows of race and class.* Minneapolis: University of Minnesota Press.

Gingrich, N., and D. Armey. 1994. *Contract with America.* New York: Random House.

Gramsci, A. 1971 [1944]. *Selections from the prison notebooks.* Q. Hoare and G. Smith, trans. New York: International Publishers.

Gregory, S., and R. Sanjek, eds. 1994. *Race.* New Brunswick, N.J.: Rutgers University Press.

Grofman, B., L. Handley, and R. G. Niemi. 1992. *Minority representation and the quest for voting equality.* New York: Cambridge University Press.

Guinier, L. 1994. *The tyranny of the majority: Fundamental fairness in representative democracy.* New York: Free Press.

Gumperz, J. 1982. *Discourse strategies.* New York: Cambridge University Press.

Harvey, D. 1989. *The conditions of postmodernity.* Cambridge, Mass.: Basil Blackwell.

Hymes, D. 1986. Models of the interaction of language and social life. In *Directions in sociolinguistics*, ed. J. Gumperz and D. Hymes, 35–71. New York: Basil Blackwell.

Kennedy, M., M. Gastón, and C. Tilly. 1990. Roxbury: Capital investment or community development. In *Fire in the hearth: The radical politics of place in America*, ed. M. Davis, 97–136. London: Verso.

Marcus, G. E., and M. J. Fischer. 1986. *Anthropology as cultural critique*. Chicago: University of Chicago Press.

Morrison, A. 1992. *The new leaders: Guidelines on leadership diversity in America*. San Francisco: Jossey-Bass.

Myers-Jones, H. J. 1988. *Power, geography and black Americans: Exploring the implications of black suburbanization*. Ph.D. diss., University of Washington.

Omi, M., and H. Winant. 1986. *Racial formation in the United States*. New York: Routledge.

Rydell, R. W. 1984. *All the world's a fair: Visions of empire at American international expositions*. Chicago: University of Chicago Press.

Sabel, C. F. 1982. *Work and politics: The division of labor in industry*. New York: Cambridge University Press.

Shull, S. 1993. *A kinder, gentler racism? The Reagan-Bush civil rights legacy*. New York: M.E. Sharpe.

Taussig, M. 1980. *The devil and commodity fetishism in South America*. Chapel Hill: University of North Carolina Press.

Terkel, S. 1992. *Race: How blacks and whites think and feel about the American obsession*. New York: New Press.

Williams, B. 1994. Babies and banks: The reproductive 'underclass' and the raced, gendered masking of debt. In *Race*, ed. S. Gregory and R. Sanjek, 348–65. New Brunswick, N.J.: Rutgers University Press.

Willis, P. 1982. *Learning to labour: How working class kids get work*. New York: Columbia University Press.

Wilson, W. J. 1978. *The declining significance of race*. Chicago: University of Chicago Press.

Winant, H. 1994. *Racial conditions: Politics, theory, comparisons*. Minneapolis: University of Minnesota Press.

Wolf, E. R. 1994. Perilous ideas: Race, culture, people. *Current Anthropology* 35:1–11.

PRISON LABOR: RACISM AND RHETORIC

PEM DAVIDSON BUCK

[T]he constabulary and the prisons are the two best educational institutions.

> Sir William MacGregor, colonial governor of Papua New Guinea,
> late 1800s, cited in Wolfers 1975, 19.

Arbeit Macht Frei ['Labor Liberates']

> inscription over the main entrance to Auschwitz,
> pictured in Laqueur and Breitman 1986, 85

The term of forced labor . . . is extended if . . . its *educational objective* is not achieved.

> Nazi administrator, cited in Yahil 1990, 162

A sound industries program has many benefits. The most important is that inmates are given an opportunity for productive work, which some people argue is the most effective rehabilitation program offered.

> comment made by Hal Farrier, a former American prison administrator, 1989

GOOD FOR THE SOUL: THE RHETORIC OF FORCED LABOR

In a display of remarkable unanimity, capitalist/imperialist rhetoric has maintained in diverse centuries and continents that forced labor is good for the soul. This rhetoric is not directed at the recalcitrant population targeted for criminalization, imprisonment, and forced labor—the use of force signals the preexisting failure of such subtle, cheaper, and less revolt-provoking ideological strategies. Instead, this rhetoric is directed primarily at those members of the nontargeted population who might object to or suffer from the effects of criminalization and forced labor, and against whom it is more difficult to employ force. It mediates the acquiescence of the nontargeted segments of the population in policies that are contrary to their own interests and ensures the compliance of people selected for the dangerous and potentially revolt-provoking work of damaging other human beings.

The British administrator, in other words, was not speaking to the local people when he made his comments about the benefits of jail education. He was speaking to the men risking their lives daily to create and control a "native" labor force for the benefit of plantation owners

133

(Buck 1991). The Nazi was certainly not trying to convince Jews, Gypsies, and dissidents that concentration camps were a good thing. He was, instead, attempting to convince nontargeted Germans that Jewish laziness and greed were the cause of declining standards of living, obscuring the substitution of free concentration camp labor for waged labor and the parallel tightening of labor and cost control policies for the remainder of the working class in a desperate attempt to maintain profit levels. Ultimately he was helping to persuade nontargeted Germans to support domestic policies that damaged the working class and to risk their lives in a war fought for the interests of German industrialists (Guerin 1973[1939]).

So, then, what of the comment of the U.S. prison administrator? Have similar conditions brought forth similar rhetoric? I will argue that this is indeed the case. As the 1980s recession deepened, unions were busted, and racism became increasingly virulent—not unrelated phenomena. Correspondingly, heightened labor-control and cost-control policies of the New World Order, as did those of the Nazi "New Order," found their logical conclusion in the criminalization of a targeted population whose constitutional rights to resist such policies have historically been weak. Gains won in the ongoing struggles for civil rights and for working-class rights are being systematically eroded, accompanied by a corresponding erosion in the standard of living of the nonimprisoned labor force.[1] This working class slide toward Third World status occurs as corporations struggle to remain "competitive" by lowering wages, cutting benefits, or turning to alternative labor forces in an attempt to wring profits from labor. Criminalization now supplies prisoners, a potentially enormous and, since taxpayers bear most of the expense, an extraordinarily cheap alternative workforce; bound labor has again become a small but growing segment of public and private enterprise. Criminalization allows for the surveillance and control of those most hurt by the slide toward Third World conditions. Furthermore, it contributes to the creation of those conditions by increasing the reserve army of labor as some jobs move from the wage labor market to the bound labor market, thus abetting a general reduction in wages. Finally, criminalization is the basis for a renewed source of profits: corrections is a growth industry (Remondini 1991) that is now second only to the defense industry (Lichtenstein and Kroll 1990, 18; Lilly and Knepper 1991; cf. Press 1990, 26).

My concern in the issues of prison labor lies in two areas. First, the world's history with the horrors of bound and racially concentrated labor is unambiguous, lying as it does in slavery, concentration camps, and convict leasing. Second, wage labor and bound labor are dialectically related: we are looking here at flip sides of prison walls.

THE RE-CREATION OF BOUND LABOR

Bound labor, except for a brief hiatus during the 1960s and 1970s (Dilulio 1988, 72) when the Civil Rights movement and unions were more potent, has been a continuous factor of varying economic significance in the United States since the invasion of this continent by Europeans. Indentured servitude, slavery, peonage, and forced labor of the Spanish *encomienda* and *repartimiento* eventually gave way to sharecropping, the chain gang, and convict leasing. Bound labor recovered from its near disappearance in the 1980s and increased as recession deepened.

Generally the legitimation for bound labor has come from divisive "we-they" rhetoric, based most frequently on race, but often snaring in its net the most vulnerable members of nontargeted racial categories as well. Since the use of bound labor damages the entire working class, not just those imprisoned, the blinders provided by the salience of race have been critical in organizing acquiescence to the superexploitation involved in the creation of Third World labor conditions outside of prison walls and of concentrated labor conditions within prison walls.

This acquiescence has been mediated partially by the construction of crack as a vicious contagion spreading from the ghetto (and from Third World growers), providing an ideological justification for the priority on law enforcement and interdiction, absorbing many billions of dollars in a nation that has serious debt problems.[2] This construction implies that, since the disease is incurable, carriers must be criminalized in order to concentrate them in "isolation wards," that is, prisons.

The hysteria promoted by this construction (Fink 1994) served for a time to deflect public attention from the actual causes of our falling standard of living. It provided legitimacy for "policing the crisis" (Hall et al. 1978) as people reacted to rising unemployment, increasingly visible homelessness, rising infant mortality and hunger, and the diminishing of benefits and job security that accompanied union busting. So long as these conditions could be passed off as drug-related, the legitimacy of the state remained unquestioned. Those most vulnerable could be jailed, welfared, or workfared; those less vulnerable could blame the nation's problems on a drugged, noncompetitive workforce, on addicts who refused to work and preferred to be homeless, and on immoral mothers who exercised the human right to bear and care for children, despite living in drug-infested ghettos or other areas where marriageable men with jobs were in short supply.

Racialized perceptions about drug use legitimize the criminalization of people of color (Gilliam 1992) and disguise the fact that incarceration rates of white superexploited ethnic groups such as

135

Appalachians are also high, and that they are high among poor whites generally (Reiman 1990[1979]). Thus, poor whites who succumb to racist ideologies that represent people of color as the country's primary criminals and therefore support tough-on-crime policies are actually working against their own interests, increasing the likelihood that they themselves will become bound labor. It is evident in the large literature analyzing the relationships between free labor, labor control, and prison labor that penal labor control policies have historically targeted ethnic and racial minorities for incarceration; it is also evident that as a minority becomes less exploitable, so that it no longer serves as an internal source of Third World labor, its representation in the prison population decreases (see Adamson 1984; Chiricos and Delone 1992; Conley 1980; Knepper 1989; Lichtenstein and Kroll 1990; Melossi and Pavarini 1981; Rusche and Kirchheimer 1968[1939]; and Weiss 1987).

The re-creation of bound labor involves three elements: the legal provision of bodies to be bound, the legalization of forced labor, and the provision of legal and profitable uses for such labor.

THE PROVISION OF BOUND BODIES

It is in the provision of convicts, the potential bound labor force, that, as has been typical historically, both the targeting of a racially defined population and the vulnerability of the least powerful of the nontargeted population become evident.

The "Drug War," targeting people of color with its "arbitrary administration of legalities" (Foucault 1979, 89), has been a major force in criminalizing a vastly increased segment of the recalcitrant working class and in producing an increasingly racialized prison population—bodies to be bound. This racialization, based on and exacerbating divisive "we-they" relationships, is critical in the legitimation that has historically accompanied the use of bound labor.

The United States' skyrocketing incarceration rate shows little if any relationship to crime rates. Numerous studies cite instead as the cause of rising prison populations the role of the "Drug War"; harsher criminal justice policies, including longer sentences and mandatory sentencing policies; and the institution of life-without-parole (e.g., Mauer 1990; Ostrow 1991; Lichtenstein and Kroll 1990; Mathiesen 1990; Nagel 1977; Harris 1987). The "Drug War" will therefore serve as a focus for the discussion that follows; it is to be understood, however, that simply ending the war would not end the inequities detailed here.

The United States now has the world's highest incarceration rate, with well over one million people in prisons and jails (Snell 1993, cover). Since the early 1980s prison populations have doubled (Ostrow

1991, quoting 1991 Sentencing Project Report). The number of drug defendants actually incarcerated rose by 283 percent between 1980 and 1990 (Bureau of Justice Statistics 1992b, 5). The proportion of prisoners provided by the "Drug War" from federal courts was 47 percent in 1990, a startlingly rapid rise from 27 percent in 1980 (McDonald and Carlson 1992, 2). The percentage incarcerated in federal prisons for drug offenses reached 59 percent in 1996, 63.5 percent for blacks (Maguire and Pastore 1997, 533).

Minority imprisonment in some areas is rapidly approaching the nearly complete racial homogeneity of concentration camps. Nationally, 60 percent of state and federal prisoners in 1990 were black and Hispanic,[3] but this disproportion reaches, for instance, 82 percent in New York State, 95 percent in New York City jails (Sharff 1990), and 76 percent in San Francisco, where they make up 20.8 percent of the workforce (Lewis 1993). Ninety-two percent of prisoners at Southport, New York State's maximum security prison, are black or Hispanic (Raab 1991), despite the fact that these groups represent only 25 percent of the state's population (Tabor 1991). Nationwide, 6 percent of the population—African-American men—provides nearly 50 percent of the prison population (Lichtenstein and Kroll 1990, 6). African Americans are incarcerated in jails and prisons at a far higher rate than are whites: 3,109 as compared to 426 per 100,000 population ("U.S. has highest rate . . ." 1991; Nagel 1977).

Together, the branches of the "justice" system now control 25 percent of the population of twenty- to twenty-nine-year-old black American men, primarily because of "Drug War" policies (Sentencing Project 1990). These racial disparities become even more apparent when looking at cities like Washington, D.C. and Baltimore. In Washington, 42 percent of the black men between the ages of eighteen and thirty-five are either wanted or already in the grip of the justice system; the corresponding figure for Baltimore is 57 percent (Jerome Miller, cited in Rothman 1994). Irwin and Austin (1994, 159–61) estimate, however, that if the various get-tough-on-crime measures proposed by the Clinton administration and other politicians are implemented, the national incarceration rate will rise to 3,015 per 100,000; they point out that, given a continuation of the present imbalance in prison populations, most black men between the ages of eighteen and thirty-nine would be incarcerated. Many of these measures are embodied in the crime bill Congress passed in 1994 (Currie 1994), and the Federal Bureau of Prisons projects a 115 percent increase in its prisons by the year 2000 over its 1991 population; many states project increases of 50 to 100 percent (Maguire, Pastore, and Flanagan 1993, 619–21). In fact, using estimates based on our present rate of increase made by the

137

Brookings Institution, Bronstein (cited in Natalizia 1992, 1) pointed out that more than half of all Americans will be incarcerated by the year 2053.

Although blacks make up about 12 percent of the U.S. population, 44 percent of those arrested for possession and 57 percent of those arrested for trafficking in 1991 were black (Coy 1991), a disproportion that has increased from 30 percent of all drug arrests in 1984 ("U.S. has highest rate . . ." 1991). Furthermore, at least in some areas, sentences for black drug "offenders" are twice as long as those for whites (Mayhan 1992).

The racialization of prison populations resulting from the "Drug War" would make sense if, in fact, blacks and Hispanic actually were more involved in drug use than were whites. However, report after report shows that this is not the case. According to the National Institute of Drug Abuse, 12 percent of drug users are black, approximately equal to the proportion of blacks in the population as a whole (Coy 1991; Gilliam 1992). Since the laws do not invoke racial quotas, but affirmative action for imprisonment is obviously at work, it is necessary to look at the formal and informal "Drug War" tactics that produce racial imbalance.

Despite being called a "Drug War," a title implying that all drugs and all neighborhoods are targeted, in actuality it is crack cocaine and minority neighborhoods that are subjected to surveillance. It is thus hardly surprising that those arrested are disproportionately people of color. Simply focusing on crack, or even on cocaine, would not produce a racialized prison population: 69 percent of all cocaine and crack cocaine users are white and 66 percent have jobs (Shannon 1990, 47). Racialization is justified by the unrelenting media discourse on crack abuse as a ghetto disease, a contagion infecting "the nation." The viciousness of the contagion is exaggerated, so that it comes to resemble AIDS, a disease without a cure. In fact, only 0.5 percent of the U.S. population uses crack; only 20 percent of cocaine users reach the point of causing serious problems; and most of them, having reached that point, cut back on their use. Furthermore, only 7.5 percent of drug-related homicides are caused by the effects of a drug,[4] and in two-thirds of those cases the drug involved was alcohol (Glasser 1989, 12). These are hardly the epidemiological patterns of an incurable disease run rampant. That crack as a drug, rather than as a valuable commodity, remains a serious problem for some individuals and some neighborhoods is probably related not so much to the drug itself as to the inadequate provision of medical services, just as is the revival of tuberculosis. The National Institute of Drug Abuse reports that 90 percent of those seeking treatment are turned away for lack of space, which is itself a reflection on the "Drug War" priority on law enforcement and interdiction (Coy 1991).

Racial disparities in criminalization have been produced not by actual drug use patterns but by the deployment of two major tactical thrusts. The first is the street sweep; the second is legal changes making it easier to imprison alleged drug offenders and to keep them in prison longer. Both these tactics, combined with racial differences in sentencing and in various forms of early release, have resulted in a vastly increased prison population that is also increasingly monochromatic.

The street sweep, which, in its violation of civil liberties, would never be tolerated in white or middle-class neighborhoods, "has become the most common anti-drug measure. . . . [They] ensnare virtually everyone present in an area at the time. Typically, all those taken into custody are 'put through the system'—that is, arrested, arraigned and detained even when the police lack evidence" (Siegel 1989; cf. Hutchinson 1990 and Sharff 1990). At this point the justice system takes over, having been efficiently provided with "offenders." Drug "offenders" are encouraged to plead guilty, and "most . . . , including most of those professing innocence, cop a plea to a lesser charge" (Siegel 1989, 4).

ABC News (12 November 1992) documented the shortage of public defenders in New Orleans and the ensuing regular miscarriages of justice: an estimated 20 percent of defendants would not have been found guilty if given a trial instead of plea bargaining; one man was in jail for eleven months waiting a trial in which the jury took fifteen minutes to find him innocent. Such procedures, combined with the street sweep, which makes no attempt to discriminate between probable guilt and innocence, virtually guarantee that significant numbers of those in prison could never have been convicted in a trial. The injustice of such tactics, however, fades ideologically before the apparent necessity to isolate the carriers of a deadly contagion. In this version of reality, the danger of infection outweighs the danger of jailing a few innocent people—and the presumption is that those who are young, black, male, and in the way of a street sweep are probably guilty regardless of a "technical" lack of evidence.

Should the suspect choose to fight back, a number of recent legal decisions can be used to limit or eliminate the resources needed for a successful fight. The Supreme Court has upheld a law allowing confiscation of an accused drug offender's assets, including both cash and property, thus limiting the ability to hire a lawyer (Your Supreme Court 1989; Cassidy 1993). Confiscation has proceeded on the basis of no more evidence than the fact of fitting a statistical profile, a practice that has particularly targeted minorities; even when the case is dismissed, reclaiming forfeited assets is difficult (Miniter 1993). While two 1993 rulings have provided some regulation of this practice, requiring proportionality to the crime of the accused and protecting the property rights of the more affluent of the accused with a hearing before the seizure of stationary property such as real estate (Roman 1993), the basic principle of confiscation before conviction remains intact. Nor is proof necessary to evict the family of the accused from public housing under HUD's streamlined eviction procedures for those suspected of drug involvement, thus diverting other family resources from possible use in a legal battle (Siegel 1989; Bureau of Justice Statistics 1992a, 184–85).

Sentences have increased dramatically as a result of minimum and mandatory sentencing laws. For instance, the average sentence for trafficking has risen from sixty-four months in 1986 to eighty-four months in 1990; an additional fifty months of supervised release may be added to the sentence (McDonald and Carlson 1992, 3, 9). Sentences for possession can be comparable to those for trafficking (Reinan 1991). The Supreme Court has upheld Michigan's imposition of life without parole for nonviolent first offenses involving 1.5 pounds of cocaine, despite the fact that an identical offense in Alabama would bring a five-year sentence. This ruling "sharply limited a 1983 Supreme Court decision . . . [which] established that the Eighth Amendment required an element of proportionality in criminal sentencing" (Greenhouse 1991b).

Once imprisoned, appeals have been sharply curtailed. Another recent Supreme Court ruling means that almost any failure in meeting a state's procedural requirements forfeits a state prisoner's right to bring a habeas corpus appeal, even when the fault lies with a lawyer who files a few days after the deadline (Greenhouse 1991a). Death row inmates no longer have a right to a court-appointed lawyer for habeas corpus proceedings (Your Supreme Court 1989), despite the fact that half of all death sentences are overturned on appeal (Greenhouse 1990). The 1994 Crime Bill provides the death penalty for an additional fifty crimes. Provisions were eliminated that would have allowed the use of racial statistics in fighting a death sentence (Mauro 1994) and would have reformed some habeas corpus injustices (Blaustein 1994). The likelihood that a convict could afford to hire a lawyer instead of relying on a court-appointed lawyer is decreased by a 1988 law curtailing or eliminating social security and other benefits to those who are incarcerated (Taylor 1988). And in January 1993 the Supreme Court ruled that even apparent innocence is insufficient grounds for a retrial if the evidence needed to establish innocence became available only after the death sentence was finalized (Wiessler 1993): Lionel Herrera, the subject of this case, was subsequently executed (Cohen 1993). Another rul-

140

ing will make the use of youth as a mitigating factor more difficult (Wiessler 1993). Defendants, in other words, are now "being *executed* on technicalities, due to the thicket of procedural obstacles in habeas corpus rulings by the Supreme Court" (Blaustein 1994). Arkansas' triple execution (Mauro 1994) shocks only because it makes explicit the political expediency of death.

If, in fact, the judicial system ever was "soft on criminals," it certainly is no longer. The tendency of these decisions is toward the efficient production of sentences that are what former president Bush called "final," so that prisoners will no longer be able to pester law-abiding folk with expectations of justice, and will no longer absorb the long-suffering taxpayers' dollars in "pointless appeals." Guilt and innocence, if we continue this trend, will no longer be accorded even the lip service they now enjoy. And in fact, even now lip service occasionally disappears. Women can be jailed for being pregnant and addicted under "fetal abuse" laws and for "delivering a controlled substance to a minor," laws that are invoked against black women far more often than against white women, even when pregnant whites use drugs at the same rate as do blacks (Siegel 1989, 4; Gilliam 1992).

Illegal detention constitutes an even more flagrant bypass of justice. One hundred inmates, or about 3 percent of the 2,800 prisoners in the Baltimore city jail, were held during 1991, several for over a year, "without being formally accused or even assigned court dates for arraignment." These illegal detentions were attributed by prison officials to "antiquated record-keeping" ("One hundred inmates . . ." 1991). If the Baltimore jails are even vaguely symptomatic, illegal detention without accusation or trial is common in the United States.

LEGALIZATION OF FORCED LABOR

The enormous and rising annual costs of producing and maintaining over one million prisoners—about $16 billion for maintenance and $12.7 billion for the "Drug War"—have become the justification for a return to forced labor in an era of budget cutbacks: prisoners are to pay the costs of their own punishment. The magnitude of these costs is overwhelming state and local budgets and is predicted to be the largest item in state budgets by the year 2000 if present trends continue (DiIulio 1988, 66). Such considerations have led financially strapped governments and prison administrations (see, e.g., Criminal Justice Associates 1985, 1), with the approval of an estimated 94 percent of Americans (Maguire, Pastore, and Flanagan 1993, 201), to look to prisoners for relief as tax revenues drop under the effects of a faltering economy and prison costs rise under the effects of a "Drug War" invoked to police the crisis within capitalism that has produced both.

The legalization of forced labor has meant legalizing the access of private corporations to prison labor, increasing state use of prison labor, legalizing the sale of prison manufactures across state lines and on the open market, shifting from "voluntary" to involuntary labor programs, and providing the state with the means to expropriate prisoners' "wages." Initiatives in the legalization of corporate access to prison labor accompanied the rapid growth of incarceration during the 1980s, followed by formal and rarely mentioned shifts toward involuntary labor as the early experiments showed the profitability of prison labor.

This legalization was in part legitimated by Chief Justice Warren Burger's pronouncement that "the U.S. needs 'factories with fences' in which inmates can make products sold on the open market," and should eliminate statutes prohibiting interstate sale of prison-made goods or restricting sale to only government agencies (Gest 1984, 46). This principle was eagerly promoted by the Reagan-Bush Justice Department (Criminal Justice Associates 1985, 82; McConville 1987, 221) and by right-wing think tanks such as the Heritage Foundation (Ryan and Ward 1989, 4). The Brookings Institution joined in sponsoring a task force that recommended "modernizing, expanding, and strengthening prison industries" and discussed paying prevailing wages so deductions could help pay costs of incarceration (Industries Task Force Report 1986). This strategy is strengthened by court rulings such as the 1993 decision that Arizona inmates working in prison industries contracting with private firms are entitled to minimum wage (Walsh 1993). UNI-COR, the Federal Corrections Industries program, is directed by U.S. code to "provide employment for all physically fit inmates in the U.S. penal and correctional institutions . . ." (Grieser 1989). As a result, laws regulating the access of private business to prison labor have eased in many states (Auerbach et al. 1988; McConville 1987, 221; Mendez 1993). In 1976 the first program in which private industry established shops run with prison labor was initiated (Criminal Justice Associates 1985, 1). Congress authorized seven experimental commercial programs in 1979, which included building satellite dishes and disk drives (Berch 1985, 43). In September 1993 the Bureau of Justice Assistance prepared a flier announcing the availability of certification for fifty such nonfederal programs (Bureau of Justice Assistance 1993). While still involving only a tiny percentage of prisoners, such programs are growing, although statistics are elusive. In 1991 65,164 state and federal prisoners were employed as a result of the massive justice system push for both public and private prison industry, more than doubling total participation since 1980 (Pinsley 1992). As such programs become more common, complaints from local businesses about unfair competition have likewise increased (Montgomery 1993; Magner 1993).

Prison industry takes a variety of organizational forms. In some cases a private corporation directly employs prison labor. Much more commonly, the local, state, or federal prison industry is incorporated and, depending on state law, either produces goods to be sold in the state-use market or on the open market, or forms partnerships, joint ventures, or contracts with private corporations (Grieser 1989).

Prison products include cotton and other agricultural products coming from the plantation-model prisons such as the Louisiana State Prison at Angola, where "farm lines" appear to have changed little since the days of slavery, and overseers on horseback direct the labor of a preponderantly black and Hispanic workforce (Snyder 1991; Vodicka 1978). However, the "industrial model" is now far more common; prison labor produces a wide range of products, from clothing to circuit boards (Duncan 1992). And, in a reflection of the nonprison economy, service and information processing are becoming common, as prisoners answer phones for state tourist bureaus, provide airline reservation services, and do data entry. As defense contractors, prison industries produce, for example, electronic cables and Desert Lightning kits. Prison industries often build prisons (Flanagan and Maguire 1992, 143). Indeed, prisoners at Angola were ordered to build a table to be used for execution by lethal injection; they went on strike until the order was withdrawn (Rideau and Wikberg 1991).

Until recently there were so few prison industry jobs available that direct coercion was unnecessary and so-called volunteers allowed the doubling of prison employment. The unavailability of basic necessities except at the prison canteen (Birch 1991; Urfer 1989), the knowledge that it was important to curry favor with guards to avoid legal punishments and the illegal beatings of which nearly all prisoners are aware (Weinstein 1990), the possible relief of the boredom and fear of much of prison life, and the desire to gain a favorable hearing from the parole board were together enough to fill prison labor positions.

During the 1990s, however, as prison costs soar and the laws change to encourage the use of prison labor, even the appearance of volunteerism is eroding. Slavery was not abolished in prisons (Hinds 1978, 328); prisoners have never had the right to refuse work (Campbell 1984, 134; Mintz 1976, 44). Therefore simple policy shifts, rather than legal initiatives, have been adequate to substitute forced for "voluntary" labor programs in many states. New York State's prison system, for instance,

> has quietly imposed one of the nation's toughest mandatory work policies, locking inmates who refuse work in their cells for twenty-three hours a day and then blackballing them when they come up for parole.

143

The new work policy was put in place over the last year when 1,071 inmates were locked in their cells until they agreed to work and another 267 had their privileges restricted, state correction officials said. . . .

Many states including New Jersey and Connecticut, and the Federal prison system, have adopted stronger work policies. . . . Daniel Dunne, a spokesman for the United States Bureau of Prisons, said that if an inmate refuses to work he risks being confined to solitary, losing "good time" that otherwise would have been subtracted from his sentence, and any chance of entering an early work-release program. (Sullivan 1992)

Prison officials can send prisoners who are unmanageable to the prison at Marion, Illinois, for indefinite disciplinary solitary confinement. The U.S. Court of Appeals has ruled that there "the prison staff can decide when a man gets out [of solitary], and sentences there can be extended, month after month, for years" (A. Rosenthal 1988). Thus fear of Marion and the ultimate penalty it extracts for infractions can serve as additional coercion for forced labor, once refusal to work is defined as an infraction. Marion, which has been criticized by Amnesty International and the National Inter-religious Task Force on Criminal Justice, was used as a model by thirty-six states in the recent building explosion of "super maximum security" institutions, leading to an expression of concern by Human Rights Watch (Miller 1993; see O'Shea 1993 for a description of the violence inflicted on prisoners in one "marionized" institution).

THE EXPROPRIATION OF VALUE FROM PRISON LABOR

Fundamental to the re-creation of forced labor has been the institutionalization of means of expropriating the value prisoners produce. State prison industries usually expropriate the value produced by prisoners directly, without the medium of significant wages. Wages in such industries are usually mere tokens, and can be as little as $0.15 an hour in some states (Lichtenstein and Kroll 1990). Moreover, these wages are simply turned back in at the canteen (see, e.g., McLoughlin 1991a), saving the state the costs of toothpaste and other necessities. Prison industries, paying token wages, may contract with or enter into joint ventures with a private corporation. In other forms a private corporation hires prison labor directly. Articles describing such arrangements usually imply that prisoners are paid the going rate for a particular skill; in fact, however, pay ranges from $0.25 to $12.25 an hour, with minimum wage being common for jobs that normally pay far more (Auerbach et al. 1988, 22). As much as 80 percent of a prisoner's wages are then appropriated by the state (Lichtenstein and Kroll 1990, 19); some additional deductions from the remaining 20 percent may be established by individual corrections departments (Bureau of Justice Assistance 1993). The prisoner pays taxes, contributes to the victim compensation fund, uses the canteen, and makes involuntary family payments, thus relieving the state of welfare costs. Twenty to 30 percent of total wages are even deducted for room and board (Lee 1991; Goodman 1990).

With such forms of expropriation available, it is in the state's interest to promote private corporate use of prison labor, and to insist on higher wages: these wages become a state subsidy, replacing tax dollars for incarceration and welfare, and that subsidy is larger when wages are higher, since the state's share is figured on a percentage basis. In addition, if higher wages serve as an incentive for docile prisoner behavior, disciplinary costs go down, and may actually permit the substitution of corporate personnel for guards during working hours (Bremner 1990).

THE PROFITABILITY OF PRISON LABOR

Prison officials generally protest that rehabilitation, not profitability, is the issue, and that prison labor is not as cheap as it appears—despite the fact that most prison industry is labor-intensive and wages may be as low as $0.15 an hour.

Corrections officials frequently claim that prison labor is neither efficient nor profitable, generally in the context of soothing labor unions resentful of the substitution of bound labor for waged labor and corporations resentful of unfair competition from corporations with access to the much cheaper bound labor force. These officials point to what they call the "hidden costs" of prison industries. These costs lie in training and supervision of prison labor, which they describe as "unskilled" and "unmotivated" (Grieser 1989, 20; cf. Skolnik 1986), in a rapid turnover of prisoners, in the short workday resulting from the interruptions due to prison discipline such as counts and lockdowns, and to the market disadvantages of using labor-intensive methods to compete with automated plants producing the same products. In support of their contention, they cite financial losses in prison industries and maintain that the importance of prison industries lies in rehabilitation, not in financial gain. However, an examination of each of these claims reveals weaknesses, often exposed by contradictory data or statements produced by other branches of the state. And, as we shall see, such claims are contradicted by the statements of private employers of prison labor.

Prisoners are not necessarily less skilled than nonprisoners; the quality of convicts as labor is attested to in numerous accounts. Data entry in Utah's state prison industry, for instance, was evaluated as having half the errors allowed by the contract (Costanzo 1990). The quality of prison manufactures "typically equal and often surpass those pro-

145

duced in the private sector" (Grieser 1989, 20). Some employers describe prisoners as model workers (McLoughlin 1991b). Auerbach and colleagues (1988, 43) comment that the prison workforce is disciplined, dependable, flexible, and relatively drug- and alcohol-free, since "prison inmates live in a tightly controlled environment." A fire captain with the California Department of Forestry, speaking of fire-fighting inmates, says, "They have the reputation of being the hardest workers" (Wilson 1988). An article on the use of prison labor by North Carolina's Travel and Tourism Bureau lauds the quality and quantity of prisoners' productive labor in this program, which now makes it possible for the bureau to keep up with inquiries, all for the cost of one dollar per day per worker, while experiencing "minimal" problems with workers (McDowell 1991). The motivation both for private use of prison labor and for the dependability of prison labor comes clear in the discussion of a program that trains inmates to work for horse trainers:

> The chief complaint one hears from trainers nowadays is the lack of skilled and eager help. The Walkill program will provide a supply of unusually skilled and motivated candidates for those jobs, if the state will license them and the trainers will give them a chance.
> "These men know what will happen if they go to the race track and screw up," Canton [an assistant commissioner for the state corrections department] said. ("Program keeps inmates on track" 1989)

Indeed, it is not clear that all prison labor is necessarily unskilled, despite comments conveying an impression of not just lack of skill, but near-incapacitation. Drug offenders who are described by a prison official as men who "were never socialized," who have led "chaotic purposeless lives," so incompetent that "they can't even make a bed" (Martin 1988), and by many others as generally lacking in the skills needed to lead successful lives, are described by an ethnographer as entrepreneurs committed to the same values and activities as are legal entrepreneurs (Gilliam 1992, citing work by T. Williams). Furthermore, some types of illegal activities may produce skilled prison labor. The skills developed by stripping cars for sales on the black market, for example, were cited in a proposal to create a prison industry doing the same type of work—legally—with cars abandoned on city streets (Martin 1988). Such skills could also be useful in prison body work shops and in refurbishing school buses. Embezzlement requires accounting skills that would certainly overqualify their possessor for working as a clerk in prison (see, e.g., Tricer 1989). Many prisoners convicted of property crimes have legal job experience (Holzman 1982).

Prisons making a committment to a successful prison industries program can alleviate many of the problems cited as causing inefficiency. Prisoner counts could be conducted at the workplace, for in-

146

stance, making possible at least a seven-hour workday. Where significant training losses would be incurred due to rapid worker turnover, prisoners with long sentences can be chosen. The women working in the North Carolina Tourist Bureau program, for instance, all have sentences of fifteen years or more and the program has a low turnover rate (McDowell 1991). Such policies should be easier to implement as mandatory sentencing limits release on parole. Another source of turnover, transfer to another prison, could be limited by administrative decisions not to transfer employed prisoners.

The market disadvantage argument, claiming that labor-intensive prison production cannot compete with automated production (Grieser 1989, 20), may also be spurious. Grieser, in pointing out the diversity of correctional industries, ranging from "products such as electronics cable assemblies for the military to ethanol fuel production and services such as travel reservations, telemarketing, and asbestos removal" (18), makes it obvious that some prison industries are in fact high-tech, and that others are labor intensive in any setting. He also points out that prison industries often choose labor-intensive areas for expansion (20). Women prisoners in twenty-five states sew for prison industries, a labor-intensive operation on the outside as well; they also reupholster furniture and do data processing and telemarketing (Duncan 1992). It is evident that not all prison industries are labor intensive, and it is not obvious that those that are will be at a disadvantage.

Finally, discussion of the profitability of prison labor is frequently so contradictory as to lead one to suspect creative bookkeeping to disguise the volume and profitability of prison labor for political reasons.[5] Some accounts of both private and public industry claim large profits, often in the context of officials displaying their improved management techniques or of convincing taxpayers that they should support programs that make prisoners pay for their own incarceration. Other accounts, particularly of public prison industries, refer instead to massive losses, often in the context of reassuring unions and businesses that there is no cause to worry about unfair competition.

The issue is further confused by unanswered accounting questions: for instance, when the value of public prison industry manufactures is cited, is it calculated using the discounted prices charged to nonprofit organizations or normal retail prices? If a cup of yogurt is sold for fifteen cents (Cheslow 1988), is the sale counted at fifteen cents or at market value? If the discounted price is used, the apparent value of prison industry production will be deflated and the apparent volume of prison-made goods minimized, perhaps allowing the industry to operate technically at a loss, frequently politically desirable outcomes. Another accounting question: how is the savings to government and

147

nonprofit organizations factored into the profitability of prison industries? The armed services, for instance, get fighter jet parts and the Marine Corps got Desert Lightning kits from people paid $1.15 per hour (Isikoff 1990). Prisoners are also building prisons, remodeling them, or building additions to them in thirty-three states, in many cases serving as skilled craftsmen, saving states millions, since they are paid as little as $0.15 per hour, with $4 to $5 per day being typical (Flanagan and Maguire 1992, 143). Are the salaries of guards counted as prison industry costs? In the case of private prison industries, how does the provision of facilities and machinery, sometimes for as little as $1 per year, fit into the accounting scheme?

Actual figures on profits are likewise contradictory in articles discussing public prison industries. Connecticut's prison industries, for instance, claimed a $40,000 profit on $7 million in sales in 1990 (McLoughlin 1991a). Considering that wages were $1.15 a day, and that prison industries usually involve labor-intensive rather than capital-intensive production, so that the major expenses are likely to be labor costs, this rate of profit seems extraordinarily low. New Jersey's prison farms alone, on the other hand, expected sales of $5 million and profits of $150,000 in addition to saving the state $850,000 in 1988 (Cheslow 1988). North Carolina's Tourist Bureau program saves the state $150,000 a year in wages and benefits (McDowell 1991). In 1988 New York's prison industries program could sell only to state or local governments, but was described as a "money maker. Nine years ago [1979] it had sales of $9 million and a loss of $8 million. Last year it reported sales of $60 million and a profit of $7.1 million" (Barron 1988). The same article reported that New York's prison industries are signing contracts with such companies as Burlington Industries, to make sheets for hospitals, and with a Canadian firm to make modular office furniture, and are working to change laws to allow sales to nonprofit organizations. The object, according to prison officials, is to treat prison industries as much like a business as possible. This would be a business with three thousand forced laborers paid an average of ninety-five cents an hour.

By 1991 total federal and state prison industry sales were well over $1 billion: without counting the approximately $60 million in New York sales nor those of three other states, the total figure was $1,105,300,000, a 139 percent increase since 1980 (Pinsley 1992). Despite such indications of the profitability of and volume of labor produced by prison industries, federal prison industries in 1989 claimed to have lost money on annual sales of $300 million (Tricer 1989). This conflicts with Lichtenstein and Kroll's (1990, 19) report that UNICOR made a net profit of $18 million on sales of $210 million. And finally,

Grieser (1989, 22) states that "In numerical terms, the average value of production per inmate is well below $20,000, which is less than one-fourth that of the production per worker in the private sector." Other figures, however, place average American productivity at only $49,000 (Nasar 1992). And again, is prisoner productivity being valued at market prices? Finally, comparing the productivity of a mainly labor-intensive set of prison industries to the average productivity of workers in the private sector will be misleading. Even taking the $20,000 figure for prisoner productivity at face value, it is important to note that prisoners in prison industries are covering the approximately $15,000 per year (Bureau of Justice Statistics 1992b, 5) it costs to incarcerate them. If they are involved in programs that pay more than token wages, so that much of what they earn is expropriated by the state, the prisoner is actually providing significant profits beyond the costs of incarceration. At least part of the disagreement in penal discourse over the most efficient and most moral use of prison labor may well boil down to fights over the distribution of profits from forced labor.

There seems to be less ambivalence on the part of private employers about the benefits to be gained from the use of prison labor, despite their frequent warnings that prison labor is not as cheap as it appears. For example, a New York State Business Council study says a $65 million construction project would cost only $15 million using prison labor, excluding prison guard costs (Eager 1994). Using prison labor may reduce the need for start-up capital, since the workshop and even the machinery may be provided by the state, sometimes for as little as $1 a year (Lee 1991). Benefits are generally minimal, and some states do not even require workers' compensation (Ripley 1991). Even where workman's compensation is required, it is usually inadequate and is not paid until the prisoner is released (Campbell 1984, 141). Savings on benefits can reduce labor costs by 35 percent even when market wages are paid (Tricer 1989). Safety regulations may not be enforced (Cullison 1990b), and unions are not a threat, although riot damage is (Bartollas 1990, 19). Prisoners "can be hired, fired, or kept inactive as needed" (Tricer 1989), providing much-needed flexibility. TWA, for instance, turned to prison labor for overflow periods in its reservation service (Malcolm 1991), as has Best Western (Goodman 1990). The president of Indiana Chair Frame Company, in discussing the company's use of prison labor, says: "some 21 states have begun making modular office systems at one or more of their facilities. . . . The big plus, of course, is the built-in sales edge correctional industries enjoy on all state contracts, which in some states can go up to $10 million. A 25 to 45 percent gross on all sales with this product is very possible" (Kaser, Wilcox, and Wilcox 1986, 13).

149

Another company reported profits of 30 percent on its sales (Funke, Wayson, and Miller 1982, 61). The increase in joint ventures, involving thirty-two prisons, forty-five companies, and fifteen hundred prisoners by 1989 (Tricer 1989), and continuing initiatives such as California's 1990 vote to increase private access to prison labor (Malcolm 1991) carry their own testimony about administrative benefits such as access to state use markets and the profitability of prison labor. This move has been described by Oklahoma's Corrections Department industrial project manager as "a slight drift back toward rehabilitation" (Malcolm 1991).

PROFITABILITY IN FOR-PROFIT PRISONS

A separate strand in private corporate profits from imprisonment comes in the experimentation with for-profit prisons. For-profit, or private, prisons such as those run by Corrections Corporation of America, while still rare in corrections, are becoming more common, with sixty-seven in operation in 1992 (Maguire, Pastore, and Flanagan 1993, 115), and a total of nearly forty-five thousand "beds" by 1994 (Ramirez 1994). The ability of for-profit prisons to limit public access to their financial records (Lawson 1990) may help to explain the lack of discussion of their labor programs. One of the rare direct references mentions that "reformative opportunities, especially in labor programs, are to be enhanced" (Durham 1989, 125). If the cost differences between public and private prisons are as small as Donahue (1989, 160–69) claims, one does wonder why corporations choose to invest in private prisons, unless perhaps prison labor provides another source of profit. It is worth noting that top officials in the Louisville-based U.S. Corrections Corporation, which received over $9 million for the operation of prisons in two Kentucky counties (Dunlop 1993a), contributed $27,500 to the campaign of Kentucky governor Brereton Jones and later received a $3.2 million contract to build and operate a for-profit prison (Voskuhl 1992).

The possible importance of prison labor in for-profit prisons is further suggested by DiIulio's comment that some advocates of privatization of prisons feel that "privatization engenders a legislative climate more receptive to the production and sale of prison-made goods. Operators of private facilities, it is claimed, have incentives to produce and sell inmate-made goods, and might help to persuade lawmakers to authorize prison industry as an effective cost-saving measure, and thus to join in efforts to transform prisons and jails into 'factories with fences' " (DiIulio 1988, 69).

Other evidence of the use of bound labor by for-profit prisons is suggestive but unclear. For instance, a private work camp in Florida produced $600,000 worth of labor (Press 1990, 39–40). Even in this reference, however, it is unclear whether this represented savings to the state, profits for the prison corporation, or both. Training programs are common and often mandated in for-profit prisons. Such training programs can double as labor programs. For instance, Louisiana's first privately run prison will take over a furniture-making operation from Angola, Louisiana's state prison/plantation. Winn Correctional Center will use this operation as a training program. The news story fails to address the question of what becomes of the furniture produced in the training program (Snyder 1991). A similar story (Ramirez 1994) mentions that Winn is starting a sixty-worker garment factory, but despite the fact that the story ran in the business section of the *New York Times*, no mention is made of the sale of the disposable hazardous waste suits the factory will make or of wages to prisoners. The growing profitability of the company is ascribed primarily to its use of a nonunion workforce that receives no pension, and to keeping prisoners so busy with rehabilitation and "training" that they have no time to cause trouble. Likewise, a news story on the takeover by Corrections Corporation of America of a state prison farm in Tennessee makes no mention of the sale of products from the farm (Fitzgerald 1986, 86). An investigation of U.S. Corrections by the (Louisville) *Courier-Journal* (Dunlop 1993b) reveals frequent allegations by prisoners and state inspectors of the illegal use of prisoner labor, ranging from cutting firewood for a prison stove to building a church and prison buildings. The state has no legal redress for such violations built into the contract; complaints have been ignored, and the newspaper alleges complicity between some state officials and the private prison corporation.

Additional suggestive evidence is the occcasional mention of private "boot camps" contracting out prison labor and of private prison farms (Durham 1989, 125; English 1990). A complaint that private prisons take the inmates who are "able-bodied and can work" (M. Ward 1991; Donahue 1989) suggests that work is done in private prisons. Petty drug dealers and casual users are being sent to private boot camps that act as labor camps where inmates perform "meaningful jobs . . . [like] digging ditches" (English 1990). The mainstream media's glowing reports on boot camps and other forms of shock incarceration make it clear that they also serve as brainwashing centers, preparing prisoners to accept authority in minimum-wage jobs and exhorting them to "work hard at Hardee's or McDonald's" (MacDougall 1993; cf. Michelmore 1991; Reiss 1989).

Analysts[6] discussing the pros and cons of private for-profit prisons focus not on the possible abuse of prison labor by private corporations, but on the morality or the efficiency of privatization of prisons them-selves, despite often starting their discussion with lip service to the past sordid abuses of prison labor (for discussions of prison labor, see Mel-ossi and Pavarini 1981; Novak 1978; Daniel 1972; Adamson 1984; Mintz 1976; Ward and Rogers 1987; Weiss 1987; Conley 1980; Hindus 1980; and Knepper 1989). Despite this dismissal of the possible role of prison labor in private prisons, and even though there is little in the foregoing discussion to prove conclusively that private prison corpora-tions are using prison labor to improve their profits, there is enough to suggest that further investigation is needed in this area. However, given the lack of evidence, this chapter has of necessity focused on prison labor in public prisons, while bearing in mind that laws dealing with public prisons are likely to eventually apply also to private prisons.

THE DIALECTICS OF LABOR: FLIP SIDES OF PRISON WALLS

Ultimately of greater import than the direct use of prison labor are the benefits that accrue to capital from the use of prisoners for union busting and for supplanting well-paid skilled labor, both processes that can reduce the general level of wages and benefits. In New York, the city government laid off a number of unionized painters and replaced them with welfare recipients, jail inmates in work-release programs, and ex-offenders. Because the replacement workers, contracted through a nonprofit agency, were paid $4.25 per hour rather than the $21 per hour paid to union painters, this arrangement meant consider-able savings to the city and, by making an alternative low-wage work-force available, could have deleterious effects on the wages of all painters, not just those replaced (Finder 1991). In Louisville, Kentucky, subcontracted inmates were employed to replace striking workers at Fischer Packing Company until union protest demonstrations forced a policy change (J. Ward 1992). According to inmates of a Kentucky county jail, since they began providing free labor on county road crews, several regular employees have been laid off (personal communication 1993). These examples underscore the dialectical relationship between free and bound labor.

Nor are employers unaware of the relationship between prison labor and the Third World. A former RCA manager commented that "RCA moved a television assembly plant from Indiana to Mexico so it could pay lower wages, but . . . [said that] such moves might be reversed if companies could bring work into prisons" (Smulevitz 1990). Con-necticut's director for private-sector prison industries, who "doesn't think the 'tedious' jobs would be easily filled from the ranks of the unemployed outside prisons" (McLoughlin 1991b), pointed out that "many of the [prison industry] projects have taken off because inmates are willing to do jobs that civilians will not" (Cullison 1990a). Prison labor, in other words, can substitute for foreign Third World labor when conditions or pay are so poor that, given the minimal safety net we have left, Americans with any choice will not accept them. And in fact some of the work being done by prisoners, either in state-run or private industry, is dangerous. Prisoners have been used to clear beaches where the debris to be removed included bags of hospital waste (King 1990). They remove asbestos (Costanzo 1990) and drop from helicopters to fight forest fires (Wilson 1988).

A perhaps larger factor than bound labor inside prison walls is the 2,475,000 people, disproportionately people of color, who are in various forms of supervised release,[7] many of whom are required to hold jobs in order to remain outside of prison, and who were referred to by Oklahoma state finance director Alexander Holmes as "the cream of the crud" (English 1990). Since losing a job could mean a return to prison, many men are being forced by the "justice" system into the kind of docility and dependability in low-wage jobs that the necessity to support children often forces on women. Participants in such programs are subject to "many requirements—written and communicated—concerned not so much with prevention of crime as with fitting people into an image of life which values hard work, not complaining, not asserting one's rights" (Diana Gordon, cited in Kennedy 1989).

In some programs the convict lives at home under intensive supervision. Work-release programs in New York State send three thousand inmates to work during the day and hold them in minimum security prisons after hours; dishwashing was cited as an example of jobs held ("Inmate is accused . . ." 1989). In New Jersey those in intensive supervision programs pay about $3,500 per year in taxes, fines and restitution payments, community service work, child support payments, and supervision fees (Kennedy 1989). Texas requires those on probation to pay fees for supervision, making caseworker evaluations dependent on their rate of fee collection (Finn and Parent 1992). Programs diverting first-time, nonviolent adults and juveniles from prison through unpaid community work are becoming more common (see, e.g., Swauger 1993; Mertens 1993).

Since labor on the two sides of the prison wall thus exists in a dialectical relationship, capital's increased access to bound labor is a small but growing factor in the immiseration of the entire working class. Bound labor within prisons relieves some employers, at taxpayers' expense, of the necessity to pay a living wage, an attraction that, as it draws employers, shifts employment away from those outside prison walls, thus increasing the reserve labor force and permitting a decrease

153

in wages and tightened labor control, of benefit to all employers, not just to those using prison labor.

While prisoners become bound, concentrated labor, labor outside the prison comes increasingly to depend on the Third World. Part of this dependence is seen in the flight of industry to foreign sources of cheap labor. Another part is seen in the importation of foreign cheap labor to the United States, for instance in the H-2 guest worker program (Wilkinson 1990) and in the use of immigrant, especially illegal immigrant, sweatshop labor (Turetsky 1990). However, conditions in the United States also indicate the increasing availability of an internal Third World, as witnessed by the explosion in child labor (Specter 1991), the revival of cottage industries, the increasingly prevalent homelessness, the development of workfare and low-wage contract and temporary labor (Feuerstein 1990; Cook 1994), and the rising unemployment among all segments of the working class, including white-collar workers, some of whose work has gone to the electronic cottage (Berch 1985) and to prisons with data processing industries. The forty-hour week is being abandoned as those still employed work longer hours (Schor 1991; cf. Kingsolver 1991; Hill and Buck 1992).

Under such conditions the "Drug War" plays a dual role. First, it provides a crime wave that helps to legitimate the state during a period of economic and social crisis (Hall et al. 1978), allowing the blame for Third World conditions to rest on drugs, and on the bad people who grow, sell, and use them.[8] Second, the same right-wing ideology and racism that allow us to believe in the "Drug War" are facilitating the re-creation, at public expense, of an even cheaper labor force, one that is provided through arbitrary laws that criminalize by definition. Association with crack rather than with alcohol, or even other forms of cocaine, criminalizes by definition, just as being Jewish rather than Aryan criminalized by definition. Being poor, especially when one is also a young man of color, appears to criminalize by de facto definition, since street sweeps are conducted only in neighborhoods with a high concentration of people meeting this definition. No one in power has ever suggested cordoning off the middle-class neighborhoods where much of the crack is used.

The able-bodied convicts produced in unending streams by the "Drug War" are now available for forced labor, and laws and Supreme Court decisions are facilitating private and state enterprise access to prison labor. Incarceration thus produces concentrated labor, an American Fourth World, whose members can be induced or forced to perform jobs refused by members of American Third Worlds. Concentration through criminalization makes forced labor practical, so that companies can pick and choose their workforce from a huge pool;

154

concentration by race makes criminalization acceptable to a large number of Americans, and concentration behind walls makes forced labor nearly invisible. The rhetoric of concentrated labor is needed only to produce the comfortable illusion for the nonimprisoned and nontargeted that those in prison deserve to be there and benefit from the experience. Such illusions appear to be validated when prisoners are found who say that they needed somebody watching over them, that forced labor was the best thing that ever happened to them (Kennedy 1989), that forced labor is for the good of their souls.

That such policies are a desperate fascistic[9] response to crisis in American capital's profit position becomes obvious only when it is understood that the two sides of the prison wall are dialectically related, so that the rhetoric of the "Drug War" becomes a rhetoric of concentrated labor. The rhetoric of concentrated labor is an ideological muddying of the increasing exploitation of all working U.S. residents, save those in the upper-income strata, and of the superexploitation of many of them.

Notes

I would like to thank David C. Buck, Faye V. Harrison, and Helán E. Page for their continuous encouragement as I worked on this paper, and Rachel Buck for help with references.

1. Numerous reports document increasing poverty, declining standards of living, rising mortality rates, and declining levels of health. For examples, see E. Rosenthal (1990); Kilborn (1991); and "Millions of children . . ." (1989).

2. Approximately three-quarters of the $10.6 billion "Drug War" budget in 1990 was spent on interdiction and enforcement (Coy 1991). An additional $2.1 billion was added by 1992, with no change of focus (Isikoff 1992). In addition, since a large percentage of prisoners are incarcerated as a result of the "Drug War," a correspondingly large percentage of the $16 billion we spend annually on incarceration (Ostrow 1991) should be included in the cost of the construction of crack as an epidemic.

3. This percentage was obtained by adding the total number of black non-Hispanic and Hispanic inmates, which was then expressed as a percentage of total prisoners, using Justice Department statistics (Jankowski 1992, 50).

4. By 1991 only 6.2 percent of homicides were listed as drug-related. Even if it were possible to argue that increased incarceration was the cause of this decrease, this represents a saving of only eighty-nine lives (see figures in Bureau of Justice Statistics 1993, 8), a saving that could easily be accomplished at far less cost in terms of both money and civil liberties by enforcement of industrial safety regulations, for instance, or by the provision of childhood immunization.

5. Khondaker Haque confirmed the implausibility of the statistics presented here and laid to rest a number of other suspicions detailed in an early draft of the

chapter. Thanks to him those inaccuracies have been deleted; however, the responsibility for any further problems in my analysis rests with me.

6. Donahue (1989, 150–78) and many of the contributors to McDonald's (1990) volume on private prisons question the reasoning behind the support for private prisons on both moral and financial grounds. Other analysts (e.g., Auerbach et al. 1988; McConville 1987) basically approve of privitization. Objections also come from labor unions, which have historically opposed the use of prison labor (see, e.g., Isikoff 1990).

7. According to DiIulio (1988, 66), "about 3.3 million Americans—roughly one white male in thirty-five, and one black male in nine—are living under some form of correctional supervision." Three-quarters of them are on probation or parole.

8. A further aspect of the dialectical relationship developed here is that the use of prison labor, by promoting the increasing immiseration of minority communities, likewise encourages people to take the risks involved in drug selling, and thus contributes to the supply of convictable conscripts for prison labor. Unfortunately, the grounding of this argument is beyond the scope of this chapter.

9. My thanks to Morton G. Wenger for an extremely useful discussion of fascism and its implications in this context.

References

Adamson, Christopher. 1984. Toward a Marxian penology: Captive criminal populations as economic threats and resources. *Social Problems* 31(4):435–58.

Auerbach, Barbara, George Sexton, Franklin Farrow, and Robert Lawson. 1988. *Work in American prisons: The private sector gets involved.* Washington, D.C.: National Institute of Justice.

Barron, James. 1988. New York prisons find new work for inmates. *New York Times*, 8 February, B3.

Bartollas, Clemens. 1990. The prison: Disorder personified. In *Are Prisons Any Better: Twenty Years of Correctional Reform*, ed. John Murphy and Jack Dison, 11–22. Newbury Park, Calif.: Sage Publications.

Berch, Bettina. 1985. The resurrection of out-work. *Monthly Review* 37:37–46.

Birch, Doug. 1991. Inmates making bay tags want a raise. *Baltimore Sun*, 26 June. In Newsbank [microform], Law 76:D12.

Blaustein, Susan. 1994. Congress's drive-by killing: Crimes against habeas corpus. *The Nation*, 20 June, 869–71.

Bremner, Faith. 1990. Program puts big business behind bars. *Reno Gazette-Journal*, 30 May. In Newsbank [microform], Law 53:E14–F1.

Buck, Pem Davidson. 1991. Colonized anthropology: Cargo-cult discourse. In *Decolonizing anthropology*, ed. Faye V. Harrison, 24–41. Washington, D.C.: American Anthropological Association.

Bureau of Justice Assistance. 1993. *Fact sheet: Private sector/Prison industry enhancement (PIE) certification program.* (NCJ#FS000046).

Bureau of Justice Statistics. 1992a. *Drugs, crime, and the criminal justice system.* Washington, D.C.: U.S. Department of Justice. (NCJ-133652).

Bureau of Justice Statistics. 1992b. *National update.* Washington D.C.: U.S. Department of Justice 2(2). (NCJ-138540).

Bureau of Justice Statistics. 1993. *Drugs and crime facts, 1992.* Washington, D.C.: U.S. Department of Justice. (NCJ-139561).

Campbell, Jamie. 1984. The prisoner's paradox: Forced labor and uncompensated injuries. *New England Journal on Criminal and Civil Confinement* 10(1):123–46.

Cassidy, Peter. 1993. Without due process. *The Progressive*, August, 2–34.

Cheslow, Jerry. 1988. Prison farms' produce: Meat and work ethic. *New York Times*, 26 June, sec. 12:4,5.

Chiricos, Theodore, and Miriam Delone. 1992. Labor surplus and punishment: A review and assessment of theory and evidence. *Social Problems* 39(4):421–46.

Cohen, Richard. 1993. Near-death experience. *Washington Post.* National weekly edition. 12–18 July, 28.

Conley, John. 1980. Prisons, production, and profit: Reconsidering the importance of prison industries. *Journal of Social History* 14(2):257–76.

Cook, Christopher. 1994. Disposable employees: Temps—the forgotten workers. *The Nation*, 31 January, 124–28.

Costanzo, Joe. 1990. Business behind bars. *(Salt Lake City) Desert News*, 19 April. In Newsbank [microform], Law 91:C8–10.

Coy, Patrick. 1991. Conscientious objector. *The Progressive*, July, 38.

Criminal Justice Associates. 1985. *Private sector involvement in prison-based business: A national assessment.* Washington D.C.: National Institute of Justice.

Cullison, Alan. 1990a. Aetna hiring workers at prison. *Hartford (Conn.) Courant*, 13 September. In Newsbank [microform], Law 103:A13.

———. 1990b. Prison fined in probe of workshop safety. *Hartford (Conn.) Courant*, 21 September. In Newsbank [microform], Law 103:A14.

Currie, Elliott. 1994. Capital gangbusters: What's wrong with the crime bill. *The Nation*, 31 January, 118–21.

Daniel, Pete. 1972. *The shadow of slavery: Peonage in the South 1901–1969.* Urbana: University of Illinois Press.

DiIulio, John. 1988. What's wrong with private prisons. *Public Interest* 92:66–83.

Donahue, John. 1989. *The privatization decision: Public ends, private means.* New York: Basic Books.

Duncan, Donna. 1992. ACA survey examines industry programs for women offenders. *Corrections Today* 54(February):114.

Dunlop, R. G. 1993a. Speaking softly, carrying no stick. *Louisville (Ky.) Courier-Journal*, 21 December. In Newsbank [microform], Law 118:C11–14.

———. 1993b. State's role: Overlooking instead of overseeing. *Louisville (Ky.) Courier-Journal*, 20 December. In Newsbank [microform], Law 118:D1–2.

Durham, Alexis. 1989. Origins of interest in the privatization of punishment: The nineteenth and twentieth century American experience. *Criminology* 27(1):107–39.

Eager, Bill. 1994. More inmates work outside prison. *Albany Times Union*, 13 February. In Newsbank [microform], Law 14:D6–7.

English, Paul. 1990. Work camps proposed for drug offenders. *Oklahoma City Daily Oklahoman*, 22 February. In Newsbank [microform], Law 21:D8.

Farrier, Hal. 1989. Secure prison industries: Getting the benefits without the risk. *Corrections Today* 51(July):110–12.

Feuerstein, Adam. 1990. Work-a-day blues. *Southern Exposure* 18(3):25–29.

Finder, Alan. 1991. New York drops painters to hire inmates, union says. *New York Times*, 5 October, I23.

Fink, Micah. 1994. Don't forget the hype: Media, drugs and public opinion. *The Best of Extra*, 45–47.

Finn, Peter, and Dale Parent. 1992. Making the offender foot the bill: A Texas program. Program Focus (October). Washington, D.C.: National Institute of Justice. (NCJ136839).

Fitzgerald, Randy. 1986. Free-enterprise jails: Key to our prison dilemma? *Reader's Digest* 128(March):85–88.

Flanagan, Timothy, and Kathleen Maguire, eds. 1992. *Sourcebook of criminal justice statistics, 1991*. U.S. Department of Justice, Bureau of Justice Statistics, Washington, D.C.: USGPO.

Foucault, Michel. 1979. *Discipline and punish: The birth of the prison*. New York: Vintage Press.

Funke, Gail, Billy Wayson, and Neal Miller. 1982. *Assets and liabilities of correctional industries*. Lexington, Mass.: D.C. Heath.

Gest, Ted. 1984. Prisons for profit: A growing business. *US News and World Report*, 2 July, 45–46.

Gilliam, Angela. 1992. Toward a new direction in the media "war" on drugs. Teaching as praxis: Decolonizing media representations of race, gender, and ethnicity. *Transforming Anthropology* (special issue) 3(1):19–23.

Glasser, Ira. 1989. Talking liberties. *Civil Liberties* (ACLU Newsletter) Fall/Winter:12.

Goodman, Howard. 1990. Seeking jobs that prepare inmates for real life. *Philadelphia Inquirer*, 8 December. In Newsbank [microform], Law 142:E4.

Greenhouse, Linda. 1990. Ideas and trends: The court cuts off another exit from death row. *New York Times*, 11 March, sec. 4:5.

———. 1991a. Court again curbs federal appeals by state inmates. *New York Times*, 25 June, A1, 22.

———. 1991b. Mandatory life term is upheld in drug cases. *New York Times*, 28 June, A15.

Grieser, Robert. 1989. Do correctional industries adversely impact the private sector? *Federal Probation* 53 (March):18–24.

Guerin, Daniel. 1973 [1939]. *Fascism and big business*. New York: Anchor Foundation.

Hall, Stuart, Charles Critcher, Tony Jefferson, John Clarke, and Brian Roberts. 1978. *Policing the crisis: Mugging, the state, and law and order*. New York: Holmes and Meier Publishers.

Harris, M. Kay. 1987. A brief for de-escalating criminal sanctions. In *America's correctional crisis: Prison populations and public policy*, ed. Stephen Gottfredson and Sean McConville, 205–20. New York: Greenwood Press.

Hill, Donna Lee, and Pem Davidson Buck. 1992. But not my soul. *Anima* 19(1):61–75.

Hinds, Lennox. 1978. *Illusions of justice: Human rights violations in the United States*. Iowa City: University of Iowa Press.

Hindus, Michael. 1980. *Prison and plantation: Crime, justice, and authority in Massachusetts and South Carolina 1767–1878*. Chapel Hill: University of North Carolina Press.

Holzman, Harold. 1982. The serious habitual property offender as "moonlighter:"

An empirical study of labor force participation among robbers and burglars. *Journal of Criminal Law and Criminology* 73:1774–92.

Hutchinson, Earl Ofari. 1990. *The mugging of black America*. Chicago: African American Images.

Industries Task Force Report. 1986. *Corrections Today* 48 (October):13.

Inmate is accused, furor is re-ignited. 1989. *New York Times*, 19 December, D20.

Irwin, John, and James Austin. 1994. *It's about time: America's imprisonment binge*. Belmont, Calif.: Wadsworth Publishing Co.

Isikoff, Michael. 1990. Does inmate labor work? *Washington Post*, 12 November. In Newsbank [microform], Law 125:A9–10.

———. 1992. Bob Martinez, the Invisible Man. *Washington Post*. National weekly edition, 2–8 March, 31.

Jankowski, Louis. 1992. *Correctional populations in the United States, 1990*. U.S. Department of Justice, Bureau of Justice Statistics. Washington, D.C.: USGPO. (NCJ-134946)

Kaser, Ronald, Nancy Wilcox, and Roger Wilcox. 1986. Modular furniture: New industries for a new age. *Corrections Today* 48 (October):12–13.

Kennedy, Nancy. 1989. More prisoners serving time outside jail. *New York Times*, 10 September, NJ1.

Kilborn, Peter. 1991. Part-time hirings bring deep change in U.S. workplaces. *New York Times*, 17 June, 1.

King, Wayne. 1990. Sweeping 20 miles of Jersey's littered shore. *New York Times*, 3 August, B1.

Kingsolver, Ann. 1991. *Tobacco, Toyota, and subaltern development discourse: Constructing livelihoods and community in rural Kentucky*. Ph.D. diss., Department of Anthropology, University of Massachusetts at Amherst.

Knepper, Paul. 1989. Southern-style punitive repression: Ethnic stratification, economic inequality, and imprisonment in territorial Arizona. *Social Justice* 16(4):132–49.

Laqueur, Walter, and Richard Breitman. 1986. *Breaking the silence*. New York: Simon and Schuster.

Lawson, Gil. 1990. Fears of expanding law on open meetings voiced. *Louisville (Ky.) Courier-Journal*, 14 December. In Newsbank [microform], Law 141:A12.

Lee, Gordon. 1991. Prisoners' pride helps lift revenue at Nyman Marine. *Seattle Times*, 28 January. In Newsbank [microform], Law 22:A9–11.

Lewis, Gregory. 1993. Blacks fill nearly half San Francisco jails. *San Francisco Examiner*, 12 July. In Newsbank [microform], Law 80:A3.

Lichtenstein, Alexander, and Michael Kroll. 1990. *The fortress economy: The economic role of the U.S. prison system*. Philadelphia: American Friends Service Committee.

Lilly, Robert, and Paul Knepper. 1991. Prisonomics: The iron triangle. *The Angolite* 16(4):45–58.

MacDougall, David. 1993. Shock gives 1st offenders opportunity for new start. *Charleston (S.C.) Post and Courier*, 8 September. In Newsbank [microform], Law 88:B14–C2.

Magner, Mike. 1993. Let inmates recycle mattresses, group suggests. *Jackson (Mich.) Citizen Patriot*, 27 November. In Newsbank [microform], Law 118:E2.

Maguire, Kathleen, Ann Pastore, and Timothy Flanagan, eds. 1993. *Sourcebook of criminal justice statistics, 1992.* U.S. Department of Justice, Bureau of Justice Statistics. Washington, D.C.: USGPO. (NCJ-143496).

Maguire, Kathleen, and Ann Pastore, eds. 1997. *Sourcebook of criminal justice statistics, 1996.* U.S. Department of Justice, Bureau of Justice Statistics. Washington, D.C.: USGPO. (NCJ-165361).

Malcolm, Andrew. 1991. Steering inmates to jobs by innovative training. *New York Times,* 19 January, I14.

Martin, Douglas. 1988. New York tests a boot camp for inmates. *New York Times,* 4 March, B1, 4.

Mathiesen, Thomas. 1990. *Prison on trial: A critical assessment.* Newbury Park, Calif.: Sage Publications.

Mauro, Tony. 1994. Triple execution in Arkansas tonight. *USA Today,* 3 August, 3A.

Mayhan, Mike. 1992. The color of justice. *Lexington (Ky.) Herald-Leader,* 19 July, A1.

McConville, Sean. 1987. Aid from industry? Private corrections and prison crowding. In *America's correctional crisis: prison populations and public policy,* ed. Stephen Gottfredson and Sean McConville, 221–42. New York: Greenwood Press.

McDonald, Douglas, ed. 1990. *Private prisons and the public interest.* New Brunswick, N.J.: Rutgers University Press.

McDonald, Douglas, and Kenneth Carlson. 1992. *Federal sentencing in transition, 1986–90.* U.S. Department of Justice, Bureau of Justice Statistics. Washington, D.C.: USGPO. (NCJ-134727).

McDowell, Edwin. 1991. Behind bars, but filling the front line for tourism. *New York Times,* 24 November, L24.

McLoughlin, Pamela. 1991a. Business booming for prison printers. *New Haven (Conn.) Register,* 28 April. In Newsbank [microform], Law 52:A4–5.

———. 1991b. For hire: Cheap labor, call prison. *New Haven (Conn.) Register,* 11 June. In Newsbank [microform], Law 77:C2–3.

Melossi, Dario, and Massimo Pavarini. 1981 [1977]. *The prison and the factory: Origins of the penitentiary system.* London: Macmillan.

Mendez, Ivette. 1993. Prison labor: Officials plan to expand program. *Newark (N.J.) Star-Ledger,* 23 August. In Newsbank [microform], Law 80:B7–8.

Mertens, Richard. 1993. First-time offenders work to avoid jail. *Pittsfield (Mass.) Berkshire Eagle,* 20 June. In Newsbank [microform], Law 56:A12–13.

Michelmore, David. 1991. Camp with an emphasis on the boot. *Pittsburgh Post Gazette,* 10 June. In Newsbank [microform], Law 71:G14.

Miller, Russell. 1993. Inside the toughest jails in America. *New York Post,* 9 August. In Newsbank [microform], Law 80:A14–B2.

Millions of children reported in poverty. 1989. *Louisville (Ky.) Courier-Journal,* 2 October, A3.

Miniter, Richard. 1993. Property seizures on trial. *Insight/Washington (D.C.) Times,* 22 February. In Newsbank [microform], Law 29:E14–F5.

Mintz, Robert. 1976. Federal prison industry—the "green monster"; part one—history and background. *Crime and Social Justice* Fall–Winter:1–48.

Montgomery, Lori. 1993. Prisons pinch profits: Businesses complain of unfairness but customers like competitive rates. *Detroit Free Press,* 27 October. In Newsbank [microform], Law 97: E6–7.

Nagel, William. 1977. On behalf of a moritorium on prison construction. *Crime and Delinquency* April:154–172.

Nasar, Sylvia. 1992. U.S. output per worker called best. *New York Times*, 13 October, D1.

Natalizia, Elena. 1992. Locking up our future. Outlook on justice. *American Friends Service Committee* 10(2):1–3. (New England regional office).

Novak, Daniel. 1978. *The wheel of servitude: Black forced labor after slavery.* Lexington: University of Kentucky Press.

One hundred inmates in Baltimore jail were detained without charges. 1991. *New York Times*, 16 August, A12.

O'Shea, Patrick. 1993. A tour through the circles of Hell. *Odyssey*. Spring:34–43.

Ostrow, Ronald. 1991. U.S. imprisons black men at 4 times South Africa's rate. *Los Angeles Times*, 5 January. In Newsbank [microform], Law 7:G9.

Pinsley, Elliot. 1992. Not-so-free-enterprise. *Hackensack (N.J.) Record*, 18 October. In Newsbank [microform], Law 109:B10–C1.

Press, Aric. 1990. The good, the bad, and the ugly: Private prisons in the 1980s. In *Private prisons and the public interest*, ed. Douglas McDonald, 19–41. New Brunswick, N.J.: Rutgers University Press.

Program keeps inmates on track. 1989. *New York Times*, 27 August, sec. 8:7.

Raab, Selwyn. 1991. Prisoners' view of riot: A reaction to brutality. *New York Times*, 26 June, B1.

Ramirez, Anthony. 1994. Privatizing America's prisons, slowly. *New York Times*, 14 August, sec. 3:4.

Reiman, Jeffrey. 1990 [1979]. *The rich get richer and the poor get prison: Ideology, class, and criminal justice.* New York: Macmillan.

Reinan, John. 1991. A regimen for reform: Convicts get a second chance at boot camp. *Little Rock Arkansas Gazette*, 10 March. In Newsbank [microform], Law 39:F4–6.

Reiss, Matthew. 1989. Gulag for drug users: "You are now the property of . . .". *In These Times* 15 (20 Dec–9 Jan): 4.

Remondini, David. 1991. Two counties look at prisons to house others' inmates for an economic boost. *Indianapolis Star*, 12 February. In Newsbank [microform], Law 20:G1–2.

Rideau, Wilbert, and Ron Wikberg. 1991. A matter of principle. *The Angolite* 16(5):21.

Ripley, Kate. 1991. Businesses question competition from prison workers. *Juneau Empire*, 11 March. In Newsbank [microform], Law 52:A3.

Roman, Nancy. 1993. Court bars seizure of suspects' assets without hearing. *Washington (D.C.) Times*, 14 December. In Newsbank [microform], Law 119:C7.

Rosenthal, A. M. 1988. In the Marion prison. *New York Times*, 23 August, A21.

Rosenthal, Elizabeth. 1990. Health problems of inner city poor reach crisis point. *New York Times*, 24 December, 1.

Rothman, David. 1994. The crime of punishment. *New York Review of Books* 41(4):34–38.

Rusche, Georg, and Otto Kirchheimer. 1968 [1939]. *Punishment and social structure.* New York: Russell and Russell.

Ryan, Mick, and Tony Ward. 1989. Privatization and the penal system: Britain misinterprets the American experience. *Criminal Justice Review* 14(1):1–12.

Schor, Juliet. 1991. *The overworked American: The unexpected decline of leisure.* New York: Basic Books.

Sentencing Project. 1990. *Young black men and the criminal justice system: A growing national problem.* Washington, D.C.

Shannon, Elaine. 1990. A losing battle. *Time,* 3 December, 44–48.

Sharff, Jagna Wojcicka. 1990. *The "American monomania": A cultural materialist view of prisons.* Paper presented at the Annual Meetings of the American Anthropological Association, New Orleans.

Siegel, Loren. 1989. A war on drugs or on people? *Civil Liberties* (ACLU Newsletter) Fall/Winter:1, 4.

Skolnik, Howard. 1986. Getting the word out: Selling correctional industries. *Corrections Today* 48(October):6.

Smulevitz, Howard. 1990. Bringing jobs to prisons under study by state, firms. *Indianapolis Star,* 21 May. In Newsbank [microform], Law 53:E12–13.

Snell, Tracy. 1993. *Correctional populations in the United States, 1991.* U.S. Department of Justice, Bureau of Justice Statistics. Washington D.C.: USGPO. (NCJ-142729).

Snyder, David. 1991. Private prison touts success. *New Orleans Times-Picayune,* 31 March. In Newsbank [microform], Law 50:F2.

Specter, Michael. 1991. Putting little hands to profitable work. *Washington Post.* National weekly edition, 22–28 April, 33.

Sullivan, Ronald. 1992. In New York, state prisoners work or else. *New York Times,* 27 January, B1, 6.

Swauger, Kirk. 1993. Paying their debts: Service replacing jail time. *Johnstown (Penn.) Tribune-Democrat,* 20 June. In Newsbank [microform], Law 56:A14.

Tabor, Mary. 1991. Judge finds bias against minority inmates. *New York Times,* 3 October, B1, 8.

Taylor, Stuart. 1988. Court rejects state claim on inmates' benefits. *New York Times,* 30 March, A22.

Tricer, Scott. 1989. The search for ways to break out of the prison crisis. *Business Week,* 8 May, 80–81.

Turetsky, Doug. 1990. Immigrants sweat it out in illegal garment factories. *In These Times,* 16 May, 9.

Urfer, Bonnie. 1989. Prisoner of conscience. *Progressive* May:18–21.

U.S. has highest rate of imprisonment in the world. 1991. *New York Times,* 7 January, A14.

Vodicka, John. 1978. Prison plantation: The story of Angola. *Southern Exposure* 6(4): 32–38.

Voskuhl, John. 1992. Floyd chosen as prison site. *Louisville (Ky.) Courier-Journal,* 28 October. In Newsbank [microform], Law 108:F2.

Walsh, Denny. 1993. Inmates suit seeks minimum wage. *Sacramento (Calif.) Bee,* February 6. In Newsbank [microform], Law 19:F9.

Ward, Joe. 1992. Inmates used as strikebreakers. *Louisville (Ky.) Courier-Journal,* 16 July, A1.

Ward, Mike. 1991. Sharp endorses private prisons as money savers. *Austin American Statesman,* 5 July. In Newsbank [microform], Law 88:E2–3.

Ward, Robert, and William Rogers. 1987. *Convicts, coal, and the banner mine tragedy.* Tuscaloosa: University of Alabama Press.

Weinstein, Corey. 1990. Study on prison discipline in the U.S.: A follow up. *Social Justice* 17(4):157–65.

Weiss, Robert. 1987. Humanitarianism, labour exploitation, or social control? A critical survey of theory and research on the origin and development of prisons. *Social History* 12(3): 331–50.

Wiessler, Judy. 1993. Death appeals dealt setback in high court. *Houston Chronicle*, 26 January. In Newsbank [microform], Law 9:D9–10.

Wilkinson, Alec. 1990. *Big sugar: Seasons in the cane fields of Florida*. New York: Vintage.

Wilson, David. 1988. Young inmates form airborne firefighter force. *New York Times*, 23 August, A14.

Wolfers, Edward. 1975. *Race relations and colonial rule in Papua New Guinea*. Sydney: Australia and New Zealand Book Company.

Yahil, Leni. 1990. *The Holocaust: The fate of European Jewry, 1932–1945*. New York: Oxford University Press.

Your Supreme Court. 1989. *Civil Liberties* (ACLU Newsletter) Summer:8.

II

POPULAR CULTURE

STRAIGHTNESS, WHITENESS, AND MASCULINITY: REFLECTIONS ON "MIAMI VICE"

BRENDA ABALOS

INTRODUCTION

During the 1980s on prime-time television, and subsequently under syndication, the weekly television police drama "Miami Vice" opened with a string of images of Miami life: Palm trees encircle the viewer; a Hispanic woman, breasts barely covered and bouncing, transforms into a man vigorously playing jai alai; horses break from the starting gate; Rolls Royces sparkle on display in a showroom; two bikinied bottoms stroll from a hotel entrance; speeding boats course through Miami waters; the city's skyline glows and sparkles in the night. The only sound accompanying these images is electronic percussion and guitar. The show's title is superimposed against the sea in hot pink and turquoise, and even though not a word has been spoken, all viewers who have watched the show before know that "Miami Vice" has begun.

"Miami Vice" is no longer part of the prime-time landscape, but it retains a special importance for several reasons. One has to do with the particular type of television drama it was: what we might call the "I Spy" type, after the earlier prime-time hit that also starred a black male (Bill Cosby) and a white male (Robert Culp). The concept of the "I Spy" type of drama is different from that of some of the series appearing since "Miami Vice," for example "In the Heat of the Night," because the black and white protagonists are colleagues and buddies, roughly the same age. They are presented as basically equals, despite

167

any niceties of actual rank or job description, which is not always fully clear in any case.

It is additionally of interest that "Miami Vice" has been the last long-running television hit of its type—prime-time, *action-adventure*, police drama. Consequently, in terms of black and white male leads and what they can tell us about the representation of black subordination to whites in society, this program is among our most recent important exemplars. (See the introduction's discussion of interracial buddies and black stereotypes in television and film.)

With "Miami Vice," although it soon became clear that Don Johnson was the real star of the show, it was also clear that the stars were intended to be peers, regardless of some inequalities in administrative authority. What draws my attention is the clear subordination of the black lead, to an extent that recalls the Lone Ranger/Tonto dyad. This subordination's particular fascination is that the more it is scrutinized, the more one discovers how strong it is: what on the surface may seem to be a drama featuring a black and a white buddy pair is revealed to be a vehicle that skirts dangerously close to being a slick, modern version of the white star/flunky-of-color narrative that litters Western literature and mass media entertainment.

This is a drama that is revealing in regard not only to ethnic imbalances, but also to those involving gender, sexual orientation, and national origin. It encapsulates its sociocultural environment. In the following discussion, my aim is to identify some of the ways in which this program reflects the society that produced it. I will begin with some background information on the show, move on to an analysis of a specific "Miami Vice" episode, and conclude with a more general discussion of some of the ideological premises underlying the show's content.

BACKGROUND

"Miami Vice," which premiered in September 1984, was a weekly, hour-long, prime-time crime series aired on Friday nights on NBC. The show was created by Andy Yerkovitch (creator of "Hill Street Blues") and produced by Michael Mann Productions in association with Universal Television. Directors for the series' segments varied, from Thomas Carter (who directed the pilot) and Bobby Roth, both well-established movie directors, to David Anspaugh and George Sanford Brown (of "Hill Street Blues"), Paul Michael Glaser (of "Starsky and Hutch"), and two actors in the series: Edward James Olmos and Don Johnson. The show is filmed in color and uses music written and performed by Jan Hammer as well as popular music by the original recording artists. The actors in the principal roles are Don Johnson as

Sonny Crockett, Phillip Michael Thomas as Ricardo Tubbs, Edward James Olmos as Lt. Martin Castillo, Olivia Brown as Trudy, and Sandra Santiago as Gina.

The plot formats of "Miami Vice" have a common thread. The typical episode opens with some wrongdoer committing a crime; the members of the Miami Vice team then seek out, sometimes undercover, the wrongdoers. In the end, the culprit is either captured or killed. The vice squad regularly combats drug dealers, illegal arms runners, and prostitution rings while often also coming into conflict with American business interests and federal law enforcement agencies such as the Federal Bureau of Investigation and the Drug Enforcement Administration. Topical issues such as the conflicting interests of American business abroad, Vietnam and its aftereffects, Haitian refugees, and the ambivalence federal agencies display toward their own employees and local police are also highlighted. Simultaneously, the plots deal with perennial concerns: greed, loyalty, the conflict between the modern and the traditional, sexism, and exploitation in general, among others. What each member of the vice team does is to act as an instrument of good combatting evil.

The show's three principal protagonists can be described as follows. James "Sonny" Crockett is a blond-haired, white male in his early thirties. Originally from Florida, he was an All-American football star at the University of Florida, but his professional career was cut short by a two-year tour of duty in Vietnam. He has been with the Vice Division of the Miami-Dade County Police for approximately seven years; before that time, he was a member of the Robbery Division. He is divorced. His ex-wife and seven-year-old son live in Atlanta, Georgia, while he resides, with his pet alligator Elvis, on a sailboat docked in a Miami marina. Even though he has the outward trappings of a sophisticate, Sonny's character is down to earth in certain ways. His outlook is that of a working-class police officer, or more accurately, this is the view he tries to hold on to as his work constantly causes him to question his values. The demands of his job as an undercover detective create a constant tension between him and reality. Apparently, he is close only to his partner Ricardo Tubbs and other members of the vice squad. The persona he typically projects is the sensitive-tough guy; he appears at times introspective and caring, but at other times callous, reactive, and volatile. Whatever the persona he is projecting, it is clear that Crockett's dedication to law enforcement is total. The impression one receives is that he is not a particularly contented person—or a happy one—in general, even though at times, when he disassociates himself from work, he can enjoy himself with friends.

Ricardo Tubbs is a black man, also in his early thirties, who is origi-

169

nally from New York City. Typically personable, he is brown-skinned with hazel eyes. He wears ties and suits, basically loose but strategically snug in places. Usually tan, grey, black, or blue, his attire contrasts with Crockett's, which is loose and almost exclusively white or a pastel color. Tubbs is single; whether he has been married is unknown. He is romantically involved at times with a black woman who is a vice detective in New York City, where he was a patrolman in the Armed Robbery Division in the Bronx. He had a brother, Raphael Tubbs, who was a detective in the Narcotics Division in Brooklyn.

Tubbs was introduced into "Miami Vice" as he searched for a Columbian drug dealer, Calderon. Tubbs had witnessed him order his brother shot to death in an undercover operation that had gone wrong in New York. Tubbs followed Calderon to Miami (with forged undercover assignment documents from the New York Police Department and his brother's gold shield), where he teamed up with Crockett, who was assigned to look for Calderon also.

Tubbs appears to take life a bit more philosophically than Crockett. There appears to be less conflict within his personality than within Crockett's regarding his work (even though this conflict does appear). In any case, Tubbs also gives law enforcement his full attention. What Tubbs seems to lack in actual Miami vice experience, his life experience makes up for.

An ex-CIA and Drug Enforcement Administration man with many years of work in Southeast Asia, Lt. Martin Castillo is the most enigmatic of the three principal characters. A Hispanic in his late thirties or early forties, he has even features and pockmarked skin. He appears currently to have no romantic attachments although he was at one time involved with a woman from Southeast Asia.

Castillo is reserved, with a commanding presence. Dressed invariably in a funereal black suit and white shirt, he always looks serious and never smiles. He is presented as someone devoted completely to law enforcement, with few if any interests outside work aside from a deep commitment to some "Eastern" philosophy. Overall, he seems most like an avenging angel, with something vaguely malevolent about him—or perhaps just deadly serious.

An Episode: "Evan"
Plot Synopsis

This episode, first shown on May 3, 1985, concerned illegal arms sales in Miami. The show opens with a scene of the interior of an empty warehouse. The only items visible are three mannequins suspended from the ceiling by chains around their necks. Two cars pull into the warehouse. An older man of about forty-five to fifty years of age, Hispanic in appearance and crippled, gets out of a white limousine, accompanied by a younger man in his early thirties who is dressed in white. The younger man, a machine gun in hand, steps over to the mannequins, caresses them, steps away, and opens fire on them with the machine gun. The footage of this scene is reminiscent of a firing squad, with the mannequins quickly disintegrating under the barrage.

Police are surveying the warehouse outside. As the police move in for the arrest, gunfire begins; the younger and older man get back into the limousine and escape. It becomes evident that the limousine is fire-, bullet-, and explosion-proof.

The scene changes to the Miami Vice squad room. Tubbs and Crockett are assigned to buy Mach 10s. Later, contacts are established to make the purchase possible. While Crockett and Tubbs are at the first meeting (with the two main characters from the first scene), the younger man, who had fired on the mannequins, acts in a particularly belligerent manner toward Crockett. After the meeting, Crockett informs Tubbs that the younger man is named Evan Fried and that he is an undercover police officer. Crockett also informs Tubbs that he and Evan do not get along.

The next day, Castillo is seen talking to an officer from the Alcohol, Tobacco, and Firearms regulatory agency (ATF). The ATF officer states that Evan Fried is part of a six-month investigation in progress on the older man (named Guzman—he is a major illegal arms dealer), and he does not want the investigation to be revealed through interference from Miami Vice. Castillo states that he will not have the Mach 10s on the streets. The police will set up the purchase of the illegal arms in order to arrest the dealers but will not take either Fried or Guzman into custody. Crockett asks Castillo to be released from his role in the setup but is told by Castillo, "The job gets done," to which Crockett acquiesces and leaves the room.

When Crockett offers no explanation to Tubbs for his hostility toward Evan, Tubbs asks Gina (a vice squad officer) to pull up the employment file on Evan Fried.

The new scene shows Fried and Guzman talking about a meeting they had with Crockett and Tubbs the preceding night. Evan is seen drinking at what seems to be quite early in the morning. He is drinking so much that Guzman comments on it, to which Fried replies that he does not like Crockett's "vibes." Guzman seems to feel that nothing is wrong with the two men and dismisses Fried's worries. Fried continues, however, and Guzman simply tells Fried that if the deal does not go through, he will kill Crockett and Tubbs.

171

The scene changes to a marina. Fried sees Crockett and greets him in a friendly manner. Crockett responds, "We're not friends, partners, or old buddies." Fried pulls a gun on Crockett, which prompts Crockett to call him sick. Fried retorts, "How does it feel to be perfect?" He then tells Crockett that the buy is on for that night and leaves. Later, Tubbs is seen finding out that Crockett, Fried, and another man, Orgell, used to be partners, and upon asking Crockett about this information, he is insulted and put off.

Crockett is seen later that night in a nightclub looking for Tubbs, who is getting ready to leave with a woman; it is obvious they will be going to his apartment to make love. Crockett tells Tubbs that he wants to talk to him and leaves, whereupon Tubbs decides to go with Crockett and, exasperated, leaves the woman in the club. Crockett then takes Tubbs to a deserted toll plaza and begins to tell him the story of Evan, Orgell, and himself.

The three men had graduated from the police academy together and were very close. During one investigation, it was found out that Orgell was gay. Both Crockett and Fried reacted to the news very strongly. Crockett reacted by denial and ostracism, but Fried reacted by embarrassing and demeaning him. Orgell, devastated by the turn of events, one night confronted an armed suspect at the same toll plaza without drawing his weapon and was killed. The guilt that both Crockett and Fried felt was enormous. Crockett for the most part internalized his guilt and became openly hostile to Fried, who, for his part, acted out his guilt by taking on especially dangerous assignments. Tubbs tries to comfort and sympathize with Crockett and to raise his self-esteem by saying, "You aren't the same person you were then."

The scene changes and Crockett and Tubbs go to the prearranged "buy place." Fried and Guzman pull up and the exchange is made. At that moment, the Miami Vice squad, in uniform, pull up and take the money and the arms from both parties. (It is not an arrest, but rather the police are setting up the criminals.) The police leave and Guzman, no doubt suspecting an internal setup, opens fire on Crockett and Tubbs. Fried gets in the line of fire and is shot. Crockett and Tubbs shoot and kill Guzman and his driver. Crockett rushes to Fried, who says to him, "Now it's your turn," and dies in Crockett's arms. As he witnesses Crockett's devastation, Tubbs can only stand behind him and place a hand solidly on his shoulder.

Toward an Interpretation

We can look at this particular episode from at least two points of view: one having to do with events that are from a sociocultural standpoint epiphenomenal, and secondly, from the point of view of events that seem to relate in some nonsuperficial way to basic themes in American culture, themes that are reflected and represented through the various entertainment media. The first point of view would have to do with, among other things, plot devices and themes that have no special connection to or shed little or no light on the sociocultural structure of contemporary America, and especially its hegemonic nature.

It is certainly true that no one episode provides one with all the material necessary to glean what the series is about from a symbolic point of view. Much hangs on the repetition and frequency of certain kinds of message. In looking at one episode for messages communicated, we have to perform a rather mechanical, unsophisticated procedure of drawing inferences, ones that may, in the context of the series over several months or years, turn out to be epiphenomenal. On the other hand, our familiarity with generalized norms (those accepted throughout much of the nation) and the history of those norms gives us a vantage point from which we can begin to draw conclusions based on the content of only one show. Our knowledge of the culture tells us, for example, whether a certain program is pushing norms in a new direction, simply reaffirming them, or clinging to norms that are on the wane.

In speaking of the "symbolic" content of the program, I will be referring specifically to actions, events, images, and so on that allude or refer to something other than themselves. This is in accord with a basic, simple definition of the term *symbol*.

The episode under consideration indicates that the men who combat crime pay a heavy price—in suffering and death. The conflict both Evan Fried and Crockett feel about their friend's homosexuality and the indirect suicides illustrate this suffering. Of course, an important question is why such suffering should be underlined, particularly since law enforcement is a service needed by society. This series seems to go beyond the depiction of dangerous adventure. It shows personal suffering that exceeds the typical domestic tension and occasional deaths of positive characters in the line of duty. One would assume that any series appearing on national television, supported by commercials bought by major corporations, would, whether directly or indirectly, validate norms that favor the reproduction of American society. Law enforcement is a vital function; why should it be presented negatively in this way?

A reasonable reply would be that it is not presented negatively; there is a positive, counterbalancing side: the glamourous side of the vice officers' lifestyle, which includes fancy cars, clothes, and access to beautiful places appointed with beautiful women. It is as though the good part is specifically being counterbalanced by the bad part. Within an ideology that claims an egalitarian society, enviable advantages in material goods and access to pleasure can be tempered by the presence of pain. The presentation of this notion in "Miami Vice"—suffering accompanies privilege, thereby making the lack of privilege more sufferable in what is often presented as a society oriented toward equality—recalls the "poor little rich girl" theme. The main point is that in this series, where the lifestyles of the policemen are especially, and no doubt unrealistically, glamourous, we witness what appears to be, for television, a new kind of psychological turmoil. One instance of this, to make the point clearer, is the emotional suffering that leads to the suicidal actions and resulting deaths.

Thus, "Miami Vice," though generally seen during its beginning years as depicting a new level of lifestyle glamour/privilege for television policemen, presents also a new level of psychological turmoil and personal suffering. This, interestingly, is a significant part of what made the series fresh. It presented a new visual style and a new content style also.

We would expect this episode's comment on sexuality to be one that, in line with what I have already stated, supports current norms or reinterprets them in the interests of our society's ruling sector—that is, in a way that assists in the reproduction of the current social order. The three characters involved in the program's comment on sexuality are Orgell, Evan, and Sonny (Crockett). Orgell is homosexual while the other two are heterosexual. Examining this trio from a digital, either/or, oppositional perspective, we get the homo-/heterosexual opposition, but leaving matters here would deprive us of the added insight that comes from considering sexuality from a more nuanced iconic, both/and perspective, which permits us more easily to confront gradient behavior.

Death in the end is not necessarily to be taken as a negative comment on a certain kind of behavior, but we know that behavior that is from the standpoint of prevailing norms questionable or censured is sometimes labeled as such through the indirect means of killing off persons who show that behavior. Looking at this episode with the homo-/heterosexual opposition, we find that one heterosexual lives, one dies, and the homosexual dies.

In terms of survival, this is a vote for the heterosexual norm. When we consider the heterosexual who dies, we find something that reinforces this vote, and that is the ambiguous nature of Evan's sexuality. The ambiguity is strongly suggested by several factors. One is his machine gun barrage of the golden mannequins at the beginning of the program, not too difficult to take as positing his negative attitude

174

toward women (not necessarily co-occurrent with homosexuality, but widely believed to be so, thereby making it symbolically effective with certain audiences). This, along with Evan's particularly strong reaction to Orgell's disclosure, does much to suggest that Evan's conflicts with himself, Crockett, and Orgell may have stemmed from a failure to accept his own latent homosexuality. If we accept the idea that Evan is latently homosexual, then we can begin to explain his extreme ridiculing behavior toward his late partner Orgell (who is what Evan does not want to recognize in himself) and the subsequent aggression and guilt he manifests after Orgell's all-but-suicide. Thus, of the two characters who die, one is clearly homosexual, and the other is tainted, so to speak, by homosexuality—a stronger comment than that which we would perceive if Evan and Crockett were simply considered as two heterosexuals without qualification.

Although the subplot concerning sexuality does reinforce the rejection of homosexuality by dominant norms, and although both Crockett and Evan react to their friend's disclosure in accepted ways, their guilt gives an indication that they do not entirely accept these norms and the ideology underpinning them. It also provides viewers with an interesting reflection of the societal conflict in this area, namely, the increasing acceptance of homosexuality in some circles, or at least increasingly less negative attitudes toward it. This is another instance of the program's willingness to confront subtlety in dealing with societal issues, conceivably an important trait leading to the program's success, and one seen much more in the nineties, no doubt partly as a result of this program's influence.

In a larger sense, the issue is not strictly one relating to sexuality, but acceptable male behavior in general and particularly the status of friendship, including all affective relationships between men. Notice how Tubbs leaves the woman in the club to comfort his buddy Crockett and how it reflects the fact that in American society male-male friendship/solidarity relationships often take precedence over male-female ones. Friendship can take precedence over romance and is typically possible between males only. Of course, one might prefer to interpret this scene as simply reflecting the precedence of an already established and important relationship over a new one that is wholly unproven in terms of value. However, in the context of the whole episode and the series in general, this particular scene would seem to gently reinforce a generalized depreciation of women.

Whether or not such is the case, women characters in the series predictably come off worse, for example, in terms of their time before the cameras and the significance of their characters in the plots. One of the only women one sees in this episode doing something productive is

175

the policewoman Trudy, who looks for a file. Later, we have Gina pointing a gun during the police setup. The tendency in this series is for women's work not to advance the plot. It would be easy to take the insignificant position of women in the series as a representation, and therefore reinforcement, of the institutionalized subordination of women in our society. There certainly are and have been women-dominated series (e.g., "Cagney and Lacy"), but they are the minority, even if we do admit that such series are an advance.

Perhaps the most telling image is the machine-gunning of the three female mannequins at the beginning of the episode, which serves not only to communicate information about Evan's attitudes toward women and suggestions about his sexual feelings, but also to communicate information on male attitudes in general toward women. It is especially revealing to consider the opening sequence with certain changes made. How would the sequence register if a group of women had machine-gunned a trio of male mannequins? I find this hard to imagine even in a series with women protagonists, and know of no scene of this kind having ever occurred on television. The main consideration, however, is that this image of male violence toward female figures, while fully reprehensible—and startling—does not strike one as strange. The analogous situation with women purveyors of violence would, and I believe this stems from the high frequency of images of male violence directed toward women and the practical nonexistence of corresponding images with female agents.

Evan dies in the end, but it is worth noting that his death does not come across as payment for his "crime" against women. The concluding segment of the episode gives indication that he dies for his "crime" against man, that is, his one-time close friend Orgell. We remember that he said to Crockett, "Now it's your turn," putting his death wholly within the framework of his male relationships. We are, consequently, left with a startling image of hostility toward that which is not counterbalanced.

THE SERIES

We would never expect a television program to present crime in any unchallenged way as paying, and "Miami Vice" meets this expectation. What is not so expected, however, is an intriguing interplay between good and bad, a kind of tension emphasized here, perhaps more than in most series, certainly more than in most series during the eighties. There seems to be an effort to remind us constantly to look beyond the extravagant lifestyles and excess materialism to the other side of life. This double focus of the series gives us on the one side a collage of whites, pinks, golds, and blues on studiedly modern and art-deco edifices accessorized by rich men and seductive women. On the other side, we see innocent men and women killed, squatters living in abandoned buildings, women exploited in brothels, and refugees being exploited.

The series is certainly not innovative with regard to visual symbolism, although its use of color overall is. Rather trite use is made of the equation of white (or heavy use of a light color) with good, represented by the good or main character, and correspondingly darker colors or black for bad, represented by bad or less central characters. Don Johnson as Crockett goes about covered in more white than either of the other two principals. Tubbs, as mentioned, wears darker colors, while Castillo is served up almost invariably in a black suit.

Physical and psychological defects are used to echo a character's negative role. If the villain does not happen to be a cripple (as with Guzman in the episode discussed), then he may be physically unattractive or have some mental pathology, as one bad character involved in an incestuous relationship with his daughter.

In the series' sound symbolism, we find distressing repetitions of well-worn devices, for example, the use of conspicuous Spanish, island (read Caribbean), and generalized foreigner accents (with little worry, apparently, about inaccuracy or stereotyping) to underscore shadiness or criminality.

The two main characters, as I have emphasized, are of particular interest since one is black, the other white. One wonders from the start of any interpretive exercise whether these characters and their relationship will point up anything interesting concerning the relationship between the two ethnic groups they cannot help but represent—at some level.

The casting of blacks in patently unflattering roles has declined significantly since the 1950s. By the 1960s, it was reasonable to say that blacks were no longer freely cast in negative or degrading roles. However, if they were, there was at least some attempt to cast whites in such roles too, in order to strike some kind of balance and to be able to successfully sidestep any charges of racism. But new issues of race have emerged. One notes, in film and on television, that where there is an interracial buddy pair, the white person is typically dominant (if not invariably so—I am not aware of any exceptions) and the only one fully drawn, if either of the two is. Typically the black character (and the same is true for other minority characters) is one-dimensional: he has a public, occupation-related life, but no private life (but note the turnaround in the *Lethal Weapon* film series, where Danny Glover's black character is shown in the context of his family, while Mel Gibson's white character has no family or social life to speak of. Yet Mel Gibson is the "admirable" one—better-looking by mainstream conventions and more complex, dashing, and intriguing). The black character is also often subordinate in terms of personality if not also in terms of official status. One often has only a vague sense that the black character is unnecessarily subordinate.

My sense that Tubbs, the black character, is subordinate to Crockett, but not in any easily stateable way, led me to do a somewhat informal analysis of the use of questions and the initiation of action. One can expect a subordinate member of a pair to ask more questions than the dominant one and to initiate actions on fewer occasions.

The show's premier in 1984 had Tubbs using questions in roughly 40 percent of his dialogue. This figure consistently climbed, to over 70 percent in the episode aired in New York City on November 8, 1985. Crockett's dialogue was roughly 1 percent questions in the 1985 season premier, and this figure was rather consistent throughout the series. For purposes of comparison, observe that Castillo, whose dialogue is mostly orders, asks questions less than 1 percent of the time. Gina, the policewoman in the November 29, 1985, episode, asks questions half of the time.

A quantitative analysis of the actors' actions also reveals another way in which Tubbs is subordinate to Crockett. When the two are together, it is Crockett who practically always initiates action. Tubbs may suggest an action, but it is invariably Crockett who drives away or states, "Let's go."

Just as Tubbs's subordination to Crockett mirrors the political and economic subordination of blacks to whites in society, so also does the subordination of the female characters to male characters mirror the female/male power relationship in society. Gina and Trudy, for example, continually look toward the male leads for eye approval. They also, unlike the males, fetch files, limply point guns, and are prone to fall into emotional and irrational behavior when confronted with criminals whose acts they find particularly offensive on a personal level. Accordingly, the women will lose their professionalism and shoot a rapist. The men, in parallel situations, are able to remain more detached and to act professionally.

Sexism is further witnessed in the series' willingness to present explicit images of the subjugation and physical abuse of women. The episode with the golden mannequins, discussed above, slow-motion scenes of attempted rapes, scenes of Trudy chained up in one episode—all exemplify this type of image. It is not any one image or set of them that allows one to charge sexism, but rather the pattern and repetition of images and also consideration of what images might have been omitted and why comparable images with male characters do not appear. To be sure, such images reflect a social reality, and one can say that the patterning of these images in "Miami Vice" reflects a social reality, so there is no reason to classify them as sexist. But this is just the issue. The series, not unexpectedly, reproduces the sexism that exists in society, and in doing so contributes, however slightly, to its reinforcement.

One feature of the series that can be seen as positive is its realism. The episodes do proceed logically with regard to time and space, and they do try to show complexities and unpleasant realities, such as the conflict between American business interests in Latin America and the U.S. government's war against drugs and the lack of cooperation between federal and local law enforcement agencies. Other shows within the same genre seldom present as realistic a picture.

I believe that it is fair at this point to ask how one should evaluate this series. Perhaps this series' most interesting feature is how novel it was at the time it came on the air—and how it broke ground in some ways that have not yet been surpassed. The minute it is placed under close scrutiny, however, it appears to present simply more of the same old content that we had been seeing on television for some time. What I am saying is that themes, patterns, relationships, and hierarchies had not changed, nor race and gender dynamics. It is the visual and acoustic elements that changed, along with elements of style—manners of walking, film editing, and related factors such as pacing, attitudes of the main characters, and so forth.

The show's producer, Michael Mann (who was interviewed on several evening magazine programs on local television) was certainly concerned with experimentation, arguably more so than other producers of similar shows. He used different writers, which no doubt made a strong contribution to the series' varied content. He exercised careful control over cinematography and music. In general, he appeared to take little for granted and actually sought fresh images and novel content. Yet—I will stress this again—when the series is examined from an ideological perspective, there is nothing significantly new about it. The one accomplishment that those behind the series definitely deserve credit for is providing many more jobs for actors of color than most other television programs. However, truthfully, this is a very small accomplishment, and it would not deserve comment if so much of television did not ignore American ethnic diversity. The greatest accomplishment of "Miami Vice," perhaps what it best demonstrates, is its ability to use a mere change in form to suggest strongly a change in content that is really not there. To the extent that it has improved television fare, it has done so as, say, fashion or advertising. It and similarly innovative programs help television better fulfill its ideological functions in society.

COLORSTRUCK AT THE MOVIES: NEW JACK CITY

DONOVAN G. WHYLIE

INTRODUCTION

In late March of 1991, apparently to precede the rush of summer films competing to become blockbusters, *New Jack City* was released by Warner Brothers. Directed by Mario Van Peebles, a young black actor and television director, it was one of a host of films debuting that summer that reflected Hollywood's wave of infatuation with black life and stories by black people. Unlike the spate of films that had been released up until that time by Spike Lee, the ice-breaking black director of his generation, this film was primarily concerned with drug trafficking engineered by black criminal entrepreneurs in poor and underclass areas of New York City.

A contemporary urban gangster epic, as described by Warner Brothers, the film is shot in a vibrant style with contemporary dance music, giving it a look and sound reminiscent of music videos. Most likely, this similarity is not a coincidence since the film was no doubt aimed at an urban, teenaged audience, from whose midst had come rap music, a key ingredient in the vitality of contemporary music videos. Among the voices on the film's soundtrack are those of Ice-T, 2 Live Crew, Queen Latifah, Keith Sweat, and Johnny Gill.

As with any film, we can approach this one with the goal of interpretation by focusing on a number of themes. Of course, we cannot assume that any one person's interpretation reflects what a film's audience will actually get out of a film. Each viewer brings her or his own

181

individual social background and psychological makeup to a film, and both of these interact with the film narrative to produce a negotiated meaning (Ellsworth 1989, 61ff).

It is crucial to remember that the consciousness of the viewer is not an artifact, in any simplistic Marxist sense, of solely the viewer's current material life and relations. That consciousness includes memory, not only of events but also of ideas and orientations placed there in many cases by the media themselves. It is important to stress, too, the media-induced fantasies (Ellis 1987) that have been placed in the minds of viewers, fantasies that interfere with a purely material-based interpretation of reality and influence the viewer's interpretation of the reconstructed reality existing in the world of a film.

In support of interpretation by the critic, though, is that there is an objective story, so to speak, a sequence of events and images, some repeated, others less so, some not repeated at all, weighted for importance in a number of ways; and together these events and images privilege certain meanings. A key issue in the study of popular culture, and of film in particular, is how meaning resides in a text (film) and to what degree viewers remain passively dominated by privileged meanings in a text or actively negotiate their own. In the black box between critical textual analysis of film and the viewer's interpretation is the psychic material, often below the level of awareness, which is key to understanding how a film is received. I will return to this issue in the following.

COLOR SYMBOLISM

One of the most interesting themes in this film has to do with the symbolic content of the various characters' skin colors. In a white-supremacist society such as the United States, skin color unquestionably has a symbolic force, which is to an important extent determined by the ideological purposes of America's dominant, white "racial" group. (See the introduction for a discussion of the ideology of film images.)

I use the term *race* and those for various racial categories, keeping in mind that, while grounded to some measure on the physical traits of individuals—more or less so depending on the society, race is foremost a sociocultural category. Racial categories, in other words, are principally the result of motives and agendas oriented toward the gaining, maintenance, and justification of wealth and power. Moreover, the internal structure of racial systems does not follow in a direct, logical way variation in physical features, including skin color. The fact that some blacks in the United States appear "white," with blond hair and blue

182

eyes, underscores this point. It is also underscored by the fact that, historically and to varying extents in the present, in much of Latin America, *el dinero blanquece*—money whitens. That is, the contribution of one's physical traits toward one's racial classification can be attenuated by the contribution of one's social traits, wealth included. (For further discussion of racism, see Harrison 1995, in addition to the introduction to this volume.)

Preferential treatment based on skin color has long been a problem within the African-American community, spurred by institutionalized three-way racial systems in some sections of the country during and after slavery (for example, Louisiana and South Carolina) and less formalized modes of color privileging in other areas. Elites in black communities have long tended to be primarily lighter skinned, and particularly before World War II, light-skinned blacks sometimes formally and informally discriminated against darker ones. Older African Americans tell of fraternity parties during their college years that allowed entry to only those women lighter than a brown paper sack placed at the door—even though some of the men inside were darker than the sack. As such reminiscences indicate, color bias has affected females more than males. In spite of the consciousness raising effected during the civil rights struggle of the 1960s and 1970s, under the banner of the Black is Beautiful movement, color prejudice has persisted in the African-American community, stronger today than twenty years ago. Two sociologists, Verna M. Keith of Arizona State University and Cedric Herring of the Institute of Government and Public Affairs at the University of Illinois at Chicago, have conducted a study that points to darker-skinned black people facing greater social and economic barriers, earning in some instances up to 50 percent less than lighter blacks with comparable education and a similar occupation ("Why Skin Color Suddenly is a Big Issue Again," *Ebony*, March 1992, 120–22).

At this point, I will turn to the issue of how skin color is structured into *New Jack City* through casting. The film's main characters are young and black. The main character, Nino Brown (Wesley Snipes), is a dark-complexioned, muscular young man who is angry-appearing and ruthless. The leader of a street gang named the Cash Money Brothers, his goal in life is to "live large and get paid," as it is put in the urban street vernacular. Nothing and no one will stand in his way. He rules his domain with an iron, merciless hand and appears to be motivated by self-gain alone. Neither friend, foe, nor innocent bystander seems exempt from his wrath.

Nino's friend from childhood and chief lieutenant is "Gee Money" (Allen Payne), a light-skinned man who introduces him to the idea of dealing crack, a new and highly profitable drug. Though intelligent, he displays none of Nino's strength or force of character. In fact, he even becomes emotionally involved with his girlfriend, which, within the value framework of the movie's main characters, is a weakness.

Their primary assistant, known as Duh Duh Duh (Bill Nunn), is an intimidating fellow of considerable girth and seemingly limited intellectual capacity, as the film seems to underscore by giving him a debilitating stutter. He is of a middling to dark complexion.

The other character of import is Scotty Appleton, played by rap star Ice-T. Light-skinned with shoulder-length braids, he, like Nino, has the look of danger. Although a police officer, he is clearly "street," and his reputation in the precinct is less than attractive. Nevertheless, he is serious and committed to his work, although he seems to be on the edge. Scotty's temporary partner, Nick Parretti (Judd Nelson), is the only important white character. He is, like Scotty, a "crazy cop." A sullen and scruffy brunette with a five o'clock shadow, he gives the appearance of having passed through a great deal of personal pain.

Pookie, played by comedian Chris Rock, is a crack addict and petty thief. He is dark-skinned and relatively short with the dry thinness of a crack addict.

Nino's girlfriend Selina (Michael Michele) is nearly a cliché as the unrealistic, naive young woman from an apparently middle-class background. Well-dressed, educated, and well-spoken, she is also attractive and glamorous, with the hair and facial features of someone who unmistakably has white ancestry. In spite of, or perhaps because of, her involvement with Nino, she hopes to settle down and marry in the future.

Her cousin Kareem, played by singer Christopher Williams, acts as the posse's accountant, and, like Selina, he has a college background and displays middle-class behavior. Like her, also, he has the look of someone with obvious white ancestry, especially with his straightish-wavy hair.

The last two characters important for my purposes in this discussion are Keisha (Vanessa Williams, not to be confused with the black singer-actress of Miss America fame) and Uniqua (Tracy Camila Johns). Keisha is the lone female member of the posse and is of average height and appearance with a medium-brown complexion. An anti-cliché, she acts as the group's rather trigger-happy executioner. Uniqua, on the other hand, is the loose, sexy vamp of Hollywood fantasy. We know little of her but that she appears to be short on conventional sexual morals but beautifully endowed with a superb figure. She is, as is said on the street, a "skeezer," just a notch above a "ho"; she "gives it up," but only for those of star quality, including heavies in drug dealing.

184

PLOT

The film's plot works on two levels. On the general level, it is a fictionalization of the arrival and rise of crack in New York's black community. More specifically, it is the story of the rise of Nino Brown and his gang from low-level cocaine dealers to crack barons. I want to retell the film's story in summary fashion, but include some pieces of it not directly relevant to my following comments on color bias, because much of what I want to discuss in the following depends on some knowledge of the narrative structure and how the characters interrelate.

The film begins with a series of fast-cut images of New York—opulent buildings, notable city sites, and other icons of the city accompanied by a powerful soundtrack of contemporary black popular music. When the camera stops, it focuses on a bridge, from which hangs headfirst a white man, well-dressed in corporate attire, held by Nino and Duh Duh. Nino is resplendent in black leather accented by the de rigueur gold chains of black inner-city drug lords. After upbraiding the man, an associate who has offended him, Nino gleefully gives the order and Duh Duh drops him, screaming and pleading, into the river.

The scene then changes to a dingy, run-down courtyard where people are milling about. Here we see Scotty in plainclothes in the process of a buy-and-bust operation, accompanied by a nervous Pookie, who in fact has no product and snatches the bag of money and attempts to escape on a child's bicycle. After a long chase, Scotty catches him by recklessly shooting after him in a crowded area, wounding him in the heel, and then tackling him.

The film then returns to the gang, recording their rise to dominance. We see Duh Duh driving Nino as they pull up alongside a playground where Gee Money is shooting jump shots and collecting money from the bets placed against him. Nino calls to Gee Money and half jokingly upbraids him for pursuing his Michael Jordan fantasy instead of taking care of business. Gee Money protests his innocence and, seating himself atop the backseat of the Jeep, begins to tell them of the new drug in town. When he tells them of the mesmerizing effect he has witnessed in people who take the drug and the easy sex he has received from crack-hungry women, Nino jokingly asks who would want to have sex with him. Although there is an apparent affection among the three—they take seriously their association as the Cash Money Brothers—it is clear from the exchanges that Nino is in control.

It is implied that Gee Money is the brain of the operation, as it is he that provides the pertinent information that neither Nino or Duh Duh have. It is also clear that, although smaller than Duh Duh, Gee Money is second only to Nino in the chain of command. He mocks

Duh Duh's speech impediment with more than a hint of disdain when Duh Duh haltingly attempts to join in their revelry about their future days as crack kings.

From this point, we begin to see the effects of the growing crack trade on the community and the gang itself. Two parallel lines develop from both sides of the spectrum as Pookie and the gang reflect one another's circumstances in reverse. Pookie, the unsuccessful criminal, is seen on the decline as he sinks into crack addiction, his clothes becoming tattered and dirty and his appearance more unstable and crazed. We also see the "board meeting" of the Cash Money Brothers, who have brought in the expert business skills of Kareem, a Wall Street accountant. When asked by Nino why he would like to join their enterprise, he says simply that $2000 a week is better than $800.

At this point also, Nino hatches the master plan to take control of the Carter Projects, in effect creating a secured business base (crack house), laboratory, and clientele base in one stroke. We see, too, the mechanization of the Cash Money Brothers' operations and a higher level of brutality within the gang and among those they deal with. Nino begins to centralize and reorganize the trade into his own hands.

In this part of the film, we are treated to two rather shocking scenes. In the first, the sparkling B-boy Jeep driven by Duh Duh pulls up to a low-level dealer in their employ. (*B-boy* is the short form of the term *banjee boy*, used in New York for young black males who display a "street" style of walking, talking, and dressing; see Yasin, in this volume, for another etymology.) Beside Duh Duh is Gee Money, relaxed, smug, and dressed in a chic jacket and sunglasses, with a portable phone in hand. Gee Money calmly informs the young man in dreadlocks that Mr. Nino Brown will no longer be needing the man's services. With that, Keisha, the executioner, bounds from the Jeep, puts an automatic pistol to the "dread's" head, and shoots him before he can move. The reign of calculated terror begins. As Duh Duh pulls away nonchalantly, Gee Money exclaims that that's the way it is done—in broad daylight.

In the second scene, we see the stunned faces of the residents of the Carter Projects as Nino and Gee Money lead a man at gunpoint in broad daylight to the front of the building. The shot is at first concentrated on the upper portion of the frame and we see Nino holding a shotgun to the man's side and gripping his neck with his other hand. When the field of view opens, we see the man from behind. He is middle-aged, with a large bald spot on the back of his head. He is paunchy and heavyset and completely naked. Nino grimaces and sneers as he leads the man into the midst of the horror-stricken witnesses. Having humiliated him, Nino then dismisses the man with a condescending laugh and a warning to stay quiet and out of the way.

In a seemingly short period of time, the Cash Money Brothers achieve their goals. As they grow, we witness a collage of images as the primary characters in the gang are measured for tailored suits and generally enjoy their new earnings. However, they begin to feel external and internal pressures as the group begins to disintegrate. Nino, having become the unquestioned leader, begins to be much less cautious and devalues his team members. He begins to verbally abuse his girlfriend and sleep with other women, indications of which were not apparent before. In one scene, as he tells her how much he despises her, she counters that she has helped him build the business. Admitting that she provided him with a few books and reading suggestions, he one-ups her with the observation that it was he who had done her the favor of freeing her from the tight grip of her overbearing, well-to-do father and providing her with the luxuries she wanted and was accustomed to.

The close relationship shared by Nino and Gee Money starts to dissolve. Functioning as the head of daily operations, Gee Money sits as the power beside the throne, apparently overseeing production, distribution, negotiations, hiring, and internal security, while Nino begins to fall into the playboy ways he had once criticized Gee Money for. Inevitably, we see the rift develop into a rupture as Nino's growing arrogance leads him to have sex with Uniqua, Gee Money's girlfriend—for whom Gee Money has some feelings. In one scene, Gee Money peers in on his girlfriend, grinding nude atop Nino.

As the gang falls apart, Pookie undergoes drug rehabilitation with Scotty's help. Here we see a tender side of Scotty as he enrolls Pookie in a drug program and personally stays with him through his withdrawal.

Finally Scotty and his fellow officers are given the go-ahead to move in on the Cash Money Brothers. Scotty and Nick go undercover to buy and bust. The rehabilitated Pookie is sent undercover with camera and hidden tape recorder to work in the gang's laboratory.

With Scotty's undercover entry into dealings with Nino's circle, we start to gain more insight into Scotty, Nick, and Nino. Most important for Nino and Scotty is that they share a past event. One day, while they are talking about their lives, Nino tells Scotty that as a youth, while running with another gang, he had gotten high on angel dust and killed a woman at point-blank range. The killing was a rite of passage in the gang. Just business, not personal.

Later, as Scotty and Nick begin to warm up to each other over a bottle of beer, Scotty explains that his mother, a school teacher, had been shot by a drugged teenager for no reason. We are given to understand that this is the reason he became a police officer. Nick shares that his life story is just a white trash version of Pookie's and, now reformed, he is on a mission to stop crime and drugs.

187

Pookie loses his cover and is killed. By the time we see Nino's group meeting again, it is obvious they are no longer the team they once were. Now a full-blown martinet, Nino vents his anger on virtually all of the inner circle, especially Gee Money, for bringing Pookie into the group's operations. He also berates Kareem, brandishing a sword blade from his walking stick and plunging it through Kareem's hand with a comment something like, "I always hated you—you pretty motherfucker." Nino threatens Gee Money by grabbing him around the neck and then wiping the bloodstained blade across his shirt. Afterward, Gee Money, apparently depressed after being belittled and humiliated, breaks the cardinal rule of drug dealers: never use your own product. He is seen shaking and sweating in his room, hitting the pipe as he talks to Nino on the phone, almost like a child hiding some misdeed from a parent.

With his sense of loyalty and self-respect all but gone, Gee Money willingly accepts an offer to cut an independent deal behind Nino's back. Nino finds out and the inevitable showdown occurs. However, it is much less than a showdown as Gee Money—it has been clear from the beginning—does not have Nino's strength and hardness of character. Again, Nino belittles him, both for selling Nino out and for becoming a crackhead, in street parlance "sucking the devil's dick." Gee Money responds with pleas for Nino to remember all they have been through together, that they are brothers in the gang, and that Nino has been disloyal and disrespectful too. Nino rejects Gee Money's pleas, in noting also that no woman should have come between them. With a final curt hug, a kiss on the cheek, and a tear of regret, Nino explains that it can never be the same again. Both have their guns drawn, but Gee Money apparently will not or cannot use his. Instead, he falls apart completely with sobs and falls to his knees before Nino calmly puts his gun to Gee Money's head and shoots him.

Afterward comes the climactic meeting between Good and Evil, Scotty and Nino. Scotty encounters Nino and beats him to a pulp in a strangely one-sided fight. He tosses the semiconscious Nino from a fire escape onto a trash heap to the tumultuous cheers of building residents who have assembled to see their tyrant's fall. In a rage, he visibly struggles to keep himself from shooting Nino. Nick, standing behind watching him, implores him not to do it, finally placing a caring, restraining hand on his shoulder. Nino is arrested.

In the final part of the film, Nino has recovered from the beating and stands trial appearing confident in an expensive-looking suit. He calmly answers the questions of the prosecutor, a youngish, quite darkskinned woman. The two have their courtroom exchange, which Nino wins rather easily. He ultimately announces that he will turn state's evidence against the Cash Money Brothers and claims that it was not he but another member who ran the organization. With that, the prosecutor is forced to accept a lesser charge, and Nino walks free for the time being.

Out of the courtroom and self-satisfied, Nino meets the press, like a cynical politician, upbeat as he mouthes platitudes designed to invoke the ideals of American ideology—success, entrepreneurship, and justice for the innocent.

Nino walks away, down a stairwell, and is shot by an elderly man we have seen before unsuccessfully trying to kill Nino in the projects turned drug headquarters. Nino dies, falling down the stairwell.

COLORSTRUCTION

Following Spears (1992), I will use the term *colorstruction* to refer to expressions, beliefs, values, and states of mind that in some way reflect white supremacy, attaching higher value to physical traits more like those associated with "white" people. This term was coined from the adjective *color-struck*, which is well established in African-American communities.

When we study the characters of *New Jack City*, we are left with a rather obvious color line that separates the more negative dark-complexioned characters (Nino, Pookie, Keisha, Uniqua, and Duh Duh) from (1) the lighter black ones (Selina, Kareem, Scotty, and Detective Stone, played by Mario Van Peebles); (2) the one important white character, Nick; and (3) the sole Asian character, a policeman named Russell Wong. This is particularly true of Nino, who is very dark and very vicious. Indeed, in the first scene, when the man is dangling from the bridge, he is decked out in full black leather, almost as if to underline his blackness, which in the context of this film might easily be taken as blackness symbolizing evil. This is an outgrowth of the long association of blackness with evil in European cultural symbolism (Hodge, Struckmann, and Trost 1975), not to mention the degradation of blackness resulting from the racialization of slavery during European colonialism and imperialism. Nino is from first to last depicted as evil incarnate, bent on power and concerned only with himself.

It is likewise plain from virtually the first scene that Nino's position in the hierarchy has less to do with his mind than with his aggressive physical presence. It is Gee Money who first recognizes the monetary potential of crack and introduces Nino to the possibilities. Additionally, although Nino is the architect of the building takeover, it is Gee Money who manages the daily business and external relations for the seemingly less adept and refined Nino.

189

Of course, it could be argued to the contrary that Nino's primacy indicates a higher level of intelligence involving an ability to formulate a vision and actualize it. However, it is not clear from anything in the film that Nino actually has a special level of insight, simply that he is able to command others who have the tangible skills for running the business. His executive style, if you will, is based primarily on intimidation. Those around him are there due, if not to intimidation, then to greed or gang/friendship ties.

In the more obvious comparison between Nino and Scotty, the same color contrast is present. Although Scotty is wild and aggressive, he is the classic independent, rule-bending, good cop cliché. He is the embodiment of the supposed freedom and individuality held so dear in much of American society. Scotty's character is actually only very sketchily drawn, and we know little of him. What little develops, though, is such that it endears him to us. Even though he is street, he is a man of morals and principles, one who would care enough to devote his time to help an addict reform, and one who, having suffered the senseless loss of his mother, hates crime and drugs.

Last, consider Kareem, with a classic mulatto look—light skin, wavy hair, and straight nose. He is also a well-dressed, educated professional, and he comes off well as such, despite the hand-stabbing, in that it does not reflect ill on his professional skills. It is telling that Nino, before stabbing Kareem in the hand, says to him that he never could stand him because he was "pretty." Nino's envy is obvious and easily imaginable, given the colorstruction that exists in African-American communities in real life. Within the framework of colorstruction, Nino, of course, would be unattractive, or perhaps just ordinary looking, simply because he is very dark-skinned; and he might be expected to resent Kareem while wishing all the same that he looked like him.

Colorstruction is no less apparent among the female characters. On one side, we have Nino's girlfriend, Selina. Another mulatto type, she is, relatively speaking, cultured. She is also educated and from an affluent background. The other two principal women characters are deep-brown-skinned. Keisha, the gang's only female member and an enforcer is strikingly atypical as a woman. From the standpoint of conventional, patriarchal ideals in our society, she is unfeminine because of her line of work, even though more and more women are entering occupations considered in the past to be reserved for men. She does not exhibit many of the feminine behaviors expected from women; this is true of her movements and style of dress. All of these qualities harden and defeminize her—from the conventional viewpoint we are discussing.

The defeminization of dark-skinned black women—along with the hypersexualization of mulatto women and the enshrinement of white women—is a key feature of racist, white-supremacist ideology (Gilliam 1988). The defeminization of the dark woman goes hand in hand with classifying her of all women as best suited for labor. Note that these work-readiness stereotypes of women based on color are found in all racial systems grounded in color. Thus, Harrison (1991, 98ff) has observed essentially the same pattern in Jamaica.

According to hegemonic conventions of morality, the other female character, Uniqua, is a woman of ill repute. In an unfeminine way, she apparently enjoys sex and uses it for power, prestige, and financial gain. She is, then, essentially a whore figure, reveling in her sensuousness, her body punctuated with black lace and garters, emblematic themselves of her demimondaine status. Uniqua has been described in street parlance as a "skeezer" and a "gold digger, jumping in and out of bed with the highest hog on the scene."

In brief, of the three main women characters, the two darker ones are presented as mannish, in one case, and a loose woman, in the other. Again, there is nothing inherently wrong with these types of women. The crucial point is that in our society they are typically seen as negative, for reasons I have sketched above.

The last black woman to be considered in the film is a minor character and the darkest-skinned of all. She ostensibly breaks the grip of the film's color bias, in that she is a prosecuting attorney, an educated, polished professional. However, she receives mixed reviews since she shows herself to be rather incompetent or, in line with another possible assessment, simply one who is a loser. Not only does she fail to prosecute Nino, she does not even seem sufficiently disturbed by her superiors' order to accept the compromise that will free Nino from full prosecution. Basically, she goes along; she is not independent; she does not cause trouble. The only black woman completely on the good side of the law, then, who is very dark, is also compliant and ineffectual. The confrontation between her, the darkest woman, and Nino, the darkest man, invites some kind of comment, given the color symmetry of the confrontation. For some, her appearance with him might seem to suggest that Nino could have been what she is, that it is not society or lack of opportunity that has forced him into a life of crime.

The black men on the good side of the law are very light-skinned and effective—they get their man. (Pookie cannot really be considered consistently on either side of the law, and he is no one's role model in any case.) All heroes are light-skinned men.

Another aspect of the film's color bias is interesting and somewhat difficult to integrate with what has already been observed. Throughout the film there is a consistent use of imagery that seems to confer impotence on the light characters, not only in terms of dominance, but sometimes also in literal reproductive terms. For example, we find out that Selina is barren.

The difference in potency between Nino and Gee Money is verbalized and symbolized in several scenes. When told of the sexual favors crack-addict women have been granting Gee Money, Nino verbally paints a picture of him as underendowed and therefore ill-qualified to attract females. In another instance, Nino lifts Uniqua from Gee Money's grasp in the midst of foreplay. In short, Nino repeatedly belittles Gee Money as a person and as a sexual presence. Practically anyone subscribing to conventional views of masculinity, as did most of the people viewing the film when I did, would see Gee Money as stripped of his manhood by Nino.

Nino's emasculation of Gee Money is also presented in the hand-stabbing scene. After stabbing Kareem's hand, Nino wipes the blood across Gee Money's shirt while threatening and intimidating him.

In their last scene together, before he is killed, Gee Money is surprisingly passive; he wilts into sobbing, eventually collapsing to his knees before Nino. Only moments before this Nino had derided him for "sucking the devil's dick" (smoking the crack pipe); on his knees, Gee Money is in position for oral sex. By this point, the audience has been beaten over the head with imagery of Gee Money's, and to a lesser extent other characters', weakness before Nino. The weakness in the male characters comes off as emasculation.

The emasculating imagery is important, if due to nothing else but its almost dunning repetition. Against a backdrop of weak gang-related characters, Nino is physically the most fierce and dominant. This dominance is expressed through physical actions and sexually allusive imagery, which ties directly into societal myths of the savage, oversexed, and "overendowed" black male. The darkest-skinned male in the film fills the oversexualized black male role, the product of the sex-color iconography in a racialized, white-supremacist society.

New Jack City is meant to portray the urban black community, and as such its symbols reflect many of the beliefs and structures of the black community, as well as those of the larger society. The structure of the film, as with all popular films, is intended to appeal to our unfounded but entrenched cultural myths, among other things. The repeated themes of blacks as negative are clearly still at play in the consciousness of many in the black community. The film references this negativity, one would suppose unintentionally, by aligning negative character traits with darker-skinned characters.

To put this differently, hegemonic discourses, in the United States or wherever we find racialized social systems or oppressive ideologies, are not the only ones we must deal with. Hegemonic discourses, as such, are typically, if not always, incorporated to some extent into the discourses of subordinate groups. Accordingly, the ideology of white supremacy and the discourses that purvey it, have in the United States have been partially assimilated into the consciousness of the African-American community, coexisting "under the veil," to use Du Bois's (1961 [1903]) term, with beliefs, values, and discourses that counter the principles of racialization and white supremacy.

However, the issue of concern is that, in the African-American community, values and beliefs derived directly or indirectly from notions of white supremacy do exist. That is, many, perhaps most, African Americans are "colorstruck" some or most of the time.

Colorstruction compels us to confront the existence of cultural domination, the incorporation into the worldviews of oppressed peoples ideas elaborated and supported by their oppressors in an effort to justify the exploitation that results from that oppression. Consequently, colorstruction is one of the ways that people who are oppressed contribute to their own oppression. Cultural domination, though always existing alongside cultural resistance, creates the necessity for culture critique, the examination of received values and beliefs as well as the discourses and symbolism that support them. Observe that culture critique is a necessity for virtually all oppressed groups, since all groups that have been oppressed and exploited for any length of time have, as a group, internalized some of the ideas used to further their oppression. Culture critique is carried out with the aim of preparing more fertile ground for liberation discourses.

Media images produced by blacks are especially powerful and worthy of attention because they generally make more of an impression on black audiences. Black creative talent (that is, producers, directors, writers, and others involved in the creative process) can fashion works that use their (typically) intimate knowledge of black culture. The incorporation of that intimate knowedge results in a work that resonates in the black viewer's consciousness, a work that has cultural specificity (Spears 1992), more so than works produced by those outside the culture, other things being equal. In the case of colorstruction, ideas based indirectly or directly on notions of white supremacy are recycled through a specifically black-culture-oriented creative process. Thus, those notions are culturally digested and nativized, so to speak, before they are presented to the black community for consumption. The prior cultural digestion, in essence, makes them more palatable for the black audience. Much the same might be said of Hispanic audiences, who in many areas of the United States have assimilated many aspects of black culture as a result of proximity.

193

In examining *New Jack City*, I have simply looked at the main characters' skin color and facial features and then ranked them according to the positiveness of the character from a conventional standpoint. Although I received a vague sense of color bias (specifically, the more whitelike characters being the more positive ones) while watching the movie, it was only after careful comparisons that I realized how much colorstruction the film conveys. I say this as someone who has thought much about color issues within and outside the African-American community. Careful analysis, then, heightened my own sensitivity to what was going on in this film. Much of the colorstruction had sneaked past me unnoticed. Conversations with friends and others have revealed that, without prompting, many detected no color bias in the film and others very little. Apparently, the African Americans involved in creating this film detected no colorstruction either.

To their credit, it should be said that they have made a commendable effort to convey some hope for ridding communities of drug infestation, although the film's premises are connected in only the loosest ways to politics and viable strategies in the real world. The bad characters do lose, and the good ones win. The creators' good intentions are so transparent and their backgrounds are such that one feels compelled to assume that they were unaware of the film's virtually exceptionless colorstruction. Although it is theoretically possible, there is no reason to believe that colorstruction was planned and incorporated into the film. That so much colorstruction can slip past so many black people is confirmation of the insidiousness of cultural domination and internalized oppression. This makes me wonder to what degree undetected colorstruction in movies and other media might reinforce notions of color bias that we have inadvertently internalized.

References

Du Bois, W. E. B. 1961 [1903]. *The souls of black folk*. Greenwich, Conn.: Fawcett Publications.

Ellis, Kate. 1987. Gimme shelter: Feminism, fantasy, and women's popular fiction. In *American media and mass culture: Left perspectives*, ed. Donald Lazère, 216–30. Berkeley: University of California Press.

Ellsworth, Elizabeth. 1989. Educational media, ideology, and the presentation of knowledge through popular cultural forms. In *Popular culture, schooling, and everyday life*, ed. Henry A. Giroux, Roger I. Simon, and contributors, 47–66. New York: Bergin & Garvey.

Gilliam, Angela. 1988. Telltale language: Race, class, and inequality in two Latin American towns. In *Anthropology for the nineties: Introductory readings*, ed. Johnnetta B. Cole, 522–31. New York: Free Press.

Harrison, Faye V. 1991. Ethnography as politics. In *Decolonizing anthropology: Moving further toward an anthropology for liberation*, ed. Faye V. Harrison, 88–109. Washington, D.C.: Association of Black Anthropologists, American Anthropological Association.

————. 1995. The persistent power of "race" in the cultural and political economy of racism. *Annual Review of Anthropology* 24:47–74.

Hodge, John, Donald K. Struckmann, and Lynn Dorland Trost. 1975. *Cultural bases of racism and group oppression*. Chestnut Hill, Mass.: Two Riders Press.

Spears, Arthur K. 1992. Culture critique and colorstruction: Black-produced media images of blacks. *Transforming Anthropology* 3(1):24–29 (Special issue on Teaching as praxis: Decolonizing media representations of race, ethnicity and gender in the New World Order).

195

Rap in the African-American Music Tradition: Cultural Assertion and Continuity

Jon A. Yasin

It's the same old song, but with a different meaning since you've been gone.

The Four Tops

Introduction

Rap music, which can be defined as the joining together of rhymes in time to a musical beat, is at least thirty years old. Rap music's beginnings, in the early 1970s, are rooted in the Black Power Movement of the 1960s and 1970s, which grew out of the African-American Civil Rights movement that began in 1955. During its first decade of existence, little or no attention was given to rap music by anyone other than its originators, the African American and Latino youths in the boroughs of New York City, although a popular rap recording, "Rapper's Delight," became internationally known near the end of rap's first decade. During its second decade of existence, only casual attention was given to rap music as a genre by anyone other than those representing youth culture. By the end of the second decade, however, the mainstream population in the United States began to take notice of this new genre of music. Mainstream Americans took notice of the violence that occurred at several rap concerts. This violence, however, was independent of the concerts and rap music. Nevertheless, partially due to the negative publicity, many people at that point began to raise questions concerning the genre's origins.

Mainstream Americans have advanced several accounts of the origins of rap music. Adler and Foote (1990, 56) wrote that "a new musical culture, filled with self-assertion and anger, has come boiling up from the streets." Then, for their *Newsweek* readers, they added, "some peo-

197

ple think it should have stayed there." This account of rap is perhaps a naive emotional reaction. Tricia Rose identifies rap music as the main feature of hip-hop culture, with the other two features being graffiti and break dancing. She locates "hip hop culture within the context of deindustrialization," leading to a postindustrial society (Rose 1994, 23). In placing rap and hip-hop within this context, she adopts "Mollenkopf and Castell's use of the term *postindustrial* as a means of characterizing the economic restructuring . . . [in] urban America over the past twenty-five years" (Rose 1994, 189). Rose discusses the redevelopment in the Bronx area of New York City, which occurred concurrently with the beginnings of rap music. She writes,

> Hip hop's attempts to negotiate new economic and technological conditions as well as new patterns of race, class, and gender oppression in urban America by appropriating subway facades, public streets, language, style, and sampling technology are only part of the story. Hip hop music and culture also relies on a variety of Afro-Caribbean and Afro-American musical, oral, visual, and dance forms and practices in the face of a larger society that rarely recognizes the Afrodiasporic significance of such practices. (Rose 1994, 22–23)

She continues,

> [In] an attempt to rescue rap from its identity as postindustrial commercial product and situate it in the history of respected black cultural practices, many historical accounts of rap's roots consider it a direct extension of African-American oral, poetic and protest traditions, to which it is clearly and substantially indebted. This accounting . . . produces at least three problematic effects. First, it reconstructs rap music as a singular oral poetic form that appears to have developed autonomously (e.g., outside hip hop culture) in the 1970's. (Rose 1994, 25)

Rose, perhaps, does not consider that the originators of rap music were motivated by the Black Power movement (see the following discussions), which was still at its peak in 1972 and 1973, the time at which the origins of rap are set. Furthermore, in a reaction against disco music, which the African-American and Latino youths in New York City did not like (Keyes 1991), deejaying became popular in the Bronx, Harlem, Queens, and Brooklyn through mobile disc jockeys, who set up turntables and other stereo equipment and played recorded music on the city streets, in the schoolyards, in the parks, at house parties, and anywhere else they could get free electricity. In addition, over the recordings that they played, they shouted phrases such as "Throw your hands up in the air." These mobile disc jockeys attracted large crowds of youths from the local communities who danced to their music and responded to the phrases that they shouted. The mobile disc jockeys played for such outside groups as a result of having seen the disc jockeys from certain radio stations broadcasting their radio programs on flatbed trucks at block parties in the various African-American and Latino communities. These radio disc jockeys, furthermore, had shouted phrases at the youths, who danced in the streets to the music they were playing. Although broadcasting outdoors in residential neighborhoods began during the 1960s, radio disc jockeys on stations featuring African-American music had been shouting rhyming phrases over the airways, while playing recorded music, since the 1940s.

By 1973, inspired by the radio disc jockeys, Clive Campbell, known as Kool Herc, who had come to the United States from Jamaica as a child, was the first and considered the best mobile disc jockey in the Bronx, for several reasons. He used two turntables and mixed records simultaneously, utilizing the heavy reggae beat called a break beat. He added other sound effects and used African-Latin percussion during the break in the recorded music. The break in the music is the point at which the singing stops and only instrumental music is heard. Using two turntables, Herc extended the break by letting one record play to the end of the break and, at that point, letting the second record on the second turntable start playing at the beginning of the break. During this extended period of the break, the instrumental percussion maintained an emphasized rhythm. Because Herc borrowed the two-turntable technique from Jamaican deejays, Rose and "many critics have drawn parallels between the development of rap and reggae, a connection that is denied by Kool Herc. 'Jamaican toasting?' said Herc. 'Naw, naw. No connection there. I couldn't play reggae in the Bronx. People wouldn't accept it. The inspiration for rap is James Brown and the album *Hustlers' Convention*' " (Hager 1984, 45).

The Hustlers' Convention was written and recorded by the Last Poets, a group of African Americans and Latinos from New York City. They began writing poetry and performing with a background of drums during the Black Power movement. Another mobile deejay, who contributed to the development of rap music, Africa Bambaataa, was inspired by the Last Poets. Bambaataa, who was from the Bronx River Housing Projects, had been a member of the Black Spades, a street gang in the Bronx, and was influenced by the neighborhood work for social change and positive messages of the African-American Muslim community, as well as the artists of the Black Power movement. In addition to the Last Poets, Bambaataa was inspired by the famous rhythm and blues singer James Brown. Known as the Godfather of Soul, Brown, in 1968, chanted, "Say it Loud! I'm Black and I'm Proud," which is considered by many to be the forerunner of rap. Many artists during the Black Power movement addressed social, political, and historical issues. El Hadi, one of the Last Poets, observed that "at that particular time everybody was angry. There was a lot of real violent actions being perpetuated against us. . . . The common enemy is ignorance and we recognized that at the beginning. . . . Our job was to reeducate our people" (Harrington 1985, C7). Those crimes being perpetrated against the African-American community, in addition to "plain, ol' ordinary racism," included the community surveillance and the counterintelligence programs of J. Edgar Hoover, then director of the Federal Bureau of Investigation (O'Reilley 1989, 261).

The Black Power movement had a primary purpose of reeducating the African-American community so that it would reorganize itself, the fundamental objective being the development of the solidarity needed to bring positive change to the masses of oppressed African Americans and to other peoples of color. The Black Power movement so inspired Afrika Bambaataa that in 1973 he organized his and other gangs in New York City into the Zulu Nation. Now one organization, the Zulu Nation virtually stopped the gang wars and invited members of different gangs to challenge or battle each other as disc jockeys, as emcees with the rhythmic rapping voice, or as B-boys break dancing to the music of the disc jockeys. *B-boys* and *b-boying*, the original terms for breakdancers and break dancing, initially were added to Kool Herc's crew. A *crew* or *posse* is that group of men who travel with the deejay, handling his equipment and performing other tasks. Herc had seen how the youths in the " 'hood" enjoyed dancing to the music that he mixed. Two brothers, Kevin and Keith, who were superb dancers and crowd pleasers, were dubbed the Nigger Twins by Herc and added to his crew. They, along with others, particularly the Latinos, eventually began doing head spins and hand spins during the break in the music.

So break dancing, which Rose considers a second component of hip-hop culture, was from its inception a function of rap music. Its origins are in the music itself. The third component, graffiti markings, was first cited around New York City during the 1960s. The origins of graffiti are with Taki, a Greek-American youth from Washington Heights. Although Herc had written some graffiti using the tag "Kool Herc," he and other African Americans used graffiti markings as part of the flyers that they used to promote club appearances and battles between deejays and their crews. Rap, then, is the continuation of an oral tradition of talking over music that comes out of African-American and African music traditions. This is discussed in more depth in the following.

According to Rose, the second problematic effect of tracing rap music to "African-American oral, poetic and protest traditions [is that it] . . . marginalizes the significance of rap's music. Rap's musical elements and its use of music technology are a crucial aspect of the development of the form and are absolutely critical to the evolution of hip hop generally" (Rose 1994, 25). Initially, much of the unique technology used in making rap music could be attributed to Grandmaster Flash, born Joseph Sadler. Flash, who began deejaying shortly after Kool Herc did, studied electronics at Samuel Gompers Vocational High School in the Bronx. Because of his knowledge of electronics and cues that could be picked up via the deejay's earphones, Flash, for example, developed the technique of backspinning, where one could repeat phrases and beats on a recording by rapidly spinning the record backward. Grandmaster also developed the musical collage, which included playing short cuts from several different records in rapid succession. Flash discovered the clock theory, which "was to 'read' the record like a clock, using the record label as the dial" (Hager 1984, 36). A thirteen-year-old friend of Grandmaster Flash's, along with his brother, invented scratching when they "noticed they could create sound effects by shifting the needle back and forth while keeping it in the [record's] groove . . . [I]t could be explosively percussive" (Hager 1984, 38).

Throughout the three decades of its existence, rap as a genre has continued to be developed technologically because of the ingenuity of the rappers or emcees and their deejays. The various deejays have continuously experimented with innovative sound and electronic techniques in an effort to win the approval of rap fans. This competitive spirit among the deejays can be traced back to the beginnings of the battles between deejays at dances held in New York City before the first commercial rap record was disseminated throughout the country and the world in 1979. In self-organized community-based competitions, deejays from different crews battled for their reputations; B-boys battled for their reputations; and, with the introduction of rapping, rappers battled for their reputations. It was for one of these battles that Grandmaster Flash wrote the first "rhyme" to be recited while music was being played. This "rhyme" was longer than the single phrases that theretofore had been recited.

At a later battle, the emcees, members of Flash's crew, began reciting "rhymes" rhythmically to the beat of the music. One of Flash's emcees, Melle Mel, is credited with beginning this rapping. At that time, other disc jockeys added emcees to their crews; however, these others only shouted words and sometimes phrases, but not rhythmically to the beat of the music. Melle Mel and Flash's other emcees, on the other hand, spoke in time to the beat of the music, pronouncing each syllable of every word in time to one musical beat, extending the pronunciation of a syllable over two musical beats, or quickly pronouncing a syllable to one-half of a beat. Also, they developed several verbal rou-

201

tines, such as alternating between emcees with each one delivering a line. This developed into alternating between emcees with each one delivering a verse or verses. Such was the beginning of the rapper, with that rhyming, rhythmic recitation in sync with a musical beat, known as the rapping voice.

In direct reference to Rose's (1994) comment, it has been the tendency in the United States for European-Americans to marginalize everything in and everything that comes out of the African-American community, until certain others can culturally appropriate it. Another tendency has been to ignore the origins of innovations coming from the African-American community, while eventually crediting such innovations to others who are from outside the African-American community. There is also the tradition of "covering," a white artist singing and popularizing before the larger white American public music originating with and originally performed by African Americans. An example is the song "Hound Dog," made famous by Elvis Presley, which was sung initially by the African-American blues singer Big Mama Willie Mae Thornton.

Rose's (1994) final problem with attributing the origins of rap music to the African-American oral tradition is that "it renders invisible the crucial role of the post-industrial city on the shape and direction of rap and hip hop" (Rose 1994, 25). That the postindustrial city affects the plight of African Americans cannot be denied; however, the problems of African Americans in the postindustrial city are fundamentally the same types of problems they have experienced since their ancestors first arrived from Africa as involuntary immigrants. People with dark skin have continuously suffered from lack of employment, in addition to inadequate housing, poor education, poor health care, police brutality, and bias crimes, to name just a few of these problems. The rapper, as have other musicians previously, simply documents this maltreatment. The rapper Ice T, as an illustration, told Siegmund that the pre-hip-hop era African-American leader

> Martin Luther King, Jr., had his dream for the future of America, and I have mine. In 1963, King said: "I have a dream that one day on the red hills of Georgia the sons of former slaves and the sons of former slave owners will be able to sit down together at the table of brotherhood. I have a dream that one day even the state of Mississippi, a state sweltering with the heat of injustice, sweltering with the heat of oppression, will be transformed into an oasis of freedom and justice." Thirty years later, those red hills of Georgia are still burning with hatred and poverty; brothers and sisters from Mississippi to New York are still fighting for justice from an oppressive system. My dream for this country's future would allow King's dream to come true. (Siegmund 1994, 185)

One of the various ways of addressing this oppression has been with music. Rap music is a new genre that continues to address such issues in the oral tradition of communicating spoken messages through music. These issues are addressed by youths who participate in hip-hop culture, but these youths are maintaining and continuing an established African-American custom that survived the middle passage during slavery. Although Toop (1984), Hager (1984), and Keyes (1991) have suggested that the origins of rap are in Africa, none have explored this in depth.

THE SPOKEN WORD IN SACRED MUSIC

The spoken word in the music of African Americans can be traced through the various musical forms back to the music of Africa for several centuries before the origins of the Atlantic slave trade, which displaced millions of Africans, bringing them to the Western Hemisphere in bondage. Nketia writes that "African traditions deliberately treat songs as though they were speech utterances. There are societies in which solo poetic recitations, both spoken and sung, have become social institutions. Instances of choral recitations have been noted, as well as the use of the heightened speech in musical contexts" (Nketia 1974, 177).

Charters writes that *Green's Collection of Voyages*, published in London in 1745, describes the griots, found throughout West Africa, as "those who play instruments . . . and seem to be their poets as well as musicians" (Charters 1981, 13). Griots were found at the court of the chief as well as in the towns and villages, acting as storytellers, clowns, genealogists, musicians, and oral reporters. As a community developer in N'Gabou, Senegal, in West Africa, I lived on a daily basis with griots, witnessing their performances and watching them train their children to become griots. The role of the griot existed in West African society before the great empires of Ghana (700–1200), Mali (1200–1500), and Songhay (1350–1600). During the Mali and Songhay Empires, the slave trade began, directed toward Europe and later the Western Hemisphere. When captured and forced into slavery, Africans were stripped of their personal and social identities. From a variety of ethnic backgrounds, they were forced to develop a new language and to accept new folkways and mores, which became the traditions of slavery. The foundations of many of these folkways and mores were a blending of West African and European traditions.

When brought to the United States, the captured slaves practiced either their own indigenous religions or that of Islam. They were generally not Christians; in fact, European government leaders and the slave traders justified slavery by saying they were bringing Africans to America to teach them about the true God. Some of the music of the African slaves underwent transfers of reference, notably African chants to the spirituals of the African Americans (Jones 1963, 18). These songs were used to carry messages and as an emotional release verbalizing the plight of the slaves. One example of a spiritual carrying a message of resistance is "Swing Low Sweet Harriet," for Harriet Tubman, which became "Swing Low Sweet Chariot" when the slave masters were in close proximity (Kellis Parker, personal communication). Sending double messages in one bit of communication is an element in signification, a widespread speech act among African Americans. Signification, or signifying, is usually related to some kind of criticism, indirect and sometimes quite subtle. In addition to its use in spirituals, it is used in other genres of music, including rap, and in nonmusical communication.

Some spirituals were and still are often sung in common meter. Common meter is a form of music that has a leader spontaneously call out or speak a line of a song, after which the church congregation sings it. This is repeated until the spiritual has been completed. For example, in "I Love the Lord, He Heard My Cry," someone (a leader) in the church congregation begins thus:

Leader says: I love the Lord, He heard my cry.
Congregation sings: I love the Lord, He heard my cry.
Leader says: And answered every moan.
Congregation sings: And answered every moan.

Many spirituals were used to teach literacy. Appearing during slavery, these spirituals are still sung in African-American churches. By the early 1930s, in addition to the several secular forms of African-American music and the sacred spirituals, Dr. Thomas A. Dorsey, a former blues singer, began writing another form of sacred music, which combined features of the spirituals, the blues, and jazz improvisation. That music was gospel. Although Dr. Dorsey wrote his first song as early as 1932, perhaps earlier, he is best known for "Precious Lord," which he wrote in 1938, following the death of his wife and his baby.

Much gospel music includes spoken words, as does the common meter of the spiritual. Often, the spoken word, a personal testimony, is spontaneous before or during both forms of sacred music. Present in secular music as well, the testimony or personal experience is a response to or comment about some event or experience and often was also the inspiration for writing a song.

In an example of talk in gospel, in a recording by the Mt. Nebo Baptist Church Choirs (1990) of Harlem, Charles Smith, talking in a rhythmic manner, gives his testimony in a style we identify as the preaching voice because he uses hemistich phrases, which are half lines of poetic verse with instrumental interruptions marking divisions:

Introduction to "I Can't Give up Now"

1. I want to tell you a little illustration
2. About a man
3. Who decided to throw up his hands and give up
4. He'd had enough
5. He couldn't take no more
6. He said, "I'm gonna backslide.
7. I'm gonna get outta the church."
8. Wait a minute!
9. Let me tell y'all what happened
10. He began to think about
11. Just how good God had been to him
12. He began to think about
13. Where God had brought him from
14. He began to think about
15. How God had made a way for him
16. Wait a minute!
17. Y'all know, I ain't studin' [don't care] about this record
18. We gon' have church here, folks
19. Uh-huh!
20. Listen!
21. He said, "I'm gon' get outta the church."
22. Something said to 'im, "Go down on your knees,
23. And talk to the Lord.
24. If you go on your knees,
25. You'll get an answer."
26. Well!
27. I can tell you about this young man
28. Because I'm talking about myself
29. Let me tell you something
30. While I was on my knees praying
31. Something said, "Read the 37th Psalm"
32. Fret not thyself
33. Because of evildoers
34. They sooon, sooon, soo-ooo-on, will be cut down
35. Oh, Hallelujah!
36. Uh-huh!
37. Something came to me, Listen!
(Mt. Nebo Choir, "I Can't Give Up Now." Nomi Records)

At this point, the choir begins singing "I Can't Give Up Now," and the song continues.

The preaching voice illustrated with Smith's illustration is not a sermon, but it takes on the sermon's phonological features. According to Davis, the phonological features or the sounds of the African-American sermon can be

> identified as a group of hemistich phrases shaped into irrhythmic metric units when performed to express an integral element in the development of the . . . theme. . . . The phrases that shape each semantic unit are not regular. They are hemistich or irregular in length. They are made metrically regular—given a sense of patterned consistency—in the performance of the sermon, and always in the environment of other hemistich phrases. (Davis 1985, 59)

The spoken word delivered in the preaching voice can appear anywhere in the song—at the beginning, in the middle, or at the song's end. Although once used exclusively with religious music, sometimes the preaching voice can be heard in talk foregrounded over secular music. The Isley Brothers' rhythm and blues song "Shout" is an example.

Use of the spoken word gradually developed into complete songs that the lead singer talks through while the background singers sing. An example is the recording by the Caravans of "Solid Rock," which was recorded in the 1960s. By the end of the 1960s and into the 1970s, the spoken word in gospel music, in addition to those types discussed above, included reciting revolutionary black poetry with a full choir singing in the background. Nikki Giovanni and the New York Community Choir produced such work on their album *Truth is on the Way*, where, for example, Giovanni recites her poem "The Great Pax Whitie" while Benny Diggs and the choir sing a gospel song, James Cleveland's version of "Peace Be Still," in the background.

from "The Great Pax Whitie"

Cause they killed the Carthaginians
in the great Appian Way
And they killed the Moors
"to civilize a nation"
And they just killed the earth
And blew out the sun
In the name of a god
Whose genesis was white
And war wooed god
And america was born

Where war became peace
And genocide patriotism
And honor is a happy slave
Cause all god's chillun need rhythm
And glory hallelujah why can't peace
     be still
(Giovanni 1970, 61)

Giovanni uses a distinct style of speaking, which we identify as the poetry-reciting voice.

The poetry-reciting voice is that voice that is used to "read" poetry with music as background. Such a voice recites poetry, which, following Webb, "is a form of organized speech" (Webb 1992, 124) that is structured around Eastman's (1951) universal attributes of poetry. These universal attributes are meter, figure or figurative language, and a preoccupation with emotions. Meter, according to Fussell, "results when the natural rhythmical movements of colloquial speech are . . . organized, and regulated so that a pattern—which means repetition—emerges" (Fussell 1979, 4). Figurative language, writes Eastman, is "using words in 'out of the ordinary' ways, calling a thing by an 'unusual' name, or applying to it an adjective that is not 'habitually' applied" (Eastman 1951, 155). The final universal attribute of poetry, a preoccupation with emotions, according to Eastman, includes making one "vividly aware of external impressions which we are not really having" (Eastman 1951, 153).

After secular rap music was introduced in New York in the 1970s, sacred or religious rap music began to be produced during the 1980s. An example of a religious rap is a part of the Christian Life Center's (CLC) Youth Choir's recording of the gospel song "I'm Not Ashamed," which was written by Glen Woodard and published by Highest Praise. After singing several verses and choruses, the rapper uses a rapping voice, which pronounces words to the beat of the music.

> So, you're sitting there wondering what I'm trying to say.
> Listen up everybody, and just let me explain.
> I was lost in sin, couldn't find my way.
> So I got down on my knees, and I started to pray.
> Well, He heard my cry.
> and changed my heart's condition.
> Gave me joy, not just a religion.
> And that's the reason I've got to explain.
> Of the Lord Jesus Christ, I'm not ashamed.
> (CLC Youth Choir, "I'm Not Ashamed," Command Records)

After the rapping, the choir continues singing the song.

THE SPOKEN WORD IN SECULAR MUSIC

The spoken word in secular music follows a developmental pattern similar to that of sacred music. Some of the indigenous African music was reference-transferred from various African cultures to the slave situation in the United States. While working, the slaves often told stories, singing parts in African fashion, explains Fisher (1953, 139),

207

indicating that the traditions of singing and narration developed simultaneously. Following is a work song, which, according to Fisher (1953, 139) subsequently became a freedom song before the Civil War. The line may have been spoken and the chorus sung.

1. Five can't ketch me and ten can't hold me,
Chorus: Ho, round the corn, Sally. Round the corn, round the corn, round the corn.
2. Here's your iggle-quarter and here's your count aquils.
Chorus
3. I can bank, 'ginny bank,' 'ginny bank' the weaver,
Chorus

The slavery period witnessed the continuation of work songs and the beginnings of the blues (Jones 1963, 50). After work, a person who played the banjo might entertain others by singing about their condition and their lives. Sometimes, slavemasters hired blues singers to sing to their slaves. Later, the guitar accompanied the spoken word as well as the singing in blues tunes. One example of the spoken word in the blues is "Don't Answer the Door," by B. B. King, which he recorded in the 1950s. In the song, King, speaking to his wife, relates why different members of her family cannot come to visit.

Blues grew and developed into country and urban blues, according to Keil (1966). In addition to blues, another type of secular music, jazz, developed before World War II. The origins of jazz

seem to have come from the arrangement of the singing voices in the early churches. . . . The . . . . religious music contained the same "rags," "blue notes," and "stop times" as were emphasized later and to a much greater extent in jazz. . . . [E]ven though ragtime, dixieland, and jazz are dependent upon blues for their existence in any degree of authenticity, the terms . . . relate to a broader reference than blues. (Jones 1963, 47)

Interestingly, jazz riffs and rhythms were worked into Langston Hughes's verse as early as the 1920s (Rampersad 1986). Jazz took another form and an additional name after World War II; it was known as "art music" as well as jazz. During the 1940s and 1950s, a synthesis of jazz, blues, and gospel forms emerged (Keil 1966, 32), and this fusion has been generally referred to as rhythm and blues music in the African-American community (and sometimes as "soul music").

Rhythm and blues, as with the other forms of African-American music, often includes speech within a given song or piece of music. For example, in the middle of a rhythm and blues tune entitled "The Bells" and recorded by the Originals in the early 1960s, the bass singer, in a speaking voice, explains to the person whom he loves that he will always be faithful to her. The spoken word in rhythm and blues has been main-

208

tained and could still be heard after the social revolution and Black Power movement of the 1960s, which brought a new identity to African Americans—an identity that was celebrated in art, music, and literature. In addition to James Brown's recording "Say It Loud, I'm Black and I'm Proud" in 1968, a forerunner of rap music, the Temptations talked in "Message to the Blackman," which was released in 1970. In their 1991 recording of "End of the Road," at one point, Boyz II Men talk to their female listeners.

As in rhythm and blues, the spoken word is a noted part of the jazz singer's repertoire. In the late 1950s and early 1960s, Nancy Wilson introduced songs with a monologue, which was often a part of the song. Wilson's song "Guess Who I Saw Today" is an example, where she tells her husband that she saw him cheating on her. The spoken text leads directly into Wilson's song. Such monologues grew in length to become complete songs with background music as an accompaniment. The spoken word seems to represent another instrument in the jazz band. Lou Rawls recorded "Street Corner Hustler's Blues" in the middle 1960s, with an entire text that is spoken. He says in the first verse,

Here's a song that's about a young man
that is widely known throughout the world,
especially in my ex-hometown,
where I used to live.
See,
This young man is a very popular young man,
and he was standing on a very well known corner
on the southside of my hometown, Chicago. . . .
("Street Corner Hustler's Blues," Lou Rawls, Capitol Records)

Rawls continues in his natural speaking voice to describe the young man, who is a hustler. Rawls and Wilson continue their monologues in a third style of the spoken word in music, using the natural speaking voice, which can be identified as the prose-speaking voice.

The prose-speaking voice is used to communicate, in prose form, both spontaneous and organized speech. Organized speech in prose form is prepared in advance of its delivery. For organized speech, the process of production occurs when the speech is being composed. When it is presented, a recitation of what was composed previously is communicated to hearers, but it is in prose form, primarily sentences.

While Rawls was becoming successful with the above monologue, the Civil Rights movement was spinning off the Black Power movement, which rapidly gained momentum, affecting all aspects of the life of African Americans, including art, music, literature, politics, and economics: "Following the big city ghetto riots of the middle 1960s . . . a

209

completely new poetry was born—new in style, content and emphasis
. . . a Black poem is not just another aesthetic happening but a searing
political statement designed to further the cause of social and political
revolution" (Barksdale and Kinnamon 1972, 661). Revolutionary Black
poetry was recited to secular music and rhythms, as well as to the sacred
music of African Americans, as discussed previously. The Last Poets
recorded several albums during this movement. "Listen to their first
records . . . and you will hear one of the essential roots of today's rap
music but with a decidedly more visceral, angry edge: belligerent voices
chanting over stark percussive accompaniment, creating astonishing
portraits and scenes from deep inside Black America" (Harrington
1985, C7).

While the Last Poets were reciting poetry with drummers in the
background around New York City, the adolescent gangs in the South
Bronx called a truce to their gang wars and began challenging each
other at mixing records or deejaying, and at break dancing or B-boying.
Individuals acquired turntables and began talking to the beat of music
in a unique fourth voice, the rapping voice.

MUSIC IN THE SPOKEN WORD

Although the revolutionary poetry of the Last Poets uses the drum
as an integral part of their recitations, poetry is primarily a verbal art
form, whereas the other art forms discussed above—blues, jazz, rhythm
and blues, gospel, spirituals—are primarily music. The tradition of the
spoken word as a cohesive integral part of African-American music has
its origins in Africa and survived the middle passage to the Western
Hemisphere. The griots, musicians of West Africa, told stories while
they sang certain types of songs, as did the first Africans in slavery in
the United States. They often told stories during the singing of work
songs. After work, many slaves in certain parts of the country partici-
pated in pattin' juba.

Pattin' juba was one type of narration current during slavery that
included one lead singer and/or a group of background singers reciting
"the words of a jig in a monotonous tone of voice. . . . Slaves . . . patted
as a way of providing dance music" (Southern 1971, 169). Apparently,
pattin' juba was a way of keeping a rhythm because the drum was much
feared by slavemasters. Pattin' juba was performed by

> striking the hands on the knees, then striking the hands together, then
> striking the right shoulder with one hand, the left with the other—all the
> while keeping time with the feet and [performing this song]:

> Harper's Creek and roarin' ribber,
> Thar, my dear, we'll live forebber;

210

Den we'll go to the Ingin Nation
All I want in dis creation,
Is a perty little wife and big plantation. (Southern 1971, 169)

The story or tale, another type of narration recited during singing,
as mentioned above, was a symbol of covert resistance to white power.
Br'er Rabbit, the trickster-hero, represents a mode of resistance to the
evils of slavery, as he displayed such qualities as "slickness, deceit, eva-
siveness and ruthless self interest" (Bone 1988, 26). In 1880, Joel Chan-
dler Harris published tales in his book *Uncle Remus: His Songs and His
Sayings*. The songs were "written, and . . . intended to be read aloud.
. . . The songs depend for their melody and rhythm upon the musical
quality of time" (Bone 1988, 46).

After the development of the narrative in song and in prose, it also
developed in another form of entertainment, as toast. Abrahams (1963)
footnotes the toast as beginning in the sixteenth century in England
and goes on to note that toasts were alive and well in Scotland in the
1870s. During the first fifteen years of this century, toasts were given
at drinking parties in the southern states. It is here that the African
American, perhaps, was introduced to the toast, as such. At this point
many of the old prose narratives and songs, such as "Stagolee," took
the form of the toast.

> The toast is a variation on the trickster . . . theme done in poetic form.
> While . . . Brer Rabbit stories are rural and older in time, the toast is a
> modern urban continuation of this tradition. While the older stories reveal
> Black power in subtle forms (such as blacks deceiving white folks), the
> toasts let it all hang out. . . . Toasts are usually kept alive in black culture
> by males. . . . You used to hear toasts quite regularly in the pool halls,
> barbershops, and on the street corners in the community; nowadays, they
> are mostly heard among black prisoners. . . . The most famous toasts [in-
> clude] . . . "Stagolee." (Smitherman 1977, 157)

"Stack-o-lee," one version of Stagolee, was printed in Baker's
(1971, 45–47) *Black Literature in America*. The toast has a definite structure, though it has no conventional length or duration; the dominant
line pattern has about four stresses.

from "Stackalee"

It was in the year of eighteen hundred and sixty-one
In St. Louis on Market Street where Stackalee was born.
Everybody's talkin about Stackalee.
It was on one cold and frosty night
When Stackalee and Billy Lyons had one awful fight,
Stackalee got his gun. Boy, he got it fast!

He shot poor Billy through and through
Bullet broke a lookin' glass.
Lord, O Lord, O Lord!
Stackalee shot Billy once; his body fell to the floor.
He cried out, Oh, please, Stack, please don't shoot me no more.

Hustlers' Convention, a toast recorded by the Last Poets, is directly related to the beginnings of rap music.

During the historical development of the toast, the ritual insult (playing the dozens) developed in the African-American community. (Playing the dozens is sometimes called "snapping.") It is believed that the dozens has its origins in Africa because of a similar tradition among several tribal groups in Ghana and Benin. In the 1950s, playing the dozens was made popular with music as a background by Bo Diddley, who made several recordings using the dozens. For example, "Say Man," includes Diddley and a member of his band exchanging insults about their mates.

While the toasts were being recited and the dozens being played in the 1950s and 1960s with music as background, the Black Power movement, growing out of the Civil Rights movement, touched all phases of African-American culture, including the literary tradition of the 1950s, which expressed

> the demand that discrimination, oppression, and second-class citizenship be immediately abolished. . . . [However, in the 1960s] a revolutionary consciousness, in short, had become the norm for the young in America. . . . The tone of black writing . . . changed to one of pride and militancy; black writers realized with pride that blackness was not the evil entity that white civilization . . . labeled it, and they spoke in bellicose voices to their brothers about the beauty of blackness and the necessity of resisting white cruelty with loaded guns and loaded words that will raise a proud nation of free black people. (Baker 1971, 304–8)

During the Black Power movement, the original rappers of the 1970s were adolescents. As teenagers, these rappers had been exposed to revolutionary poetry and the spoken word of the traditional African-American secular and sacred music. Experimenting with music rhythms and the spoken word in poetic form appears to be a typical development in African-American music; however, rap music, with its new form, continues to be, as is all African-American music, "a rich source of aesthetic-spiritual emotion, in church pews, concert halls, and family living rooms [that] strengthens the cohesion of social groups offering security and support for their individual members. Black expressions uplift the downhearted and express the joys and sorrows of the black situation" (Pasteur and Toldson 1982, 122).

212

Rap: The Spoken Word as Music

There are, as would be expected, several types of rap. One of the more prominent types, which I will focus on in the following, is message rap, much of which has as its function presenting messages about racism and discrimination, as well as offering solutions to these problems and other problems of the world, as rappers view them. Message rap, as well as perhaps most other types, is an integral part of the maintenance of the oral tradition in African-American culture, in that it is used to transmit themes of the past to the present. Vansina (1985) takes up this theme, stating that the oral tradition is a verbal message that reports from the past to the present generation; thus, the oral tradition involves both a process and a product. The process is the transmission of messages by word of mouth over time until the disappearance of the message. The product is an oral message based on previous oral messages passed by word of mouth for at least one generation. The past-in-the-present element of rap can easily be seen in the way rap music samples (taking bits or chunks of earlier songs and musical styles) and in its heavy engagement in historical remembrances, notably of Malcolm X (which to a great extent accounts for his high level of name recognition among urban, African-American youth).

Although there are many messages that are repeated in the oral tradition, two major types are news and interpretations of one's experience or of an existing situation. Rap music interprets primarily experiences or existing situations. It is important to stress that the performance (or recitation for one's own enjoyment) of rap is not limited to paid performers. Rap is an integral part of the culture of the urban areas where it flourishes. It is not uncommon to hear young men, particularly, walking down the street reciting their own raps or those of others. Stated differently, rap is organic in its cultural context. Rapping skills are developed throughout the full social fabric of people's lives. Many, if not most, young people are rappers at some moment, and they recite raps for all the reasons that anyone anywhere engages in stylized communicative behavior "free of charge."

I examine below a rap entitled "We' Lackin'," by Chris Miles, a twenty-year-old student at Bergen Community College in New Jersey. The first verse is as follows:

It's a shame
I see people gettin' shanked up
Mugged up on the basis for a can of Seven Up
Now, who's the man who gets caught in the act
With an illegal substance better known as crack
Well! Well! Look a here, Miss. La-De-Da

213

With her fishnet stockin's
Sellin' her meat for a fee that's free
Which is [w]ho[re] hoppin' for a livin'
Come on America! How we' livin'!

In an interview, I attempted to get from him an idea of the thoughts and motivations present during the process of creation. Following is a brief passage from the interview, followed by comments on some of the poetic and general discursive devices used in this verse.

> *Jon:* Now, this piece you wrote, "We' Lackin'," tell me about it. What made you write this piece?
>
> *Chris:* I was home watching TV, and I'm just tired of news, you know, kids out here stealing. You got these prostitutes doing what they have to do to make a living, and it shouldn't have to be like that. And I just put it down in my pad, in my rhymes and stuff, that as a community, we're lacking. People getting shanked up, mothers and fathers out here working hard to get these kids the best that they can give them and they're out there behind their back doing wrong, which is hurting the mother and the father. And it's like we don't have to live like this, you know what I'm saying? There's no need for it.
>
> *Jon:* Yeah, I hear you. So, it's just a combination of what was going on out there that made you put this together.
>
> *Chris:* A combination of that and on how I felt about it and I just had to do it. I just had to write about it.
>
> *Jon:* Is that what most rap people do, people who do message rap?
>
> *Chris:* Yeah, that's what some people usually do, but I can't speak for, you know, how they do it because I'm not them. But some of them probably feel the same way that I feel and they just feel like they just have to do it. You know, they just have to do it.

Message rap includes a social or political message or a message that is designed to educate the listeners. As a product of the oral tradition, it presents performed messages, conveyed through oral performance, even though, as is the case with rap, the lyrics are usually written beforehand. A variety of rappers write or rhyme in paragraph form. The written text may seem closer to prose; however, the performance of the rap brings out more clearly its metrical structure, which in turn makes its rhymes more prominent. Indeed, several poetic devices are incorporated into rap music, devices that heighten cohesion and thus assist in conveying the message of the rap. Following are some of the devices used in the first ten-line verse of "We' Lackin'." On the phonological level, that which deals with sounds and their interrelationships, we find the patterns itemized in Table 1.

One sees several instances of parallelism, that is, words, phrases, and clauses structured in such a way as to highlight equivalences within

214

TABLE 1

1. Assonance (a recurrent pattern of vowel sounds). Examples follow:

/ʌ/ as in up	line	1	a
		2	a
		3	mugged up of up
/æ/ as in at		4	act
		5	an as crack
/i/ as in bit		7	with fish
/I/ as in beat		8	meat fee free

2. Consonance (a recurrent pattern of final consonants).
   Some examples are:

	line	7	stockin'
		8	sellin'
		9	hoppin' livin'
		10	livin'

3. Alliteration (a recurrent pattern of initial consonants).
   Examples of this follow:

sh	line	1	shame
		2	shanked
s		3	basis seven
w		5	with
		6	well well
		7	with
h		6	here
		7	her
		8	her
		9	ho (whore) hoppin'
		10	how
f		7	fish
		8	for fee free
		9	for

4. Rhyme (a recurrent metrical or measured pattern of sounds).
   The following are examples:

	line	2	shanked up
		3	Seven Up
	line	4	act
		5	crack

215

the structure of the verse. Two prominent types of parallelism in "We' Lackin' " involve free (or independent) clauses, on the one hand, and bound constituents (dependent clauses or phrases) on the other. Basically, a free clause is one that can stand alone and make a complete sentence. Bound constituents (here, dependent clauses and phrases) cannot stand alone as complete sentences; thus, they are parts of sentences. With this in mind, one can break the first verse down as in Table 2.

What is interesting for my principal point, that rap is highly structured as we would expect of poetry, is the rather intricate structure of this verse. First, we see that the verse can be broken down into sections, each of which contains minimally a free constituent and maximally several bound ones in addition to the free one. If there are bound constituents, the free one begins the section; thus, the free constituents mark the structure of the verse. These sections are presented below in terms of their syntax (bound, free) and their function (meaning):

1. Intro—evaluation
2. Observation—action
   Description of action
3. Observation—action
   Description of action
4. Observation—person
   Description of person
   Description of action
   Interpretation/Elaboration
5. Conclusion—exhortation

The verse is bounded by an introduction, which evaluates an existing situation, and a conclusion, containing a generalized exhortation to look at what is wrong with the situation. There are five sections, con-

TABLE 2

Line	1	free	It's a shame
	2	free	I see people gettin' shanked up
	3	bound	Mugged up on the basis for a can of Seven Up
	4	free	Now, who's the man who gets caught in the act
	5	bound	With an illegal substance better known as crack
	6	free	Well! Well! Look a here, Miss. La-De-Da
	7	bound	With her fishnet stockin's
	8	bound	Sellin' her meat for a fee that's free
	9	bound	Which is ho hoppin' for a livin'
	10	free	Come on, America! How we' livin'!

sisting of one, two, two, four, and one line(s) each, providing a crescendo effect, longer and longer sections, until the drop back to a one-line section, the conclusion. The use of the spoken word is incorporated into most forms of African-American music and is an integral component of rap music. The spoken word in music is one of the ways in which African Americans communicate. In rap music, the most recent development of this element of the tradition, we witness a strand of cultural continuity. Rap, however, is a new development of this tradition because of its uniqueness: combining musical rhythm with poetic speech, but without melody. It is the first music of its kind in the United States.

RAP AS MESSAGE

Rap communicates to a specific group of people, African Americans and a number of other youths of color, who have little if any access to communication via the mass media, certainly not news programs or talk shows. Rap is written primarily by adolescent and young adult African-American males, while the media in the United States are controlled almost exclusively by adult European-American males. However, some few radio and television stations feature music of African-American rappers, providing some access to rappers to communicate with many more members of their community than those few with whom they are in personal contact. Chris, the composer of "We' Lackin'," said, "When I write music, I'll write on reality . . . [for] the [African-American] community and the world. And you know, you got a lot of stuff out here, you got drugs out here, you got alcohol. And that's just, as a person, myself, I feel that I just have to write about it. I know it's not going to change the world, but I . . . have to write about it. Give the people my own point of view on how I feel about it."

Members of the community listen and respond to message rappers, their modern-day griots. A group of professional rappers, for example, in 1987 organized the Stop the Violence Movement, whose goals were

1. to raise public awareness of black-on-black crime and point out its real causes and social costs
2. to raise funds for a charitable organization already dealing with the problems of illiteracy and crime in the inner city
3. to show that rap music is a viable tool for stimulating reading and writing skills among inner-city students (George 1990, 3)

The movement composed, produced, recorded, and sold a rap recording, "Self-Destruction," made a music video, and organized other programs to promote their theme of stopping the violence at rap con-

217

certs and in African-American communities in general. The movement's efforts were financially successful; all proceeds were donated to the National Urban League. Also successful was the message of the rap lyrics, which had a positive effect on many members of the African-American community. Chris relates the story of a personal friend from the same community who was positively affected:

> *Chris:* Well, he was doing bad things out there, messing with drugs and stuff, doing bad things, until one—to make a long story short—one day he just finally realized that he had to go straight. He was into rap music and he listened to the song "Self-Destruction" [from the Stop the Violence Movement], and just made up his mind, POW, I got to do what I gotta do.
> *Jon:* What else was he doing besides not—was he doing crack and such?
> *Chris:* Dealing and stuff, yeah.

The young man of whom Chris spoke is now a productive person in his community and still an avid rap fan. It is unfortunate that we do not have any way of assessing on a broader, more detailed basis the effects of the movement. In any case, given its financial success, which we can asssume had a significant impact (mediated by the Urban League), any direct postive effect the message had on people was a noteworthy bonus.

In addition to providing advice, as does "Self-Destruction," some rap messages have an educational function and, incidentally, are not created for commercial reasons. In Boston, at the Thomas Edison Middle School, a number of African-American students were having problems learning their multiplication tables. Their teacher, Susan McGinnis, noted that several of these children had memorized a popular rap tune "word for word, syllable for syllable" (Franklin 1990, 36). She, another teacher, and four of their students then wrote the lyrics for "Tough Times: A Multiplication Rap." This rap was so successful with their students that they "agree that rap . . . is getting a bad rap" (Franklin 1990, 36). Moreover, raps have been written to teach students about English language structure and used in projects dealing with critical thinking skills.

It is well known that much of rap music goes against mainstream norms and institutions, and, given its source, this is something that we would expect. It is also to be expected that the anger of African Americans as an oppressed group will be expressed in popular cultural production, if it is not censored. Rap is, of course, to some degree censored; and one of the principal sources of censorship is the music companies, often susidiaries of conglomerates, with whom rap artists have contracts. What is striking about rap as an African-American institution is how much forceful, untempered, and direct criticism it contains of white supremacist values, behaviors, and institutions, criticism that larger, traditional institutions typically fear to communicate. One example of this strand in rap is Ice T's album *Body Count*, which included a selection entitled "Cop Killer."

A majority of African Americans who have had experiences with the police have had negative ones; this is true for African Americans in all socioeconomic classes. The brutal beating of Rodney King by four Los Angeles policemen in 1991 is but one instance of such negative experiences. These policemen struck King, who was on the ground, more than fifty-six times in eighty-one seconds in reaction to what they reported as speeding, driving while intoxicated, and refusing to stop when directed to do so. The joke in some quarters of the African-American community was that King could not have been too intoxicated, because he had sense enough to flee after realizing some of Los Angeles's notoriously violent police were after him.

Commenting on the album in a *Rolling Stone* interview (12 August 1992), Ice T observed, "this album's mentality is a progressive mentality against racism. It's hate against hate, you know. It's anger. It's not necessarily answers, it's anger with the same force of their [the police's] hate. It scares them when they see it being kicked back at them" (Light 1992, 30).

Thus, far from reaffirming hegemonic discourse, much of rap serves as a countervailing discourse and furnishes one of the very few sites in popular culture where unbridled culture critique of diverse kinds reigns. Thus, Levy writes in the *Village Voice* that in Sister Souljah's album *360 Degrees of Power*, the "unjudgemental representation of several viewpoints [in the lyrics] . . . is as uncommon in journalism as it is in pop music" (Levy 1992, 73). Many rap lyrics do not glorify European-American traditions; neither do they denigrate them. They simply address issues important to the African-American community, such as survival, or how to meet one's physical and psychological needs in this society; and in so doing they fill a void that the mass media are virtually incapable of contemplating.

It is interesting that rap has spread to other countries where alienated groups have identified with it, bought music of American rappers, and produced rap in their own languages. In Japanese, for instance, rap "lyrics range from sentimental tributes to the victims of the atomic bomb at Hiroshima to messages of greed" (Weisman 1992, 22–23). Rap sustains and builds the critical powers of oppressed communities, but its usefulness outside the United States is perhaps primarily in providing an additional area for the expression of interests—sometimes emancipatory and sometimes not—typically for groups outside the ramparts of power. Its role in the United States in creating a forum outside the corporate and mass media world (but increasingly co-opted by it) has been observed by groups in other countries, and they have adapted rap for their own often counterhegemonic purposes.

A FINAL WORD

One of my principal focuses in this discussion has been what we might call an archaeology of genre. The aim has been to examine rap from a historical standpoint, by concentrating on (1) form, rap's unique style of foregrounding highly rhythmic, poetic speech and (2) content, rap's frequently sharp criticism of American society and flouting of mainstream values. Rap is the contemporary way station of a long-standing African and African-American oral tradition, and its overtly and sharply politicized strains reflect the anger and suffering that its creators witness in their social environment.

Often strongly assertive of blackness, rap may seem to be especially aggressive in its confrontation with mainstream values and precepts, but we must remember that the historical record often does not retain African Americans' most bitter and aggressive commentaries, not to mention violent reactions. There is almost a complete absence of mentions of black resistance and rebellion during slavery (especially in American history textbooks), successful episodes in particular. Resistance, in its widest sense, has many fronts: political, economic, and cultural. Given its form and usual content, rap can perhaps best be understood in a general sense as a form of cultural resistance, even while recognizing that some forms of rap fall into a second category. They are basically about reactionary misogynist and/or homophobic themes, or they mix in such themes, producing controversial products. Some forms of rap seem to have no other but a commercial motivation. Into this second category would fall 2 Live Crew's highly controversial recording of the early 1990s, "As Nasty as They Wanna Be."

Given rap's cultural aggressiveness and content, which is often directly or indirectly political, it is not hard to figure out why it generates such intense (and no doubt frequently strategic) interest across a broad spectrum of people outside the African-American community, where it originated and established its primary base. We probably could have expected that mostly depoliticized, crossover versions would develop and that unfanged versions of the genre would flourish among European-Americans. Examples to mention here are Hammer (originally MC Hammer) and European-American rappers such as Vanilla Ice, whose popularity is (was?) primarily outside of communities of color, and who is now seldom heard.

One reason that rap music has thrived in the black community is that, although a new genre, it has a foundation in African and African-American musical and oral traditions, combining as it does rhythm, words, and music. All oral traditions communicate to a specific group of people in a way that resonates with their overall cultural experience. The rapper accomplishes this communication by incorporating poetic elements into a message while imposing an extralinguistic rhythm onto the message. Certainly not detracting from rap's success in the African-American community is that much of it is in African-American Vernacular English (hereafter AAVE), the language of most African Americans. The language of rap is primarily AAVE not only in a grammatical sense, but also in the broader sense of language that includes discourse, what people actually use a language to say and the verbal routines they use in saying it.

It is important to remember that rap is used not just for entertainment and critique, but also for education and the spread of information. Over the last thirty years, it is the messages of rap, as well as other forms of poular music, that young people have listened to, as opposed to messages emanating from mass media, books, public speeches, and so forth. Willis (1990) concluded that popular music is the main cultural interest of young people; therefore, popular music is an important site of common culture that includes individual and collective symbolic work and symbolic creativity. This is especially true of rap, with its music form just twenty years old. The message in the rap looked at above illustrates the kind of symbolic creativity at issue, which, according to Willis, is

> the multitude of ways in which young people use, humanize, decorate and invest with meanings their common and immediate life spaces and social practices—personal styles and choice of clothes; selective active use of music, TV, magazines, . . . subcultural styles; the style, banter and drama of friendship groups, music-making and dance. Nor are these pursuits and activities trivial or inconsequential. In conditions of late modernization and the widespread crisis of cultural values, they can be crucial to the creation and sustenance of individual and group identities, even to cultural survival of identity itself. There is work, even desperate work, in their play. (Willis 1990, 2)

This symbolic creativity has produced the more overtly critical messages of rap as well as the more covert messages in spirituals and trickster tales. These messages play a role in communicating the need for African Americans to resist the almost four-hundred-year-old matrix of oppression imposed on their communities.

221

JON A. YASIN

References

Abrahams, Roger D. 1963. *Deep down in the jungle*. Chicago: Aldine.
Adler, Jerry, and Jennifer Foote. 1990. The rap attitude. *Newsweek*, 19 March, 56–59.
Baker, Houston. 1971. *Black literature in America*. New York: McGraw-Hill.
Barksdale, Richard, and Kenneth Kinnamon. 1972. *Black writers in America*. New York: Macmillan.
Bone, Robert. 1988. *Down home*. New York: Columbia University Press.
Charters, Samuel. 1981. *The roots of the blues: An African search*. Boston: Marion Boyers.
Davis, Gerald L. 1985. *I got the word in me and I can sing it, you know: A study of the performed African-American sermon*. Philadelphia: University of Pennsylvania Press.
Eastman, Max. 1951. *Enjoyment of poetry with anthology*. New York: Charles Scribner's Sons.
Fisher, Miles Mark. 1953. *Negro slave songs in the United States*. New York: Russell and Russell.
Franklin, M. 1990. It's so fine rappin' 8 times 9. *Learning Magazine of the Boston Globe*, 15 June, 36–37.
Fussell, Paul. 1979. *Poetic meter and poetic form*. New York: Random House.
George, Nelson. 1990. *Stop the violence*. New York: Pantheon Books.
Giovanni, Nikki. 1970. *Black talk, black feeling, black judgement*. New York: Morrow.
Hager, Steve. 1984. *Hip hop: The illustrated history of breakdancing, rap music, and graffiti*. New York: St. Martin's Press.
Harrington, Richard. 1985. The Last Poets: Roots of rap. *Washington Post*, 25 June, C7.
Jones, Leroy. 1963. *Blues people*. New York: Morrow.
Keil, Charles. 1966. *Urban blues*. Chicago: University of Chicago Press.
Keyes, Cheryl Lynette. 1991. *Rappin' to the beat: Rap music as street culture among African Americans*. Ph.D. diss., Indiana University.
Levy, Joe. 1992. Blues for generations. *Village Voice*, 30 June, 72–73.
Light, Anthony. 1992. Ice. *Rolling Stone*, 12 August, 28–31.
Nketia, Kwabena. 1974. *The music of Africa*. New York: Norton.
O'Reilley, Kenneth. 1989. *Racial matters: The FBI's secret file on black America, 1960–1972*. New York: Free Press.
Pasteur, Alfred B., and Ivory L. Toldson. 1982. *The roots of soul*. New York: Doubleday.
Rampersad, Arnold. 1986. *The life of Langston Hughes*. Vol. 1. New York: Oxford Press.
Rose, Tricia. 1994. *Black noise: Rap music and black culture in contemporary America*. Hanover, N.H.: Wesleyan University Press.
Siegmund, Heidi. 1994. *The Ice opinion: Ice T as told to Heidi Siegmund*. New York: St. Martin's Press.
Smitherman, Geneva. 1977. *Talkin' and testifyin': The language of black America*. Detroit, Mich.: Wayne State University Press.
Southern, Eileen. 1971. *The music of black Americans*. New York: Norton.
Toop, David. 1984. *The rap attack: African jive to New York hip hop*. Boston: South End Press.

222

Vasina, Jan. 1985. Oral tradition as history. Madison: University of Wisconsin Press.

Webb, Edwin. 1992. *Literature in education*. London: Falmer Press.

Weisman, Steven R. 1992. The many accents of rap around the world: Japan. *New York Times*, 23 August, 22–23.

Willis, Paul. 1990. *Common culture*. Boulder, Colo.: Westview Press.

Recordings

CLC Youth Choir. "I'm not ashamed." *Whatever it takes*. Command Records, ET 48000.

Mt. Nebo Choir. "I can't give up." *Gospel from Mt. Nebo, Vol. 1*. Nomi Records.

Rawls, Lou. "Street corner hustler's blues." *The best of Lou Rawls*. Capitol Records, 4N 16096.

AFTERWORD:
THOUGHTS FOR
A PRAGMATIC THEORY
OF RACE/RACISM

ARTHUR K. SPEARS

The chapters in this volume cover a large territory. After spreading out, it would be well to narrow our focus, orienting our thinking to the main implications of the foregoing pages. As I stated in the introduction, it is my belief that thinking on race/racism should focus on fundamental, liberation-oriented questions in order to build a pragmatic theory of race/racism. Answering fundamental questions allows us to establish the range of possible liberation strategies. Much of the huge, recent production of writings on race/racism has been excellent, but nearly all of it is narrow and specialized in terms of basic questions such as, Where do we go from here, people of color, whites, and ex-whites (see the introduction on the abolition of whiteness), in seeking greater freedom for realizing our potential?

The idea of America, the American Dream if you will, has always been that one can make it here—gain financial security and success and all the things they entail. I have always thought that anyone with a good education, ambition, good interpersonal skills, and a will to set goals and plan can become rich in the United States, or attain other (perhaps more worthy) forms of success. But, of course, one of the central American ideas is that success is measured financially. The problem, though, is that gaining all of these qualities is a tall order. Where will the average American get a good college education (or even high school education, for that matter)? Without an educational system that by some stretch of the imagination provides equal educational opportunity, most students in the United States, and especially those of color, will not have access to an educational foundation for functioning successfully out in the world. The horror of large city public school systems simply must be seen firsthand to be understood. Classroom practice simply must be observed to understand how the public schools' primary accomplishment is to dull the intellect, diminish self-esteem, and destroy any sense of order and progress, the few excellent public schools notwithstanding. Most of the very bad behavior of public school students is merely an acting out of their hatred for an institution that despises and degrades them, a hatred that they do not know how to name and channel into something positive. Teaching in a large city public college, I meet many charming, and as I often discover, brilliant students in whom the public educational system has managed to instill irresponsibility and an embrace of ignorance. For several years, I was somewhat irritated when students asked me what their grade was at different points during the course. After all, they had all their grades and the simple grade calculation presented in the syllabus (25 percent for this, 25 percent for that, etc.). I found out, however, that many simply did not know how to calculate their grade—and weren't interested in learning how. In a word, the basics one needs for success, or what we might term financial, psychological, and occupational comfort, are off limits to probably most Americans, and certainly most people of color. So it will not do to state, as has the sociologist Orlando Patterson ("The News Hour with Jim Lehrer," 13 November 1997, Channel 13 [Public Broadcasting System], New York City), that the skills problem is greater than the race problem. This is a misanalysis of the situation. Racism greatly hinders access to skills, and this is more the case as we descend the social scale to the poorer strata.

The fundamentals we can draw from the preceding pages are several. First, racial categorization and racism play a fundamental role in U.S. society: they prop up the entire system of social stratification and exploitation of working whites and people of color, with ethnicity as a secondary hierarchizing principle. Note that one's blackness in the United States is more determinative of how one will be touched by policemen than one's Ethiopianness, Cape Verdeanness, African-Americanness, or Haitianness. The Ku Klux Klan does not inquire into multiracial matters and ethnic particulars before proceeding with lawn decoration and the suspension of "strange and bitter fruit." American discourse on ethnicity has not even provided us with a useful term for distinguishing the long-term resident, Anglophone black population from others. (Haitians, Ethiopians, and so on are *all* African Americans, as descendants of Africans.) Racism is the foundation of ruling elite power. Thus, the power sector of U.S. society will not allow for the elimination of racism without a suitable replacement. Only a replace-

226

ment of the current power sector with another would eliminate this obstacle to racial progress.

Much indeed has been made of the progress of African Americans since World War II and the significant growth of the black middle class. The claim in the introduction is that the condition of possibility for post–World War II civil rights progress was realpolitik, the capitalist-socialist struggle embodied in the U.S.-Soviet cold war struggle for hearts and minds, but, above all, resources. Many statistical presentations indicate that the black condition has improved relative to that of whites. Even if we assume that such statistics speak the truth, the "facts" they reveal are superficial from a holistic, social system perspective.

As stated in the introduction, ruling elites are mainly interested in maintaining ruling elite power, not white power or any ethnically based power specifically. Mexican elites in California after the Mexican-American War intermarried with and otherwise joined the new American conquerors, as did Canadian French elites after the British conquest of Canada. U.S. elites themselves have accepted new additions, and not under conditions of conquest: the American power sector has gone from being predominantly White Anglo-Saxon Protestant to a more broadly defined whiteness, as various ethnic groups have assimilated into whiteness (the Irish, Eastern Europeans, Jews, and so on).

One could read the putative progress of blacks as indicating that they will eventually join the power sector of American society in significant numbers. Their doing so, however, would profoundly disturb the racial order. Another basic mechanism for maintaining control qua social stratification, something other than racial hierarchy, would have to be put in place before blacks could ascend in important numbers to the ruling elite. Highly influential and often wealthy blacks, the Colin Powells, Ron Browns, Vernon Jordans, Bill Cosbys, and Oprah Winfreys, are isolates; thus, in the full sense they are tokens. Taken together, such individuals do not create a collective thrust capable of changing the *structural* position of blacks.

What such individuals do reveal is the biggest story in the history of race in the United States, one that has gone virtually unreported. This brings up the second point: the United States is experiencing a shift from a (primarily—especially on the symbolic level) two-way, black-white racial system to a three-way one, composed of blacks, whites, and a third, in-between group of medium and lighter-range skin colors, including Asians and Hispanics (symbolically conceived of as lighter-skinned people of color—a false view, but one rigidly enforced by media discourses and images). Three-way systems, such as are found throughout most of Latin America, are notable for their category leak-

227

age: racial status is based on phenotype (physical appearance) and consequently can change more easily on the level of the individual and intergenerationally. It is not based on lineage, and thus is not fixed, as lineage is. Three-way systems also allow for a broader range of factors to be used in assigning racial status, including social and economic ones. They allow, in other words, for more whitening based on wealth and prestige. Stated differently, there is a greater leak of relatively darker-skinned persons out of lower-status racial categories into higher ones. The possibility of "honorary" lightening or whitening makes struggle to improve the condition of one's race less compelling; co-optation becomes more attractive when it can facilitate color promotion also.

The officialization or cultural and media recognition given to in-between groups in the middle color ranges reinforce distinct identities in those groups, thereby making cross-group, and consequently, cross-class political mobilization more difficult. (There is a strong color-class correlation.) Three-way systems also have the effect of reinforcing the desire of people of color to lighten their offspring: if families become lighter but still remain black, there is less incentive to lighten than if lightening increases racial rank in ways certified by hegemonic institutions, whether formally or informally. There is already significant color stratification in communities of color, and the move toward a three-way system grants it evermore recognition, primarily in the media, as exemplified by the greatly expanded media discourse of multiracial persons. Another way of expressing this fundamental shift in the United States is by saying that the United States is changing from a racist order with discrete categories into a colorist one allowing seepage, both, of course, structured by white supremacy.

The leakage in a colorist, three-way racial system allows for some black, elite isolates who are "honorary" whites, but the transitional stage that the United States is in allows only almost "honorary" white status. Thus, O. J. Simpson, a black man acquitted and convicted of murdering his white ex-wife, in separate trials, was never a full honorary white because there were still possible situations that could strip his ostensible honorary whiteness from him. His alleged murder of his white ex-wife, whatever else it may have been, was also treason against the racial order and exposed him as a nonbearer, in reality, of rich, white, male privilege. It is quite conceivable that if he had been truly white and rich enough, he could have "beat the rap," whether actually guilty or not.

Promotion to whiteness (e.g., of the Irish and Jews), in the context of a diminishing white population (in the United States and worldwide) has played itself out, based as it is on European ancestry. (Basically, all European-descent Americans are now white, in other words, members of the highest ranking racial or subracial group.) Besides, shifting to a leaky, colorist, three-way racial system fixes the problem of white population decline permanently (see the introduction), it would seem, while satisfying a basic regime-maintenance imperative—the maintenance of a white-supremacist racial order.

Racism, with its relatively unleaky, fixed categories, will not be the problem of the twenty-first century and the third millennium. "Colorstruction" will be.

CONTRIBUTORS

BRENDA ABALOS is a student in anthropology at the City College of the City University of New York (CUNY). Gender issues in the production of entertainment is the focus of her research.

LEE D. BAKER is a professor of anthropology and African-American studies at Columbia University. He has written on race discourses in anthropology and African-American political history and legal activism. He is the author of *From Savage to Negro: Anthropology and the Construction of Race, 1896–1954.*

PEM DAVIDSON BUCK is a professor of social sciences at Elizabethtown Community College (Kentucky). She has written extensively on prisons, the American Right, and neofascism. Her current project is a book on fascism in the United States.

YVES DEJEAN, an internationally recognized authority on adult literacy and bilingual education with respect to Haitian Creole, is currently director of the Creole Language Bureau of the Secrétairerie d'Etat à l'Alphabétisation, Port-au-Prince, Haïti. He has taught in the bilingual education programs of Long Island University; Teachers College, Columbia University; Bank Street College of Education; and the State University of Haiti. He is the author of *Comment écrire le créole d'Haïti.*

ANGELA GILLIAM is a member of the faculty at the Evergreen State College, Olympia, Washington, and has done research in Mexico, Brazil, and Papua New Guinea. Professor Gilliam also taught at the University of Papua New Guinea from 1978–80, during which time she organized the first two international film festivals in that country. She is the coeditor of *Confronting the Margaret Mead Legacy: Scholarship, Empire, and the South Pacific.*

IAN HANCOCK is a professor of linguistics at the University of Texas, Austin. He is a leading creole language scholar and is widely known for his writing on Rom (Gypsy) affairs. He has represented the Rom before the United Nations and spearheaded many projects seeking to present an accurate image of the Rom. Among his many publications is *The Pariah Syndrome: An Account of Gypsy Slavery and Persecution.*

231

ARTHUR K. SPEARS is chair of the Anthropology Department at the City College (CUNY) and a faculty member in the linguistics and anthropology programs at the Graduate Center (CUNY). He specializes in pidgin and creole languages (particularly French-lexifier creoles of the Caribbean); African-American English; and race and ideology. His most recent book is *The Structure and Status of Pidgins and Creoles* (coedited).

DONOVAN G. WHYLIE is a student in the Anthropology Department at the City College (CUNY). He is particularly interested in race, religion, and culture and has recently completed his first screenplay.

JON A. YASIN is an English professor at Bergen Community College and is an organizer of the Conference on African-American Language and Communication at Teachers College, Columbia University. He was formerly the director of the Centre d'animation Rurale in N'gabou, Senegal, and has taught at the University of the United Arab Emirates.

Index

233

ruling, 32, 33, 39–40, 41, 226, 227; subordinate, 40
Cleveland, James, 206
Clock theory, 201
Cockney dialect, 67, 68
Code-switching, 75–76, 123
Coercion, 16
Cohn, Werner, 108
Cold War, 23, 28–29
Colonialism, 80, 86, 90
Colorstruck, 49
Colorstruction (colorism), 11, 17, 49, 50, 229; in *New Jack City*, 189–94
Commando, 51
Common meter, 204
Communicative competence, 77
Concentration camps, 137
Confiscation, 139–40
Consonance, 215
Constraining ideologies, 36–37
Contextualization cue, 127
Contract With America, 130 n.1
Convict leasing, 135
Co-occurrence, 123, 126, 127
Coons, 47
Co-optation, 32, 33, 228
"Cop Killer," 219
Corrections Corporation of America, 150, 151
Corresponding settings, 121–22
Cosby, Bill, 48, 117, 167, 227
Cottage industries, 154
"Covering," 202
Crack cocaine, 47, 135, 138, 154
Creed, Apollo, 51
Creolizing language, 45, 84
Crew (posse), 200
Crime Bill of 1994, 140
Criminalization, 134, 135, 139, 154, 155
Cuba, 14, 45, 102
Culp, Robert, 167
Cultural critique, 80, 193
Cultural deficit, claims of, 12, 13
Cultural domination, 33, 34, 80, 193
Cultural self-critique, 17
Cultural specificity, 49, 193
Culture capsules, 76

Danish, 69, 70
Death penalty, 140
Debt peonage, 22, 24, 29

Dejean, Ives, 44, 45
Democracy, illusion of, 38
Denmark, 45
Dialects, 66; Nonstandard, 67, 68; Standard, 68, 69–70
Diddley, Bo, 212
Die Hard, 48
Diggs, Benny, 206
Diglossia, 123
DiIulio, John, 150
Dillard, J. L., 68
Disc jockeys, mobile, 198–99, 200
Discourse Strategies (Gumperz), 127
Discrimination: employment, 130 n.5; reverse, 115
Disfranchisement, 38
Disparate impact, 130 n.5
Disparate treatment, 130 n.5
Diversity: ethnic, 116–17; institutionalized, 129
Divide-and-conquer strategy, 28
Divine descent, 41
Divine right, 41
Domestic Fourth World (captive) labor, 46
Dominant class. *See* Ruling elite
Dominant ideology thesis, 31
Dominicans, 54 n.17, 62
Donahue, John, 150
"Don't Answer the Door," 208
Dorsey, Thomas A., 204
Double negatives, 67–68
Dougherty, James, 107
Doukhobors, 105
Dravidians, 18
Drug use, racialized perceptions about, 135–36
Drug War: budget, 155 n.3; dual role, 154; and foreign policy, 47; and racialization of prison population, 29, 47, 136, 137, 138–41, 155; and U.S. military intervention abroad, 47
Du Bois, W. E. B., 11, 15, 52 n.1, 80, 193
Dunne, Daniel, 144
Dutcher, Nadine, 95
Dutton, T. E., 84

Eastman, Max, 207
Ebonics controversy, 43, 44, 72–74
Ebony Magazine, 117
Educational system: inadequacy of, 226;

235

Books in the African American Life Series

Coleman Young and Detroit Politics: From Social Activist to Power Broker,
by Wilbur Rich, 1988

Great Black Russian: A Novel on the Life and Times of Alexander Pushkin,
by John Oliver Killens, 1989

Indignant Heart: A Black Worker's Journal, by Charles Denby, 1989 (reprint)

The Spook Who Sat by the Door, by Sam Greenlee, 1989 (reprint)

Roots of African American Drama: An Anthology of Early Plays, 1858–1938,
edited by Leo Hamalian and James V. Hatch, 1990

Walls: Essays, 1985–1990, by Kenneth McClane, 1991

Voices of the Self: A Study of Language Competence, by Keith Gilyard, 1991

*Say Amen, Brother! Old-Time Negro Preaching: A Study in American Frus-
tration,* by William H. Pipes, 1991 (reprint)

*The Politics of Black Empowerment: The Transformation of Black Activism
in Urban America,* by James Jennings, 1992

*Pan Africanism in the African Diaspora: An Analysis of Modern Afrocentric
Political Movements,* by Ronald Walters, 1993

*Three Plays: The Broken Calabash, Parables for a Season, and The Reign of
Wazobia,* by Tess Akaeke Onwueme, 1993

*Untold Tales, Unsung Heroes: An Oral History of Detroit's African American
Community, 1918–1967,* by Elaine Latzman Moon, Detroit Urban
League, Inc., 1994

*Discarded Legacy: Politics and Poetics in the Life of Frances E. W. Harper,
1825–1911,* by Melba Joyce Boyd, 1994

African American Women Speak Out on Anita Hill–Clarence Thomas, edited by Geneva Smitherman, 1995

Lost Plays of the Harlem Renaissance, 1920–1940, edited by James V.
Hatch and Leo Hamalian, 1996

*Let's Flip the Script: An African American Discourse on Language, Litera-
ture, and Learning,* by Keith Gilyard, 1996

*A History of the African American People: The History, Traditions, and Cul-
ture of African Americans,* edited by James Oliver Horton and Lois
E. Horton, 1997 (reprint)

Tell It to Women: An Epic Drama for Women, by Osonye Tess Onwueme,
1997

Ed Bullins: A Literary Biography, by Samuel Hay, 1997

Walkin' over Medicine, by Loudelle F. Snow, 1998 (reprint)

Negroes with Guns, by Robert F. Williams, 1998 (reprint)

A Study of Walter Rodney's Intellectual and Political Thought, by Rupert
Lewis, 1998

Ideology and Change: The Transformation of the Caribbean Left, by Perry
Mars, 1998

"Winds Can Wake up the Dead": An Eric D. Walrond Reader, edited by
Louis Parascandola, 1998

Race and Ideology: Language, Symbolism, and Popular Culture, edited by
Arthur K. Spears, 1999